SYMPHONIC MUSIC

SYMPHONIC MUSIC

ITS EVOLUTION SINCE THE RENAISSANCE

HOMER ULRICH

COLUMBIA UNIVERSITY PRESS

NEW YORK AND LONDON

TO ERIC DeLAMARTER

PREFACE

THE BOOKS which deal with symphonic music are numerous; their approaches to the field are as varied as their purposes. Some provide analyses of the orchestral works of a single composer; a few are briefly concerned with but a single musical form. Others resemble minor encyclopedias and, with their alphabetically arranged program notes, do not pretend to be continuous. Still others, more venerable ones, are of lesser value to the present generation because of age, inaccessibility, and outmoded content.

The present book attempts to survey this large field afresh, and to do so in connected, chronological fashion. It takes notice of the fact that concertos, overtures, ballets, and suites—often overlooked or minimized in other books on symphonic music—are also parts of the literature. It endeavors to provide the reader with an account of the form and style of the compositions that constitute the various orchestral repertoires; to present information about the origin and content of significant works in those repertoires; and to facilitate the musical and historical understanding—as well as the enjoyment —of the entire field.

Nevertheless, this book is not a history of all music composed for orchestral ensembles. Such a history could scarcely be compressed into one volume and still do justice to the great number of works that exist. My choice of material may be questioned in geographical regions where native sons are duly honored, and I may, in some instances, have slighted the reader's favorite composer. I can plead only that I have attempted to observe proper proportion in the space at my disposal and to avoid writing a book for the specialist in any particular historical period.

A brief explanation of the principle which underlies the treatment may be made here. A musical composition may be discussed from several points of view. Analysis discloses its technical elements but may fail to make it come alive as an artistic entity. Critical evaluation provides the basis for an aesthetic response to the work but may throw little light upon the compositions that surround it. Historical commentary places a work in a chronological frame but may overlook the musical factors that make it unique. Biographical discussion of its composer may reveal the circumstances of its inception but may say nothing about its qualities as a piece of music.

I venture to assert that a composition can be completely appreciated and understood only if all these points of view—analytical, critical, historical, and biographical—are brought to bear upon the music itself. Only then can a musical work be seen as one which has both individual and type characteristics, which bears a relationship to the culture that surrounds it, and which reflects to some extent the psyche of the human being who composed it. To a particular author, obviously, one aspect of a work may seem to be more significant than another. The treatment in this book will vary, consequently, from composition to composition and will reveal my own feeling about what is especially noteworthy in individual works.

I record here with deep satisfaction my indebtedness to the late Frederick A. Stock, under whose baton large portions of the repertoire first came alive for me. Dr. Stock's extensive knowledge of and great insight into orchestral music made my years of professional association with him a rare privilege. Similarly, my long friendship with the late Max Reiter was fruitful. A fresh understanding of many musical problems and a familiarity with many compositions off the beaten path were for me among the valuable results of that friendship.

Dr. Otto Kinkeldey's generous help at early stages of the book's growth, his points of view, and his stylistic suggestions are gratefully remembered. The knowledge as well as the orchestral library of Dr. Fritz Oberdoerffer were drawn upon liberally; my sincere thanks go to him. Professors Dalies Frantz and Kent Kennan contributed valuable factual information. Professor Paul A. Pisk read the entire manuscript; his many suggestions were cheerfully and generously made. Dean E. William Doty's long-standing interest in my writing projects smoothed over many difficulties encountered in the course of preparing this manuscript. Miss Jean Cassel was of great assistance in all bibliographical matters. My appreciation for the considerable help that these and other friends gave me, and for the interest they expressed in my efforts, is acknowledged with thanks.

The action of the University of Texas Research Council in recommending, and of the Administration in granting, a research leave of absence greatly expedited the completion of the manuscript. I am deeply appreciative of their timely assistance. The staff of Columbia University Press receive thanks for their patience and technical help. Mr. J. Christopher Herold, of that staff, at all times revealed a keen interest and complete editorial insight into the problems the manuscript presented; his professional help far transcended the duties of an editor. I am indebted to Alfred A. Knopf, Inc., for permission to quote from the *Memoirs of Hector Berlioz;* to The Haydn Society, Inc., for supplying details about the orchestration of several Haydn symphonies; to Mr. Wilhelm Hansen for permission to reproduce a passage from the fifth symphony of Sibelius.

All such technical help, however copiously given, would not have availed me without the constant encouragement, stimulation, and understanding provided by my wife. Her many patient suggestions, made from the reader's point of view, are largely responsible for whatever clarity this book possesses. To her goes my sincerest gratitude.

HOMER ULRICH

Austin, Texas
April 28, 1952

CONTENTS

TABLES AND CHARTS

MUSICAL EXAMPLES

SYMPHONIC MUSIC

I

THE SEVENTEENTH CENTURY

THE EXPANSION OF the orchestra from a modest group of scarcely two dozen players in the mid-eighteenth century to a complex and highly organized ensemble of a hundred or more in the early twentieth is one of the outstanding developments in the history of western music. Each succeeding generation of composers from the time of Haydn to that of Stravinsky made greater demands upon orchestral resources, and performers and instrument makers were often hard pressed to meet those demands. The musical form in which this development most clearly came to light is, of course, the symphony. That form has challenged the majority of instrumental composers for over two centuries and has become the repository for their most significant musical thoughts. The symphony, consequently, forms the principal category in the extensive literature for symphony orchestra.

Even before the symphony came into existence, however, another orchestral form—the concerto—had held a high place in that literature. At first characterized by a kind of texture, later by the presence of solo instrument or instruments playing in competition with the orchestra, the form developed three main types: orchestra concerto, solo concerto, and concerto grosso. These types reached their highest development in the early eighteenth century and subsequently declined in importance; but out of them grew the modern solo concerto, a type which constitutes another important category in the orchestral literature.

In the second half of the nineteenth century a number of composers transformed the symphony into a new form variously called tone poem and symphonic poem. Symphonic textures were retained in most of these works, along with the serious purpose and high standards of craftsmanship that had marked the parent form; but the abstract character of the symphony was abandoned in favor of a pictorial or programmatic ideal. Since about the 1850s the symphonic poem has represented yet another category of orchestral music.

A number of single-movement forms exists also; of these, the concert overture is perhaps the most significant. Other musical literatures have been drawn upon to provide the orchestral field with shorter compositions, with pieces that may serve special functions on the concert stage or that may provide the orchestral literature with the lighter moments it requires. Occasional excerpts from the music dramas of Wagner, arranged for concert performance, selections from ballets, opera overtures and suites made out of portions of operas, arrangements of organ compositions, and the like—such works may be grouped together in a large and varied category of miscellaneous forms.

Symphonies, concertos, symphonic poems, a number of single-movement forms, and a variety of selections and arrangements of music drawn from other fields—these, then, are the compositions which may fairly be understood under the term "symphonic literature." And these are the works with which this book will be concerned.

There are obviously many other musical forms which employ the orchestra's resources but which can scarcely be included in the present account. Such monuments as Handel's *Messiah*, Bach's B-minor Mass and his *Passion According to St. Matthew*, Beethoven's *Missa solemnis*—to name but a few outstanding choral works—are often performed in orchestral concerts, it is true. Yet the instrumental portions of such works are not their principal elements. The composer's attention in writing for voices and orchestra is necessarily fixed mainly on the texts and on the full utilization of his vocal forces, and the orchestra's function is that of accompanying or, at best, that of enhancing the resources of the vocal group. The very expressive purpose of a vocal work differs from that of an orchestral composition in that the one illustrates or illuminates a text while the other presents abstract musical materials in purely musical forms. Thus it seems proper not to discuss vocal or choral compositions in the following pages. When a work is both choral and orchestral—as are, for example, Beethoven's ninth symphony, the third of Debussy's *Nocturnes* for orchestra, and Stravinsky's *Symphonie de psaumes*—it will receive due notice, of course.

It is understandable that not all the items included in the extensive symphonic literature have survived, and that even the survivors are not all equally vigorous today. One large group of works, of wide and lasting appeal, enjoys repeated performances wherever orchestral music is heard; this group may be termed the "standard repertoire." Another group, perhaps somewhat smaller, has a restricted or specialized appeal and comes to less frequent performance; here the term "restricted repertoire" is appropriate. A few items drawn from the vast quantity of almost-forgotten music come to the concert stage on rare occasions and hence deserve the term "fringe repertoire." It may be said parenthetically that contemporary music, when it comes to performance, quickly finds its level; it either takes its place in one of the above repertoires or is forgotten entirely.

When the compositions that constitute the standard repertoire are arranged in chronological order, one finds that the years about 1720 are the earliest represented. The "Brandenburg" concertos and two of the suites by Bach are from those years. If works from the restricted and fringe repertoires are included, a slightly earlier year emerges: concertos and suites by Handel and Arcangelo Corelli now take precedence in time. But scarcely ever does an orchestral composition of the seventeenth century come to performance today. Except for a few works by the men mentioned, the large mass of Baroque orchestral music has been virtually forgotten by those responsible for concerts today.

Immediately, then, an almost sixty-year gap in the standard repertoire comes to light. Contemporaries of Bach and Handel are largely ignored; important groups of composers who wrote in the years between 1720 and about 1780 have been virtually forgotten. And even the greater amount of the orchestral music by the two great masters of the late eighteenth century has slipped into oblivion. For in the standard repertoire after Bach come about a dozen symphonies by Haydn and perhaps ten by Mozart—late works, written in the last quarter of the eighteenth century. From the nineteenth century, then, the picture changes. Each generation is well represented, and music from each decade since about 1800 is heard with great regularity.

Thus the standard repertoire, beginning with works from the first quarter of the eighteenth century and leaping immediately to those from the last quarter, customarily omits just those works that would give it historical continuity. More importantly, it omits that portion of the past which alone allows the achievements of Bach, Haydn, and Mozart to be seen in their full measure. Bach represents the culmination and perfection of a musical development that began in the 1600s; Haydn and Mozart brought to completion a whole series of events and stylistic impulses which began even in Bach's lifetime and served to undermine the style of which Bach is the greatest exponent. The standard repertoire does not allow one to become aware of the true position of Bach's music, nor does it enable one to appreciate the real extent of Haydn's departure from Bach. A brief account of the music upon which the respective masters built becomes desirable, then, in order that the relationship of Bach and Haydn to the standard repertoire may be appreciated fully. That account will be attempted in this and in the following chapters.

The field with which this book is concerned is one of the youngest branches of music. Instrumental music for large ensembles became an important and independent branch of the art as late as the middle of the seventeenth century. But instruments had existed and had been cultivated assiduously long before that time. In various secular and military pursuits small ensembles had flourished far back in the fifteenth century. Toward the end of the sixteenth, such ensembles received extensive employment in supporting and augmenting choral groups. And through much of the interval between those times, ensembles of wind instruments were employed by municipalities in various outdoor capacities. These town bands existed far into the Baroque period; they were called upon to perform suitable music for dances, town festivities, and assemblies, and they assisted at weddings, christenings, and birthday celebrations as well.

Other types of festivities required more elaborate music. Especially in the Italian cities, large and brilliant motets and other choral works were played by instruments, often in conjunction with voices; and in connection with them, fanfares which served notice that something was about to begin. Among Italian cities, Venice was probably the most festive and colorful. Civic and patrician pageants and similar displays were important elements of that city's proud and noble life. Certain musical forms of the day reflected that Venetian ceremony and were likewise influenced by the trumpet fanfares and by contemporary developments in the ensemble canzone. The "sonatas" and "symphonies" of Andrea Gabrieli (c. 1520–1586) and his nephew Giovanni (1557–1612) emerged in the last decades of the sixteenth century to set the Venetian stamp upon instrumental music for more than fifty years.

This type of orchestral music flourished throughout the seventeenth century. Its festive character and its broad majestic moods are reflected in many opera overtures of the early 1600s, and as late as 1700 the one-movement form was still alive. But with the rise of the Neapolitan school of composers, toward the century's end, the form lost favor. The light humorous works of the Neapolitans brought a new air into the theater and into music generally; this survivor of Renaissance pomp and dignity fell by the wayside.

The word "symphony," which appears in the titles of some of Giovanni Gabrieli's works, requires closer attention. Like the term "sonata," it has had many different meanings. For the classic Greeks, "symphony" was a musical interval. In the Middle Ages, the term "symphony" was applied to certain musical instruments, notably the hurdy-gurdy. By the late sixteenth century it had become the title of a composition, and thus approached its later meaning. It appeared in Gabrieli's "sacred symphonies" and in similarly named works by his German pupil, Heinrich Schütz; in Waelrant's "angelic symphonies," Banchieri's "ecclesiastical symphonies," and in other works after 1600. But a symphony in this sense was not necessarily an instrumental piece: Gabrieli's *Sacrae symphoniae* include many motets and canzoni, along with sonatas for several instruments.

After the turn into the seventeenth century, the term was employed in yet another context. The operas of the first decades sometimes contained instrumental interludes, to which the Italian term *sinfonia* was given. These single movements, for instruments alone and often with a rich and poetic content, appeared separately or were inserted into the middle of an operatic act or into an oratorio; there they enjoyed a vigorous life until well into the eighteenth century. Prime examples are at hand in the *sinfonie* of Bach's *Christmas Oratorio*, of Handel's *Messiah*, and of numerous other choral works of the time.

Toward the end of the seventeenth century, a fifth use of the word appeared in connection with the overtures to the Neapolitan operas. But since that use of *sinfonia* is related directly to the present-day meaning of the word, the elaboration of this point more properly belongs in a later chapter.

In the last years of the sixteenth century, a series of speculations and experiments on the part of a group of aristocratic and professional musicians in Italy led to a radically new style of vocal music. For a variety of reasons, all of which lie outside the scope of this book, that group, known as the Florentine Camerata, abolished polyphony in their compositions and developed a texture in which a single line of half-spoken melody, supported by chords over a continuous bass line, became the principal element. The new style had an enormous effect upon music of all types, and was quickly adopted by many of the instrumental composers of the time. In its wake came many technical innovations, which soon began to appear in all manner of ensemble compositions. The most important of these, and one which influenced the course of all music for almost two centuries, centered around the new emphasis upon the bass line.

The composers, both instrumental and vocal, who embraced the new style were concerned primarily with the melody and the sustained or continuous bass; inner voices were left to be filled in by performers in a free, improvisatory manner. To guarantee, however, that the improvised harmony of the middle voices did not depart too radically from the composer's intentions, a system of notating chords was developed. Certain numerals, along with flats and sharps, were placed below the bass notes to indicate the spacing and the quality (whether major or minor) of the intervals in the desired chord. Thus, a note G with a $^6_4$ placed below it implied a chord of G–C–E. A sharp written below the note D implied a major third, namely F sharp.

The process of "realizing" the symbols of the figured bass—for so the system was called—into actual harmonies became an important part of the keyboard player's duties until the middle years of the eighteenth century. To enhance the sonorities of the ubiquitous keyboard instrument, one or more melody-instruments of bass range duplicated those figured-bass notes upon which the harpsichordist or organist erected the chords; the cello, the bass viol, the bassoon, and the trombone were often employed in this capacity. The aggregate, then, of keyboard and melody instruments supplied with a bass line containing symbols, was known as the *basso continuo* or, briefly, the continuo.

The early decades of the seventeenth century witnessed the flowering of an extensive and significant literature for large and small instrumental ensembles. That music no longer imitated the melodic style of vocal music, as much of the earlier instrumental music had done. The technical and individual characteristics of the various instruments—viols, flutes, *cornetti*, and, later, violins—were now taken into account, and one may speak of the beginning of idiomatic writing. A type of figuration that was suitable, let us say, for a string instrument was seen to be unsuited to a woodwind. The violins especially profited from this concern with instrumental idioms; and although violin style was not perfected until the end of the century, notably in the sonatas and concertos of Corelli, its evolution began in the variation sonatas of Salomon Rossi as early as 1613.

The early literature embraced a large variety of musical forms. Certain of them, notably the canzone, enjoyed a brief life span before they were absorbed by newer formal plans. Others quickly established themselves and lasted—with many changes, of course—into the following centuries. The cantata and the opera are examples. The orchestral field is indebted to the seventeenth century for two of its representatives: the dance suite, which began its development in the early 1600s, and the instrumental concerto, which emerged just before 1700. It is in those two forms that the most significant changes in Baroque instrumental music took place, and it is with them that the remainder of this chapter will be concerned.

After a long period of suppression at the hands of the church authorities, dance music emerged with renewed vitality in the sixteenth century. Patrician society and humble villagers alike danced to the music of the rudely schooled instrumentalists of the day, whose tunes were of two widely contrasting kinds, one usually slow or moderate in tempo and most often in duple meter, the other fast and sprightly and in triple meter. It became customary to alternate examples of these types; a slow, duple-meter dance tune was followed by its triple-meter associate, which usually contained great melodic similarity to the first dance. This pair of melodically related, metrically contrasting tunes, then, was repeated many times. And out of it emerged the dance suite of the late sixteenth century.

Over fifty years of concentrated activity on the part of composers in all sections of western Europe led to the creation and abandonment of many types of dance suites. One factor, however, was common to all—the element of a unifying tonality. Regardless of the internal arrangement or dance type, each suite customarily contained movements in but one key. Through the entire early period of suite formation to about 1650, this unity of tonality was seldom if ever violated. Not until developments in the French version of the suite swept aside all other types of assembly did movements in a contrasting key appear. Those developments may be summarized as follows.

Early in the seventeenth century, instrumental composers in France wrote both for the patrician dances and for the staged *ballets de cour*. They customarily added a second pair of dances to the original pair, unrelated to each other and in a triple-meter, duple-meter sequence. Toward the middle of the century, when the instrumental suite was taken over by the harpsichordists, the typical suite included an allemande, a courante, a sarabande, and a gigue.

Meanwhile, the single dances in these French suites were undergoing considerable internal transformation. In the early 1600s, the various dance tunes had been solidly rhythmical, and each form had its characteristic mood and rhythmic pattern. Carried forward in note-against-note textures, mainly, the regular pulse of the dance had come to clear expression. Toward the 1650s, several factors caused the dance to lose its pristine rhythm and to acquire a stylized character. Among such factors were the use of contrapuntal devices which tended to obscure the rhythm; the adoption of the continuo, which allowed a greater amount of rhythmic diversity and a rich figuration to develop in the upper parts; the development of self-contained melody to such a point that lyric expression became a part of instrumental style. The end result of these transformations was to remove the suites from the realm of pure dance music and to make them into miniature concert suites.

The dance movements remained virtually unchanged in a formal sense, however. Each movement consisted of two parts, and each part was designed to be repeated. A group of phrases without noteworthy melodic contour was presented in the tonic key, another group appeared in or gravitated toward the dominant, and the whole part was repeated. The second part, most usually concerned with still other melodic materials, reversed the sequence of harmonies. Seldom did these phrase-groups reveal sufficient melodic distinction to allow them to be called themes; and rarely did material heard early in the movement recur in later sections. In general, the following diagram was characteristic:

||:tonic–dominant:||:dominant–tonic:||

As mentioned above, it was customary before about 1650 to place all the movements of a dance suite in the same key. Under the influence of the variation principle, successive movements had been essentially rhythmic variants of the first dance, and as such had no need of appearing in contrasting keys. After that date, however, French composers often added to the suite a pair of dances in the same form, and in the pattern Minuet I–Minuet II–Minuet I; the second was then placed in a contrasting key, most usually the dominant. In the latter half of the century, this practice of contrasting tonalities was adopted by composers in other countries and was extended to other movements as well. The compositions of Corelli provide an example; almost half of his seventy-two trio sonatas and concertos, written between 1681 and 1712, contain at least one movement, usually a slow one, in a related key. By the turn of the century the practice was general, and any sonata or suite with all its movements in the same key was distinctly old-fashioned.

The addition of nondance movements to the suite, after about 1650, became another of the factors which enabled the dance suite to approach the field of concert music. Of prime importance among these additions was a new type of movement added at the beginning of the set. Various types had been so attached: Johann Rosenmüller, in 1667, had composed a type of movement that combined the fragmentary pattern of the canzone with the chordal pomp of the Venetian opera overture; Corelli had often employed a prelude consisting largely of broken-chord patterns. But the most important of these added first movements, and one which was destined to drive its competitors from the field, was the so-called French overture.

The French *ballet de cour*, about 1640, was often preceded by an orchestral introduction. It became customary to divide such an introduction into two parts, slow and fast, and to employ stately

dotted rhythms in the first part. One may assume that the cere-
monial entrance of the king during the overture required a pompous
or dignified kind of music. These introductions, called overtures,
became the models upon which Jean Baptiste Lully (1632–1687)
formed the overtures to his ballets (from 1653) and his operas (after
1673).

The *ballets de cour*, with their added overtures, were a feature of
the court of Louis XIII (reigned 1610–1643). They were performed, insofar as their instrumental portions are concerned, by the
Grande Bande, the "Twenty-four Violins of the King," a string
orchestra of violins, violas, and basses. Now one can speak of an
orchestra in terms approaching the modern sense: in this group the
concept of orchestral doubling appeared for probably the first time.
Earlier "orchestras," in Italy and elsewhere, had in general been
made up of solo players, each of whom played a different part. Now,
in the "Twenty-four Violins," each instrumental voice in the five-
voice compositions was reinforced: six players on each of the outer
parts, four on each of the inner. And the *Grande Bande* had continuity; it became the first permanent orchestra of the Baroque period.

The Lully overtures, then, made use both of the ballet's introductory movement and of its instrumental medium. Lully retained the
slow first part with its stately measure and its dotted rhythms. The
fast second part, however, became fugal in texture, generally was
set in triple meter, and often closed with a few measures in slow
tempo. But it remained a two-part form. With this slow-fast formula, and with the contrast provided by majestic first part and fugal
second, Lully created a form that was widely imitated in fields other
than the opera.

Now, just in those countries where dance suites were most popular, namely in France and Germany, no collective name for the set
was in use. Italians had employed the term *partita* since 1603, and
sonata da camera since 1637. German composers had often taken
refuge behind fanciful titles, as in Schein's *Banchetto musicale*, or
avoided any kind of collective title, as in Neubauer's manuscript,

"Newe Pavanen, Galliarden, etc." Later in the century, the Germans adopted the term *Partita* or *Partie*, and by the century's end the French had settled upon "suite." Finally, in the early decades of the eighteenth century, the terms *ordre* and "overture" came into general use as collective names for the dance suite with the Lully-type first movement. The term "overture" points to the dominating position enjoyed by the first movements of the suites. In that sense one must understand the four "overtures" of Bach when those sets of movements are discussed.

The significant developments in the evolution of the dance suite took place largely on French and German soil and spanned the entire seventeenth century. But simultaneous with those developments were the stylistic changes to which vocal music was subjected. Out of those changes, in turn, grew a new style and a new series of instrumental forms—the *concertato* style and the *concerto* forms. Both of these new elements played important roles in the progress of instrumental music through the entire Baroque period and beyond. It is necessary to examine them briefly; to do so, we return to the last decades of the sixteenth century.

An essential element in the music of St. Mark's in Venice during that period was the use of the double chorus. Ranged on opposite sides of the church, the two choruses engaged in antiphonal singing and echo effects, and were often provided with organ and instrumental accompaniment. Inevitably, under the influence of the concept of contrast, alternations of instrumental with vocal groups appeared also. To further the requirements of the new manner, vocal parts were written in a melodic style which differed widely from the usual late-Renaissance style. The smooth, flowing melodies of the earlier period gave way to short, rhythmically diverse melodic fragments which were intertwined, imitated, and overlapped; and which were well suited to instrumental performance.

To this new style, the name *concertato* was given. Probably derived from the Italian verb *concertare*, to compete, the new term neatly characterized one element of the new style: that of competition between the vocal group and its instrumental accompaniment. But the other stylistic elements—rhythmic diversity in the tonal lines and contrasts established by the presence of two dissimilar tonal bodies—were equally important in an understanding of the term. And a work written in the new *concertato* style was sometimes called a *concerto*.

Not until late in the seventeenth century did purely instrumental forms based upon that style emerge. It is to those forms that the present-day meanings of the term "concerto" properly apply. Arcangelo Corelli's twelve concertos of Opus 6 are probably the first works of this type, although earlier works by Alessandro Stradella (c. 1645–1682) had anticipated such forms to some extent, notably in the use of a divided orchestra.

Corelli's compositions include several sets of chamber-music works and the one set of concertos mentioned above. In the trio sonatas (Opus 1, 1681, to Opus 4, 1694) and in the solo violin sonatas (Opus 5, 1700), Corelli had laid the foundations for violin style. Idiomatic writing suited to that instrument is everywhere present, along with a refined expression and a contrapuntal excellence unmatched in earlier instrumental music. The set of twelve concertos, published as Opus 6 in 1712 or 1714, but reputedly performed at Rome as early as 1682,[1] contains another marked stylistic innovation which the full title of the work reveals: *Concerti grossi con due violini e violoncello di concertino obbligato, e due altri violini, viola e basso di concerto grosso ad arbitrio che si possono raddopiare* (the last phrase freely translated: the parts may be doubled at will).

The innovation consists of dividing the orchestra into two unequal groups: the three soloists, called concertino; and the concerto grosso proper, consisting of two violins, viola, and bass (with continuo understood), and sometimes called the tutti or the ripieno (i.e., the full group). That instrumentation is found in all twelve concertos of the set. Each group is provided with its own continuo, in order to make complete independence possible. Thematic differentiation between the concertino and the concerto grosso occurs seldom. Both

[1] Bukofzer, *Music in the Baroque Era*, p. 223.

groups are concerned with similar phrases and figurations, and contrasts are achieved largely by changes from loud to soft.

In content, the twelve concertos of Opus 6 parallel the chamber music of Corelli's time. Nos. 1 to 8 are analogous to the *sonate da chiesa*, or church sonatas; they were probably employed, like the latter, to accompany the celebration of High Mass. Nos. 9 to 12, on the other hand, are similar to the *sonate da camera*, or chamber sonatas; each of them contains a prelude and six dance movements. Thus one may differentiate, in the works of Corelli and many other composers, between *concerti da chiesa* and *concerti da camera*.

It is the texture of these works, however, that points most directly toward the future and toward the solidification of the instrumental concerto style. Two textures are discernible, one contrapuntal and the other homophonic. The first is confined largely to the slow movements and to the fugal fast movements of the *concerti da chiesa*. Occasionally a contrapuntal texture appears also in the preludes and in isolated passages in the dances of the *concerti da camera*. In all these places the counterpoint reveals how strongly Corelli had embraced the concept of tonality, a concept that had been evolving since the beginning of the century, that came to full realization about the 1680s, and that stands in strong opposition to the modality which reached its highest point of development in the music of Palestrina, Vittoria, and other composers near the end of the sixteenth century.

The essential element in tonality is the presence and awareness of a key center to which melodies and chords can be related. The function of the various chords is to establish that key thoroughly. Different degrees of harmonic tension in the different chords make cadence feeling possible, and various formulas of chord progression enhance that feeling. Corelli, in these contrapuntal passages, employs such harmonic tensions, enriches them through series of suspensions—in which the mild dissonances create still more tension—and provides a considerable amount of tonal feeling. Especially noteworthy is his skillful avoidance of cadential feeling through long passages, an effect which increases the ultimate tension (and interest) and establishes a real sense of harmonic motion.

The other—that is, the homophonic—texture that may be distinguished in Corelli's concertos also arises out of his employment of tonal resources. Important as his melodies are, their harmonic structures or harmonic accompaniments are even more important. The chord structure underlying compositions such as these was played, as we know, by the keyboard member of the continuo aggregate. In fast movements the harmonic changes transpired quickly; often the chord changed with every rhythmic beat, and the continuo player improvised an accompaniment that reflected the rapid changes. Above this solid chordal texture, the melodies freely developed characteristic rhythmic patterns, and often dissolved into rapid scale passages or broken-chord figurations; all these melodic devices were idiomatically written for the violins. To this texture, Bukofzer has given the name "continuo-homophony"; that term aptly describes it.[2] The texture later spread to other countries and was employed in forms other than the concerto.

The twelve works of Corelli's Opus 6 differ so markedly from earlier instrumental forms in their consistent exploitation of the characteristic texture that one may speak of them as having established a true concerto style. The new texture made practical a fast interchange of chords, and a choice of melodic lines and chord progressions that thoroughly established tonal feeling. The far-reaching rhythmic energy of the concerto grosso became identified as one aspect of Italian style, and was adopted in other musical forms. Corelli's melodic lines are composed in large part of sequence repetitions of broken-chord patterns. Usually a particular pattern with a characteristic rhythm is repeated over one of the harmonic formulas that became almost a trademark of the concerto: a series of chords of the sixth, as in Example 1; a series of suspensions which create consecutive seventh chords, as in Example 2; or a segment of the circle of fifths, as in Example 3.

Parallel to Corelli's activity in the field of the concerto grosso was that of another composer in an allied field, Giuseppe Torelli (c. 1650–1708), of San Petronio at Bologna. Among Torelli's early

[2] Bukofzer, *Music in the Baroque Era*, p. 221.

EXAMPLE 1

CORELLI, Concerto Grosso, Op. 6, No. 1
Largo, meas. 13-15 (condensed)

Concertino Vl. I / Vl. II

Viole da ripieno

Basso e continuo

6 6 6 6 6 6 6 6 6♮ 6 6♮ 6 6♯ 6

EXAMPLE 2

CORELLI, Concerto Grosso, Op. 6, No. 2
Andante largo, meas. 11-14 (condensed)

Concertino Vl. I / Vl. II

(Ripieno omitted)

Basso e Continuo

7♭ 7♭ 7

7 7♭ 7 ♮
♮ ♭ ♮

EXAMPLE 3

CORELLI, Concerto Grosso, Op. 6, No. 2
Allegro, meas. 84-88 (condensed)

works were some not unlike Corelli's, namely his Opus 2, *Concerto da camera a 2 violini e basso* (1686), and his Opus 4, *Concertino per camera a violino e violoncello* (c. 1690). But his later works firmly established the three-movement, fast-slow-fast sequence which was to dominate the concerto for two hundred years. And in his Opus 5, *6 Sinfonie a tre, e 6 concerti a 4* (1692), he clearly differentiated between the respective styles without employing any of the usual tutti-solo contrasts that are often thought to be the only distinguishing marks of the concerto style.

The last six works in Torelli's Opus 6, *Concerti musicali a 4* (1698), established a new form—the concerto for orchestra without solo instruments. The term concerto is justified here, for these works employ the stylistic devices of the concerto grosso: continuo-homophony, inexorable rhythms, and rapid harmonic movement.

But even here, in these orchestra concertos, short passages for solo violin point to another, and perhaps more important innovation in which Torelli played a leading part. That is the form of the solo concerto.

Among the very first solo violin concertos are the six contained in Torelli's Opus 8, published posthumously in 1709 but possibly written before the similar concertos of Tommaso Albinoni (1674–1745) emerged in 1700. At the very beginning of its career, the violin concerto exhibited the opposition between solo part and orchestra that still characterizes the form. Each is given its own material: rapid passage-work and florid figuration for the violin, as against repeated rhythmic patterns and melodic fragments in the orchestra.

The work of Corelli, Torelli, and Albinoni culminated in the many concertos of Antonio Vivaldi (c. 1675–1741), Venetian priest, violin virtuoso, and prolific composer. Less than a third of Vivaldi's three hundred concertos have yet been published. They include works for one to four solo violins, concertos for solo flute, and many concertos for orchestra built on the Torelli pattern. Many of them have descriptive titles: one collection, Opus 8, is called *Contest between Harmony and Invention*, and contains four concerti grossi, *The Seasons*. Descriptive devices, too, abound in these works; sounds of nature are depicted, along with fanciful passages that correspond to the somewhat bizarre titles of the pieces.

But in a formal sense, the Vivaldi concertos are not affected by these programs. The three-movement form that Torelli had introduced remains basic; occasionally a slow introduction is added. The movements themselves, especially the fast ones, are characterized by an alternation of tutti and solo elements, analogous to the alternation of two contrasting ideas in the rondo forms. But whereas the rondo's basic idea usually returns in the tonic key (in the form ABABA; the "A" section is in the tonic), the corresponding section in the concerto movement was permitted to return in a variety of keys. The movement, however, always ended in the tonic. This section in a contrasting key became known as the "ritornello," and characterized the majority of eighteenth-century concertos.

In every sense, the concertos of Vivaldi are more satisfactory than those of Torelli. The mannered rhythmic patterns of the tutti are employed more consistently and lead with relentless motion toward the cadences. Occasionally a fragment of the tutti's musical material is used in the solo refrain and serves to unify the movement. As many as five returns of the tutti are found, with a consequent expansion of the movement, opportunity for a wider range of key contrasts, and greater diversity in the brilliant solo passages. Vivaldi's rhythmic patterns, while stereotyped, have vitality and a character that allows them to be recognized easily in successive ritornellos. And the close relationship between the style of tutti and solo sections allows the movements to exhibit a high degree of cohesiveness. Finally, the rhythmic drive of these works is enormous.

Inevitably, the well-organized forms and the effective writing that characterized the solo concerto influenced the concerto grosso and the orchestra concerto also. Conversely, the contrapuntal textures of the larger ensembles were taken up by the solo concerto. Early in the eighteenth century, the Italian concerto style was adopted by the Germans, notably by Telemann and Gottlieb Muffat, who had been similarly eclectic in the matter of the French dance suite. The way was then prepared for the culminating works in the style: the concertos of Bach.

II

BACH AND HANDEL

THE HIGH ESTEEM in which Johann Sebastian Bach's music is held today does not go back in continuity to his own time. Even before his death in 1750, Bach had long been considered an old-fashioned composer of scarcely more than provincial importance. His fame rested more upon his accomplishments as an organist than as a composer. In the years after 1750, his small reputation declined quickly in the memories of all but his sons, his pupils, and his few devoted admirers.

More than fifty years were required for the public at large to rediscover his music. A Bach revival began in the early decades of the nineteenth century; its first success was the famous concert performance of the *Passion According to St. Matthew* under Mendelssohn's direction in 1829—almost a century after that great work had been written. At the height of the revival Schumann uttered the remark that "music owes Bach the same debt that a religion owes its founder." The implication was clear: Bach was to be considered the first in a line of composers which included, presumably, Haydn, Mozart, and Beethoven. The historical facts, however, point to a different conclusion, one that Schumann, in his ignorance of Baroque music, could not have reached.

Bach represents the culmination of the musical development which began in the 1600s; Bach's music is the greatest monument of the entire Baroque period. The contrapuntal texture which is the outstanding characteristic of his style was derived from a long line of Flemish and North German predecessors; his musical forms are those which the seventeenth century had developed. Probably no composer had his musical roots so deeply embedded in the past and owed so much to those who came before him. Rather than being the founder of a new music, Bach represents the peak toward which generations of composers had been striving.

In 1717 Bach was called from his post at Weimar, where he had been court organist, to direct the music at Cöthen. The Cöthen court was a small one without a theater, with virtually no vocal resources, and with a minimum amount of music in its Reformed church service. A small but competent group of musicians, most of them string players, supplied the music for the concerts which were a notable feature of the life at court.

Bach was ever able to adapt himself to the requirements of a new position. At Weimar he had composed a large number of organ works; later, at Leipzig, where his responsibilities included the writing of church music, the majority of his choral works were written. Just so now at Cöthen, faced with an interest in orchestral and chamber music, Bach devoted himself wholeheartedly to those fields. The greater number of his orchestral compositions were written between 1717, when his Cöthen service began, and 1723, when he moved to the position at Leipzig that he was to hold until his death, twenty-seven years later.

Perhaps the most important orchestral work of this period was a collection of six concertos. The set was written as the result of a wish expressed by Christian Ludwig, margrave of Brandenburg, that Bach provide some music for his private orchestra. The works were completed early in 1721 and were sent to the margrave with an elaborate dedication in French under the title, *Six concerts avec plusieurs instruments*. . . . They are at once Bach's earliest large orchestral works and his finest accomplishments in this field. In style, content, and expressive intent they are as diverse as their instrumentation. No two are alike, and they contain virtually a summary of concerto developments up to Bach's time.

The first concerto, in F major, is scored for two horns (*corni da*

caccia), three oboes, a bassoon, and a *violino piccolo* [1] in the concertino; the concerto grosso includes string instruments and continuo. The three regular movements of the concerto form (allegro,
adagio, allegro) are followed by a long, compound movement in
dance meters: a minuet heard four times, with two trios and a
polacca interspersed between the repetitions of the minuet.

The instrumental resources employed here are considerable, and
Bach makes full use of them. A variety of bustling figures, in the
two allegros, are distributed among the various instruments in turn
and provide an ever-changing pattern. But a real division between
soli and tutti seldom takes place; the texture is more that of a full
orchestra enriched and vitalized by numerous obbligato phrases
given to solo instruments. The second movement, without horns,
is dominated by one oboe and the *violino piccolo;* a broad melody
is heard first in alternation, later with imitations, over a slowly
pulsating accompaniment. The fourth movement employs the instruments in yet another fashion. The minuet, on each appearance,
is played by full orchestra. The first trio is for two oboes and bassoon, after which the minuet returns. The polacca is scored for
strings and continuo; again the minuet intervenes. The second trio
is for two horns, with three oboes supplying the bass; and the movement ends with yet another return of the minuet. Thus Bach made
full use of the instrumental combinations available to him.

The first Brandenburg concerto reveals a characteristic that is
seldom absent in Bach's music: usually symmetrical in an external
sense, the various compositions contain internal relationships that
repay the closest analysis. Single movements display an amazing
variety of formal plans. The first movement of this concerto, for example, consists of seven sections. Each of the sections begins with
the identical figure, after which extensions and elaborations carry
it in an individual direction. The key relationships provide the internal balance and much of the symmetry:

---

[1] A small violin tuned a third higher than normal. Here, in the F-major concerto,
its part is notated in D major.

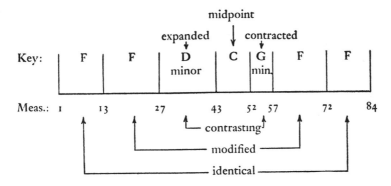

A similar plan is encountered in the concerto's third movement.

The second concerto, also in F major, is considerably more elaborate. Now four instruments are required in the concertino: trumpet, *flûte à bec* (recorder or block flute), oboe, and violin; the concerto instruments are, as usual, strings and continuo. The presence of the trumpet here, and the special use to which it is put, require an explanatory note about brass instruments in general.

In a day when trumpets and horns were no more than tubes of fixed length, only the natural overtones could be played on them. The normal range of the large trumpet then in use (i. e., its two middle octaves) included only the tonic triad plus one imperfect note. Toward the end of the seventeenth century, however, the topmost octave (the "clarino" range) of the instrument was cultivated, with the result that the diatonic scale which the higher overtones form now lay within the grasp of players thus specially trained. The large trumpet of Bach's day was often pitched in F; that is to say, the length of the tube was such that the following tones, the natural overtones of the F series, could be produced (see Example 4).

But the instrument existed in other sizes also, notably in D. It

EXAMPLE 4

was desirable to adjust the notation of the trumpet parts so that the visual aspect of the various overtones corresponded in the different sizes: the fifth overtone, for example (counting above the fundamental), which was C on the F trumpet and A on the D trumpet, was made to read G as if for a hypothetical trumpet in C. This practice, called transposition, made it possible for the player to shift from one instrument to another without upsetting the delicate lip adjustments upon which clarino-range playing depended.

Examination of the score of Bach's second Brandenburg concerto will reveal that the "tromba in F" is notated in C major, a perfect fourth below its actual sound. Thus the passage in measures 21–22 of the first movement reads as follows (see Example 5):

EXAMPLE 5

J. S. BACH, "Brandenburg" No. 2

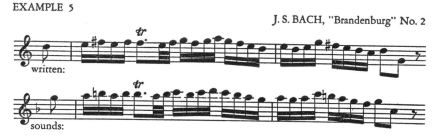

Transposition of certain instrumental parts has, since the time of Bach, become a fixed practice of composers, even though much of the need for transposing has disappeared. Much could be written about this important technical branch of orchestration. It suffices here, however, to resolve the apparent contradiction between the notes shown in Example 4 as being possible for the trumpet, and the notes revealed by an inspection of the trumpet parts in this and similar works.

To return to the second concerto: Bach employed a three-movement form quite on the Vivaldi model. While the fast movements are externally similar to the corresponding movements in Vivaldi in that an alternation of soli and tutti elements takes place, the power of Bach's imagination provided here an intricate internal arrangement of phrases that is beautiful in its logic and in its aesthetic effect (see diagram, page 29).

The significant thing, and one that can never be lost sight of in Bach's music, is that the formal plan reveals no mannered, stereotyped arrangement of phrases and sections. Working with unpretentious materials, within a tightly circumscribed set of key relationships, and in a well-defined idiom, Bach succeeds in providing a maximum amount of aesthetic pleasure in a logical and intellectually satisfying form.

Consider the outward symmetry of beginning and end (measures 1–9 and 103–118, respectively); the balancing of the two groups of solo phrases (measures 9–23 and 60–68); the approximate balancing of the two development sections (measures 31–60 and 68–103). But consider also the fact that the first solo-phrase group is expanded by the addition of tutti interludes, while the second group is compressed; and that the C-minor development passage (measures 68–103) is more extended and freer than the D minor (measures 31–60); and that the short transitional development (measures 23–29) is in effect the first of three developments (namely, 23–29, 31–60, and 68–103) which increase in scope and climactic effect. But the first and second of these passages, taken together, are exactly as long as the third: thirty-five measures in each case. Thus there is perfect internal balance after all.

While these inner relationships are perhaps lost sight of in the sheer joy of hearing this music, they are nevertheless integral parts of Bach's musical processes. Expansion, sense of direction, cumulative growth toward the final cadence—in the midst of perfect proportion, symmetry, and balance: that is one of Bach's great achievements. Similar cases abound in his music: the five-voice motet, *Jesu, meine Freude*, *The Musical Offering*, and *The Art of the Fugue* provide outstanding examples of the formal perfection of Bach's works. In each case the plan is adapted to the musical or textual requirements of the composition; and in each case the result is satisfying to the utmost degree. One additional formal plan may be examined here, with the observation that scarcely a work of Bach's is without a beautifully calculated yet spontaneous internal arrangement of details.

The third movement of the second Brandenburg concerto differs from the first movement, for here the principal musical interest is supplied by the solo parts. A series of five phrases on one motive, alternately six and fourteen measures long and alternately in tonic and dominant keys, is first heard in a variety of solo-instrumental combinations. Not until measure 48 does the tutti appear with a bit of accompaniment below a new motive in the solo quartet. Then comes a section (measures 57–86) in which the soloists, again in different combinations, return to a development of the first motive; now the cello and bass are entrusted with the solo motive also and lead into a series of sequence modulations for full orchestra. Out of this the quartet emerges briefly (measures 86–98) to manipulate a third motive derived from the first. The tutti returns (measure 98) and the development continues. Then (measures 107–136) comes a return of the soli section first heard in measures 57–86; similar melodically to that section, it now contains harmonies that prepare for and lead toward the final cadence. The last four measures (136–139) bring back the first motive, but now for full orchestra.

Again an involved formal plan is concealed in this brief description (see diagram, page 29). Now there is merely a bow to outward symmetry, for only the last four measures contain what forty-seven had contained earlier. In place of symmetry is a greatly expanded cadence from tonic and dominant to relative minor, through subdominant back to dominant and tonic. But there is also an exact balance of two internal divisions: measures 48–86 and 98–136; each begins with a nine-measure tutti passage and continues with twenty-nine measures of soli and tutti. While these two sections correspond melodically, they differ widely in their harmonies. Thus Bach again achieves balance and contrast simultaneously, and demonstrates for all time that intellectual activity, and even mathematical exactness are vital components of musical expression.

Perfect proportion is likewise revealed. The first section of forty-seven measures is exactly one third of the movement's total length; the middle section (measures 48–98) of fifty measures is slightly longer than the final section (measures 98–139) of forty-two. But

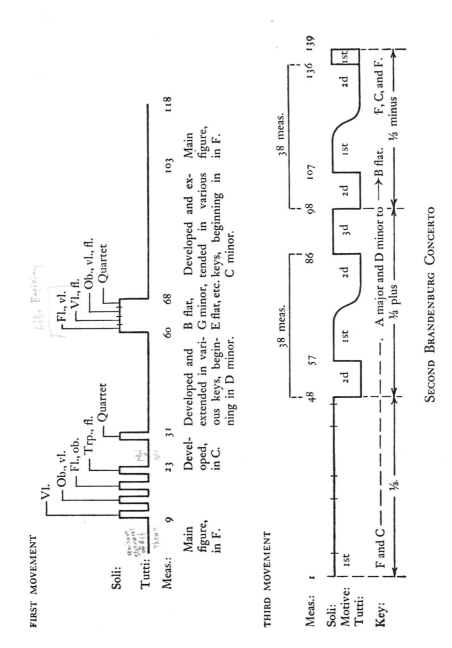

FIRST MOVEMENT

Soli:

Tutti:

Meas.: 9   23   31   60   68   103   118

Main   Devel-   Developed and   B flat,   Developed and ex-   Main
figure,   oped,   extended in vari-   G minor,   tended in various   figure,
in F.   in C.   ous keys, begin-   E flat, etc. keys, beginning in   in F.
               ning in D minor.   C minor.

THIRD MOVEMENT

Meas.: 1   48   57   86   98   107   136   139

Soli:

Motive:

Tutti:

Key: F and C   A major and D minor to → B flat.   F, C, and F.
          ⅓.   ⅓ plus   ⅓ minus

SECOND BRANDENBURG CONCERTO

the harmonic freedom of the middle part requires more room than the cadence-forming, direct closing section. Bach is no pedant, to insist on formulas; when he adopts a three-part form, as in this case, he is aware of the expressive requirements of his plan and modifies it accordingly. Thus the final, more concentrated section is proportionally shorter than the freer, more leisurely second.

If proof were needed that great art includes the organization of its material, such proof is plentifully available in the works of Bach. Dozens, perhaps hundreds of different internal plans lie concealed in that music. The present author will forego any additional examples, with the hope that interested readers will find their own and come to realize that in spite of all the veneration showered upon Bach, he is still a vastly underrated composer.

The third Brandenburg concerto, in G major, presents a radically different instrumentation. Here we have to do not with a concerto grosso, as in the first two works of the set, but with an orchestra concerto akin to the works contained in Torelli's Opus 6, of 1698. It is scored for three violins, three violas, three cellos, and continuo. Nowhere else in the Brandenburg set is the continuo-homophony texture so joyously exploited as in the G-major concerto. The first movement breathes vigor and youthfulness from start to finish. Solid blocks of tone alternate with sections in which the instruments appear group-wise: three violins, followed by three violas, then three cellos. Sonorous unisons tie the richly varied texture together. A diversity of motives, a variety of instrumental combinations, and an inexorable rhythm shape the movement and bring it to a powerful climax. At the end Bach employs merely a Phrygian cadence, one measure long, to serve as a transition between the movements.

The second movement, even more than the first, is alive, sparkling, and vigorous. Rising and falling scale figures in rapid sixteenth notes dominate the texture. The momentum and driving exuberance of the musical lines are nowhere relaxed; every measure carries the listener along with relentless force. And then, by the addition of the tiniest of details, the exuberance is increased; in measures 15–16 and again in 35–36 an unaccented passing note compounds the rapid motion (see Example 6). Here is an example of Bach's Jovian humor, of his ability to invest a well-defined texture with his personal touch, and to provide a heart-warming, enjoyable detail in the midst of this powerful movement. Youthfulness, zest, and drive place the third Brandenburg in a category all its own.

EXAMPLE 6

J. S. BACH, "Brandenburg" No. 3
meas. 35-37

The remaining concertos of the set differ greatly from each other, especially in instrumentation. The fourth, in G major, is essentially a concerto for solo violin and orchestra. The fifth, in D major, requires a concertino of violin, flute, and harpsichord. The sixth, in B flat, is scored for two *viole da braccio*, two *viole da gamba*, cello, bass, and continuo; in modern performances, violas and cellos usually replace the obsolete instruments.

The outstanding characteristic of the Brandenburg concertos, however, is their great variety of textures, forms, and moods. It is difficult to exaggerate the technical perfection of these works; yet their ability to provide listening pleasure is equally great. The sheer exuberance of many of the movements, and the restrained dignity of others, combined with their richness in instrumental color and texture, make this set of works unique in the literature. Among Bach's first attempts at writing for instruments alone, they represent an amazing accomplishment. In no later orchestral works did he transcend the expressive levels he attained here, and seldom did he equal them.

Many other concertos are found among Bach's works. First is a concerto in A minor for solo violin, two violins and viola obbligato, and continuo. This work contains the customary three movements, but is a bit more conservative in form than the works discussed above; the old distinction between tutti motives and solo episodes is clearer here than was usual in the Brandenburg set. The A-minor concerto is attributed to the Cöthen period, as is another solo-violin concerto in E major. In the E-major concerto, the accompaniment is for full string orchestra plus continuo; again the three-movement form is employed. In content, the work resembles its A-minor companion: solid tutti alternate with characteristic solo passages, a sonorous continuo-homophony underlies the whole, and vital rhythms drive the movements forward.

There exists also a concerto for two violins, in D minor, again in three movements with full string-orchestra accompaniment. The presence of two solo instruments of equal range permits Bach to exploit imitative devices. A rich polyphonic texture results, with antiphonal effects and full unisons to supply contrasting episodes.

In a day when instrumental media were fluid and when a work could appear in several guises, it was natural that arrangements of these violin concertos should be made. All three are found also among Bach's fourteen concertos for one, two, or three keyboard instruments; [2] in each case the new version was transposed down one tone and made to undergo the necessary instrumental modifications. And there is considerable evidence that several others among the fourteen keyboard works were based upon violin con-

---

[2] Bach used the term *Clavier* in his titles. In his day this term referred to harpsichord and clavichord alike.

certos that have been lost.[3] Still others are arrangements of choral or instrumental works (see the tabular summary, pages 34–35).

Within the orchestral ensemble, the presence of a clavier employed to realize the figured bass and thereby complete the harmonic structure was always implied. The term "continuo" reflects the cooperation of keyboard and bass-range melody instruments. This employment of a clavier, necessary in a work for string and wind ensemble, was also necessary in the solo-clavier concerto. In works of the latter type, it was Bach's general practice to figure only those portions of the bass part that underlay the tutti, and to leave unfigured the bass of the solo passages. Thus the clavier's function was actually a dual one: at times to support the ensemble, at other times to engage in solo playing.

It was customary to employ two claviers for this dual purpose: the soloist omitted the passages which were figured, while the other player confined himself to just those tutti passages. It was no great problem for Bach to conceive of the second part as a soloistic one and to provide it, on occasion, with the same material that the first part contained. Thus the concerto for two keyboard instruments came into being; in works of this type there was no need of figuring the bass, for both solo parts were now usually written out in full.

The first work of this type may well have been Bach's C-major concerto (No. 11 of the fourteen). It has the usual three movements, but there are notable deviations from the usual concerto texture. The first movement is concerned with developments and imitations of a pair of motives, and it proceeds as though the orchestra were also on the solo level, that is, without the customary tutti-soli opposition. The second movement contains a series of lyric phrases in tight imitation and is played by only the two solo instruments. The third is an energetic and masterly fugue distinguished by long episodes for one or the other clavier alone. The C-major concerto is among Bach's most successful and imposing instrumental works.

There remain two concertos for three keyboards and string or-

---

[3] In this connection, see Wilhelm Rust, in the introduction to Vol. XXI of Bach's works (Bachgesellschaft edition).

chestra, in D minor and C major, respectively; they are ascribed to the year 1733. In that year Bach's sons Karl Philipp Emanuel and Wilhelm Friedemann were still under the parental roof at Leipzig. Both sons were accomplished performers; the evidence is strong that Bach wrote the concertos for himself and the two young men. These works are full of unison passages to a degree unusual in Bach, and the accompaniment likewise is given an unusually minor role. At no time in the D-minor, and rarely in the C-major concerto, is the tutti entrusted with anything more important than a doubling of the solo part or an unobtrusive chordal accompaniment. These are primarily display pieces; there is in them little of the soli-tutti interplay that makes Bach's other concertos at once so fascinating and so rich in expressive content.

A tabular summary of Bach's keyboard concertos is made here in order to show the relationships that exist between original works and arrangements. A number of other concertos found among Bach's works are transcriptions of music by other composers. Thus, sixteen solo-violin concertos, including several by Vivaldi, were arranged for clavier and orchestra (Vol. XLII); Vivaldi's quadruple violin concerto, Opus 3, No. 10, was made into a work for four claviers (Vol. XLIII); and four works by others were transformed into concertos for organ alone (Vol. XXXVIII, Part 2).

Concertos for One Keyboard
(In Vol. XVII of the Bachgesellschaft edition)

No. 1, D minor, c. 1730. Based on the lost violin concerto in D minor (Vol. XXI).

No. 2, E major, c. 1731–1732. The first and second movements are from the Cantata No. 169 (Vol. XXXIII); the third movement is from the Cantata No. 49 (Vol. X).

No. 3, D major. A transcription of the violin concerto in E major (Vol. XXI).

No. 4, A major. An original work in this form.

No. 5, F minor. Based on the lost violin concerto in G minor. Its second movement, the famous "Arioso," is also employed in the Cantata No. 156 (Vol. XXXII).

No. 6, F major. A transcription of the G-major Brandenburg concerto, No. 4 (Vol. XIX).

No. 7, G minor. A transcription of the A-minor violin concerto (Vol. XXI).

No. 8, A minor, for clavier, flute, and violin. Its first and third movements are from the Prelude and Fugue for clavier, c. 1725 (Vol. XXXVI); the second movement is from the organ sonata of c. 1727 (Vol. XV).

No. 9, D minor fragment (in Vol. XVII, Preface, p. xx). In complete form in the Cantata No. 35, c. 1731 (Vol. VII).

Concertos for Two Keyboards
(In Vol. XXI, Part 2, of the Bachgesellschaft edition)

No. 10, C minor, c. 1736. Based on the lost concerto in C minor for violin and oboe.

No. 11, C major, c. 1727–1730. An original work in this form.

No. 12, C minor, c. 1736. A transcription of the concerto in D minor for two violins (Vol. XXI).

Concertos for Three Keyboards
(In Vol. XXXI of the Bachgesellschaft edition)

No. 13, D minor, c. 1733. An original work in this form.
No. 14, C major, c. 1733. An original work in this form.

One category of Bach's works remains to be discussed: the four suites or "overtures" for orchestra. The first and second were written at Cöthen for Bach's own orchestra; the third and fourth at Leipzig, probably for the Collegium Musicum which Telemann had established there in 1705 and the conductor of which Bach became about 1729. These facts of origin are reflected in the instrumentation of the works. The first two require only string instruments and continuo, with bassoon plus oboes in one case, and a flute in the other; the last two specify oboes and trumpets in addition to strings and continuo. These suites were among the last to be written in the eighteenth century; virtually none were printed in the period after 1750.

The first suite is in C major; beginning with a massive French overture, it continues with six dance movements: courante, gavotte, forlane, minuet, bourrée, and passepied. The now familiar compound form of Dance I, contrasting Dance II, and *da capo* repetition of Dance I is found in four of them. The overture, following its Lullyian prototype, contains a stately adagio and a lively fugue; but at the close the slow section returns. Thus the French overture in Bach's hands becomes a three-part form unlike its two-part predecessor. Certain of the fugal episodes in the middle part are noteworthy, in that a concerto-like alternation of tutti and soli passages occurs: the solo group consists of two oboes and a bassoon. Fugal texture by no means dominates in this fast middle part. The second suite is in B minor and emphasizes the solo flute. Here again are a three-part overture and six dance movements. The entire piece is lighter and brighter than the rather heavy and dark C-major suite; the style of the whole is in keeping with the nature of the solo flute which dominates throughout.

The third suite, in D major, is a larger work in all respects. It employs the full orchestra of Bach's time; the presence of three trumpets and of tympani adds a festive note to the suite, and rich sonorities and imposing tutti are characteristic. The first movement is again a three-part symmetrical overture. But here are none of the tutti-soli contrasts that marked the C-major suite; the texture is compounded of imitative and homophonic passages, always in company with the forceful rhythm that is seldom absent from Bach's music. Then follows a movement of rare lyric beauty, the well-known "Air," popular in dozens of transcriptions—none of them by the composer. The paired gavotte and the single bourrée that follow are distinguished by solid writing which does not obscure the lively dance rhythms. The closing gigue is a masterpiece in its relentless progress toward the cadences and in its consistent sonority.

The fourth suite, again in D major, adds a third oboe and specifies a bassoon among the continuo instruments. Again Bach writes a three-part overture, more grandiose than before and also character-ized by richer instrumental effects. A long passage for three oboes and bassoon contrasts with passages for string orchestra and adds something of the soli–tutti, antiphonal style to this massive move-ment.

The overture to this suite was used also in the Cantata No. 110, *Unser Mund sei voll Lachens* (in Vol. XXIII). But there, in the middle section of the piece and without any change in the instru-mental parts, Bach superimposed a four-voice contrapuntal chorus upon the orchestra. The woodwind trio passage is augmented by a vocal trio; the corresponding string-orchestra passage, by a florid solo for bass; and elsewhere the full chorus is employed. This con-trapuntal addition to a preexisting piece that is already in polyphonic style is a technical tour de force and a musical masterpiece at once.

One more orchestral work remains: a *sinfonia* in F major for two horns, three oboes, string orchestra, and continuo. This composition contains the first two movements and the minuet of the first Branden-burg concerto, but the part for *violino piccolo* has been eliminated. In omitting the concerto's third movement and shortening the minuet by excising the polacca, the arranger (Bach himself?) brought about the three-movement form which characterized the *sinfonia*—fast–slow–fast. The concerto elements, the alternations of concertino and ripieno, remain; thus the form of this *sinfonia* is a hybrid. The mere existence of this arrangement from Bach's own time suggests that the concerto grosso had become an outmoded form. The *sinfonia* had become popular, was soon to drive concerto and suite from the musical scene, and was to emerge with a domi-nant literature of its own.

Since that was destined to be, it is fitting that the works which mark the end of the Baroque period should be among its finest fruits. Baroque style tendencies were summarized and refined by Bach in these works; the period expired in a final flare-up of rare technical perfection and expressive worth. What Bach achieved here could not have been done earlier; and no possibility existed of repeating his accomplishment at a later time.

Bach was fortunately placed, historically speaking. Ever since the monodic revolution at the beginning of the seventeenth century, composers had been faced with the conflict between harmonic and melodic elements. The virtual abandonment of counterpoint about 1600 had laid bare the melody, and had provided it with the sketchiest kind of harmonic support. Such a procedure was perhaps adequate in the vocal music of the time; but it provided no firm basis upon which the emerging instrumental music could flourish. A return to modal counterpoint was unthinkable; generations of Baroque composers struggled with the problem.

It remained for Bach to find the solution. At a time when harmonic (vertical) and melodic (horizontal) elements were equally balanced, he arranged his chordal progressions so that they created real melodic parts; and at the same time he composed melodies that were firmly and logically tied to a functional harmonic scheme. Harmonic inner parts became independent melodies; contrapuntal textures were harmonically conceived. Thus a fusion of vertical and horizontal elements resulted.

In still another sense does Bach represent a summation of the period's struggles. During the course of the seventeenth century, various style elements had taken on national characteristics. The concerto forms, with their extreme affections and their variety of moods, had become the cultural heritage of the Italians; the suite, with dance elements prominent and facile ornamentation characteristic, stood for France. Bach, now, with dance rhythms and lyric grace in his concertos, with soli-tutti episodes and solid continuo-homophony in his suites, resolved these national differences and superimposed upon the product the contrapuntal texture and logical harmonic sense that represented the German style. But even more importantly, he impressed upon this Italian-French-German fusion the power and universality of his own creative genius. New forms developed, compounded of older formal elements; a new style emerged, one that contained elements of all these national styles, yet one that was uniquely Bach's own.

In formal variety, in expressive power, in technical accomplishment, in honesty of purpose, in musical effect—in short, in all the essentials, Bach stands alone. The logic of his formal developments does not falter, nor does the expressive intention of his works suffer through its consummate craftsmanship. After Bach there could be no progress; there could be only a new beginning in a new style.

It is one of the ironic facts of music history that Bach, the greatest figure of the late Baroque, should have brought that period to its highest point even after the style which the period represents had crumbled around him. But strange, too, is the fact that another composer of equal worth, exactly contemporary with Bach, should have pursued a similar course of isolated development and summarized the period in his individual way, a way that was strikingly different from Bach's. Above the Baroque tower not one, but two lonely peaks.

The reputation of George Frederick Handel (1685–1759) is thoroughly established. Few composers are revered as greatly as this Italianized German who spent the greater part of his creative life in England. Yet, one may ask, upon what is this reputation founded? Upon intimate knowledge of all his important works, as is the case with Beethoven and Brahms? Or even upon a familiarity with a judicious selection of his latest ones, as happens with Haydn and Mozart? No; it is founded upon one major work, perhaps a dozen small ones, and a few portions of others—a tiny fraction of Handel's enormous output. *The Messiah*, two or three violin sonatas, a concerto or two, and an occasional aria are the compositions with which the present generation is familiar. And these few works have sufficed to keep Handel's almost legendary fame alive.

In his own day, matters stood differently. Many of his forty-six operas lived past their first seasons; impressive performances of some of his thirty-two oratorios found favor year after year; his chamber music and his orchestral works were widely performed during his

lifetime. His organ concertos were particularly popular and contributed a full share in enhancing the reputation of the composer.

Today the great majority of those works have disappeared from
the standard repertoire, and information about their origin and content is not readily available. In the interest of restoring Handel's orchestral works to public notice and of assembling the most significant facts about them in one place, the attempt is made here to discuss those works which are still performed; and to mention a few of
the more significant forgotten compositions. The total published
list includes fifty-three works and fragments, as follows: [4]

1 concerto for oboe and orchestra, G minor, c. 1703 (Vol. 21)

1 sonata for violin and orchestra, B flat, 1710 (Vol. 21)

Water Music and an allied fragment, 1717 (Vol. 47)

6 concerti grossi, Opus 3, c. 1720 (Vol. 21)

3 concerti grossi of Walsh's *Select Harmony*, c. 1736–1740 (Vol.
21)

1 movement of a concerto grosso, F major, c. 1736–1740 (Vol.
21)

6 concertos for organ and orchestra, Opus 4, c. 1738, Walsh's *First
Set* (Vol. 28)

12 concerti grossi, Opus 6, c. 1739–1740 (Vol. 30)

2 organ concertos arranged by Handel, 1739, and

4 organ concertos arranged by Walsh(?), 1740; these six items are
included in Walsh's *Second Set* (Vol. 48)

6 concertos for organ and orchestra, Opus 7, c. 1740–1750,
Walsh's *Third Set* (Vol. 48)

1 movement of a concerto for two organs and orchestra, c. 1740–
1750 (Vol. 48)

2 concertos for organ and orchestra, D minor and F major, c.
1740–1750 (Vol. 48)

3 concertos for double wind choir and orchestra, c. 1740–1750,
Arnold's *Fourth Set* (Vol. 47)

Firework Music and two allied fragments, 1749 (Vol. 47)

[4] The volume references are to the Deutsche Händelgesellschaft edition.

In 1712 Handel took up what was destined to become permanent residence in England. Despite an inauspicious beginning with a mediocre opera, he quickly became well-known. Three successful operas wiped out the memory of his first failure, and a number of other compositions added to his standing with the fickle London public.

The widely circulated legend about the origin of the *Water Music*, which invented a quarrel between Handel and his king in 1715, has been proved false.[5] The documented truth reveals merely that King George I wished to have a concert on the Thames River on a July evening in 1717. The plans were made by a Baron Kielmansegge, who engaged Handel to compose music for the occasion. The latter wrote a suite of twenty movements, utilizing for the eleventh and twelfth movements a partially completed concerto grosso he had composed a few years earlier. The older fragment was considerably transformed in content and instrumentation to meet the new conditions.

The *Water Music* is scored for two horns, two oboes, two violins, viola, and continuo. A pair of trumpets appear in several movements and a flute is called for in one. The suite begins with a massive, imposing two-part French overture quite on the Lully model. Then follows a series of dances, airs, and movements in imitative style; F major dominates through half the suite, with D major, G major, and G minor prominent in the last half. These pieces vary greatly in length, some being as short as eight measures; and their content varies as greatly. In fact, variety is the chief characteristic of the suite.

The diversity of tonalities, of styles, and of textures becomes noticeable whenever the *Water Music* is attempted as a concert suite. But imagined in its original setting, as outdoor music performed on a barge floating down the Thames, with long pauses for conversation and refreshments certainly taking place between movements, the lack of unity is not perceived. One sees the suite then in its proper light: not as an organized set of pieces arranged according to a certain pattern, but simply as a quantity of music designed for outdoor

[5] See Flower, *George Frideric Handel*, pp. 122–25.

entertainment and brought together under one title. One must not believe, however, that Handel failed to exercise care in his selection. A comparison of the two versions of the eleventh and twelfth movements, for example, reveals how carefully he considered the purposes for which the music was intended. Further, the thematic use of the trumpets and the quasi-echo effects produced by the horns in several passages are beautifully calculated for their effect in the open air.[6]

The years from 1717 to about 1727 marked Handel's great success as perhaps the foremost opera composer in England. Many of his most popular operas were written during those years for performance at the Royal Academy of Music, of which he was a director. In 1724 he had published his Opus 1, a set of fifteen sonatas for various instruments, and began work on a set of six (later, nine) trio sonatas, published in 1733 as Opus 2. By that time his operatic successes had temporarily come to a halt, and he turned to oratorio composition. In 1734 his first set of six concerti grossi was published as Opus 3. The works had probably been written as far back as 1720.

Handel had become acquainted with the concertos of Corelli during a trip to Italy in 1708. He was struck by the vigor and nobility of Corelli's style, and to a great extent he succeeded in recapturing elements of that style in his own music. Opus 3 was published under the lengthy title of *Concerti grossi, con due violini e violoncello di concertino obligato e due altri violini, viola e basso di concerto grosso ad arbitrio, da G. F. Handel. Opera Terza*—very similar, it will be noticed, to the title of Corelli's Opus 6, (see page 15). But in addition to these specified instruments, the score calls for a pair of oboes in all but the third concerto of the set; the latter includes a part for one oboe or flute; and the first concerto requires a pair of flutes in addition to the oboes. The presence of bassoons, along with cellos, basses, and harpsichord, was taken for granted in the continuo; but in several cases the bassoon is specifically mentioned. Thus, Handel's Opus 3 is by no means merely a composition for string orchestra.

[6] Chrysander, "Händels Instrumentalkompositionen für grosses Orchester," in *Vierteljahrschrift für Musikwissenschaft*, III (1887), 6–11.

The prominence of the oboe part in many movements of the set has given rise to the nickname, "oboe concertos"; but the nickname is scarcely justified in view of the predominant solo violins.

The concertos differ considerably in internal arrangement and contain from two to six movements. The textures and instrumental combinations vary as greatly as the forms. Several movements contain double fugues; imitative passages and canonic devices are much in evidence. Contrapuntal writing, in fact, is rather prominent in the set. As a consequence, a consistent continuo-homophony texture seldom persists throughout even a single movement.

The works of Opus 3 reveal a characteristic that is often present in Handel—self-borrowing. Thus, the final allegro of No. 3 is adapted from the second of his six fugues for organ; and the last allegro of No. 6 appears in the third keyboard suite of about 1733. But seldom do borrowings appear unchanged; usually they are appropriately modified to fit the new instrumental conditions.[7]

It had become customary in Handel's day to play an occasional movement or even an entire concerto in connection with opera or oratorio performances. Now, great as was Handel's reputation as a composer, his fame as an organist was even greater. A long series of oratorio performances took place in the spring of 1735. Handel conceived the idea that a combination of his music and his organ playing might prove attractive to his oratorio patrons; and thus the form of organ concerto with orchestral accompaniment originated.

The first such work was heard at a performance of the oratorio *Esther* in April, 1735; the practice became general thereafter. For these performances Handel composed a set of six concertos for organ and orchestra during 1735 and subsequent years. They were published by Walsh as a first set of *Six Concertos for the Harpsi-*

---

[7] It may be mentioned in passing that the three well-known "cello sonatas" by Handel are based on the concertos. The first sonata, in G minor, is an arrangement of the oboe concerto of 1703. The second, in D minor, is drawn from Opus 3: four movements of No. 5 and one of No. 4. Likewise the third sonata, in B flat; it contains the first movement of No. 6 and the three middle movements of No. 2. The sonatas, arranged by August Lindner, have been published in Paris by Heugel (n.d.).

chord, Opus 4, in 1738. Five of the six are scored for organ solo, two oboes, the usual strings, and continuo; the third concerto contains parts for solo violin and solo cello in addition; and the sixth, without oboes, is for harp or organ solo, with strings and two flutes.

Here, in contrast to the concertos of Opus 3, formal regularity is at hand. All but the sixth concerto of Opus 4 contain four movements, usually in the customary slow-fast sequence. And again in contrast to Opus 3, contrapuntal textures are noticeably absent. Only one movement contains imitative devices to any extent, and fugues appear nowhere. The period 1735–1740 marked Handel's shift from opera to oratorio, in the course of which his style took on added elements of drama and lyricism. Perhaps those factors bring with them a lessened use of counterpoint; the concertos of Opus 4 indicate as much.

In point of style, Italian elements predominate in these concertos. Counterpoint is replaced by a loose, improvised texture full of arpeggios and stereotyped accompanying figures—the Alberti bass, for example. These factors, plus the virtual absence of pedal parts (the small organs moved into the theaters for Handel's performances were seldom equipped with pedals) and the free nature of the themes, bring the Italian harpsichord style into the concertos. Thus, Walsh's title had specified harpsichord or organ for Opus 4.

Handel's composition of operas and oratorios continued; almost a dozen such works were written and produced in London between 1737 and 1739, and his older works were also performed. In spite of this never-ending activity, Handel succeeded in completing twelve concerti grossi in a five-week period—September and October, 1739. (A few movements of the ninth of that set had been written a year earlier.) These massive works, among his greatest accomplishments in the field of instrumental music, were published as Opus 6 in 1740. They are scored for two solo violins in the concertino and a full string orchestra with continuo in the concerto grosso; occasionally a solo cello emerges from the larger group to provide a bass for the two solo violins.

The formal plan of Opus 6 is as free as the plan of Opus 3 had been almost twenty years earlier. Sequences of four, five, and six movements appear, with five-movement works in the majority, and the movements differ widely in content. In several of them, Handel departed widely from the concept of two solo violins. Broad unison passages serve to destroy the integrity of soli and ripieno; virtual orchestra concertos emerge. In other cases, the second solo violin is all but ignored; brilliant passage work is confined to the first violin, and a solo concerto for violin and orchestra is the result. And even in those movements which contain a well-defined soli–ripieno opposition, the texture changes so often that all three concerto types are present in part.

These works enjoyed considerable acclaim when they were first performed in the winter of 1739 and the spring of 1740; the presence of Handel, with his dominating personality, made their success sure. But removed from the excitement engendered by the composer's nearness and forced to stand on their own merits, they disclose certain weaknesses. Chief among them are lack of unity and an improvisatory tone. The range of moods in the twelve concertos is great: from the large double fugue of No. 4 to the sketchy chordal patterns in the introduction of No. 9; from the delightful and humorous finale of No. 1 to the dignified and serious larghetto of No. 6; from the march-like andante in No. 8 to the brilliant finale of No. 11. Every shade of expressive intention is touched upon in this set, and almost every movement contains passages of real worth. Yet the overall effect of these concertos is disappointing.

A Second Set of organ concertos, without opus number, was published by Walsh about 1740. The six works contained in that set are arrangements, however; the concerti grossi of Opus 6 contributed many of the movements. Two arrangements were made by Handel, the other four presumably by Walsh.

The last four, of course, shed no light upon Handel's methods of arranging. But the first two, as transcribed by the composer, are revealing. They show merely a framework upon which the organist improvised, and embellished, and expanded the musical material, in keeping with the custom of the time. This custom, it may be said, must be observed in performing any of Handel's organ concertos. In all these works harmonic skeletons and a few figurations alone are given; the organist must freely ornament the bare tonal lines if he is to approach the degree of richness that Handel intended these works to exhibit. The Handel organ concertos become a test of the organist's improvising ability and good taste.

The intention of Handel to exploit all the possibilities of the concerto form without, however, transcending its limits is borne out by the presence of three concertos for two solo-wind choirs with string orchestra and continuo. Nothing is known about the exact origin or date of these works, but it is likely that they were composed in the years between 1747 and 1750. The first, in B flat, is scored for two solo groups each containing two oboes and a bassoon. The second and third, both in F major, require horns in addition. It is probable that these works were intended for outdoor performance, and they are in large part based upon choral movements from Handel's oratorios.

The three double-wind concertos, along with the *Firework Music* (to be discussed below), were written at a time when the aristocrats of London made considerable use of Vauxhall, the famous outdoor recreation park. The gardens of Vauxhall were the scene of concerts and other performances; a bust of Handel had been placed there, and that composer's music was heard on all occasions. It seemed appropriate to include in the concertos, then, such movements from his oratorios as had found favor with the influential audience on other occasions. Thus one may account for the presence of so many oratorio-derived movements in the concertos.

In the spring of 1749 Handel was commissioned to write suitable music for a firework display, held belatedly to celebrate the conclusion of the War of the Austrian Succession. Designed to be massive and impressive, the celebration required unusual music. Handel established an orchestra (rather, a band) of three trumpet and three horn sections, with three players to each section; three oboe sections, with eight players each; two bassoon sections of six players each, one contrabassoon, and three tympani. For this imposing group of fifty-eight instrumentalists he composed a large overture in four sections; its first two sections are derived from the first two movements of an earlier D-major concerto of undetermined date.

The overture, designed to be played before the fireworks began, was followed by five movements of varying content. Three movements—bourrée, *La Paix*, and *La Réjouissance*—accompanied allegorical pictures made by the fireworks; and two minuets ended the festivities. From the second movement to the sixth, twenty-four violins were specified; this fact has led to the speculation that these movements, too, along with the two sections of the overture, might have existed in earlier versions. The success of the entire work, both at a dress rehearsal a week before the display and at the event itself, was great; repeat performances were demanded. For the later performances Handel added string parts to the overture; thus, as a fully scored suite for orchestra, the *Firework Music* of 1749 took its place among his principal orchestral compositions.

This large array of fifty-three concertos, suites, and fragments occupied Handel from about 1703, his eighteenth year, to 1751, when blindness put an end to his creative activity. While it is true that some compositions are apparently counted twice or even oftener, one need not object to including his arrangements in this account of his orchestral compositions. For with the exception of the four "concertos" arranged by Walsh in his *Second Set* of 1740, the arrangements constitute essentially new compositions. Thematic material is often identical, and the same formal structure is adhered to, in both the original and subsequent versions. Yet so subtly does Handel alter the harmonies, the figurations, and the instrumentation that the later composition is given qualities all its own.

Handel, according to Chrysander, was a composer who worked from models. Seldom concerned with novelty for its own sake, he strove constantly for objective expression, for a quality of writing that was true and natural. The model, whether taken from his own works or from other men's, served mainly to guide his power of invention and his enormous technique along traditional lines. He was little concerned with "improving" upon a model, or with advancing in a formal or technical sense. His arrangements deserve the term "transformations"; and no greater transformer of compositions can be named, unless it be his contemporary, Bach. A careful comparison of any of Handel's subsequent versions with its original will reveal how each of the two is eminently suited to its new instrumental dress and to its new expressive purposes.

A study of Handel's orchestral works discloses that they are essentially melodic. Even in the most polyphonic sections the dominance of one melody over others is assured; the middle voices remain relatively less important than the outer ones at all times. The melodies are most often cast in regular periodic structures; four- and eight-measure phrases are characteristic, and Handel's inexorable rhythms carry the successive phrases forward relentlessly. There is a single direction in this music: onward. Seldom does Handel allow any deviations to obtrude and to halt the flow of the music.

As a consequence, this music is enjoyable in the way that vocal music is enjoyable; both are compounded of chains of melodies over a supporting bass. But at the same time the orchestral music is somewhat devoid of that intellectual content which alone can make music stimulating and interesting as well as enjoyable. The manipulation of thematic material, the rise and fall of significant inner voices, the growth and transformation of motives and of rhythmic patterns, in short, all the many elements that denote the activity of a musical intellect—these are largely lacking.

It is precisely this characteristic that gives Handel's vocal writing its charm and power. His melodies are written for the human voice; the full range of the voice is employed, and its colors and dramatic expressive qualities are exploited. Melodic intervals in Handel are singable and lie easily in the human throat; massed effects are carefully or intuitively arranged to bring out all the possibilities of vocal expression. And the technical limitations of the voice are reached without being exceeded. But the same processes are employed in the instrumental music, in a medium that requires more than beautiful melodies for its fullest realization. The possibilities of that medium are not fully exploited; and what is thoroughly significant in a vocal context becomes merely enjoyable in an instrumental one.

In a formal sense, the orchestral works of Handel do not reveal a high level of organization. Various sequences of movements suggest that Handel's purpose was to combine the important instrumental forms of his youth without transcending their inner structures. Elements of the dance suite, of the four-movement trio sonata, of the contrapuntal *sonata da chiesa*, of the two-part French overture—all are present, but present in a rudimentary form. Seldom does a single concerto attain the formal unity of even a Corelli composition, and almost never does it approach the tight three-movement form of Vivaldi. At a time when other composers—notably Pergolesi, Sammartini, and various obscure Viennese musicians—had progressed far on the path of the three-movement *sinfonia* and had instituted the formal innovations that were to lead to Classical sonata-form, Handel was content to look backward along the path and to keep the old forms alive. Like Bach, he seemed loath to leave Baroque formal elements and textures behind him, but unlike Bach, he was satisfied with the forms and textures that a generation of composers had prepared for him. Handel remains, in his instrumental works, a conservative, retrogressive composer.

III

THE ROCOCO AND THE STYLE GALANT

WE HAVE SEEN THAT the early decades of the eighteenth century brought forward those elements of Baroque music which loom so large in the music of Bach and Handel. Succeeding decades up to about 1750 saw the development and culmination of the monumental Baroque style. But even while that style was attaining its peak, a number of sociological, political, and musical events were setting the stage for its quick decline. Thus, the musical history of the period about 1720 to 1760 develops in two parallel streams. The present chapter will be concerned with that stream of events which, though contemporary with the two great Baroque masters, touched them briefly in passing and influenced their own stylistic development in minor respects only.

Among the important sociological events of the period was the gradual decline in the importance of the Church as a cultural center. The popularity of secular music, especially manifested in the phenomenal success of operas in many parts of Europe, doubtlessly contributed to a growing disinterest in the strict forms and the severe, stylized content of the period's church music. A number of philosophical works emanating from France minimized the place of authority and tradition in human life and stressed freedom of thought and conscience. John Locke's *Essay on Human Understanding* (about 1690, but known in an abridged form in France from 1688) and Pierre Bayle's *Historical and Critical Dictionary* (1697) contributed to a new philosophy of rationalism which was to animate the period of the Enlightenment, roughly three quarters of the eighteenth century.

The death of Louis XIV (1638–1715), king of France for seventy-two years, provided the artists and courtiers associated with the court at Versailles with an opportunity to express themselves in a new way. They departed, in the fields of art and architecture, from the formalism of the Baroque and emerged with a new ornamental style. That style was based on the use of artificial rockwork, decorated and sculptured shellwork, profusion of detail in color and carving, and extravagance of proportion. Enthusiastically imitated in Germany and Italy, the new style left its mark upon other art forms, particularly music and literature, in the shape of elaborate attention to insignificant detail, delicacy of structure, and choice of frivolous subject matter. The period in which the new style developed is the Rococo; the term, derived from the French *rocaille*, "rockwork," calls attention to the leading place that architecture had in the formation of the style. The limits of the Rococo may be placed roughly at 1720 and 1760.

Late Baroque music had been strongly influenced by the doctrine of the affections. Affections, in the old sense, are emotions or states of feeling (compare the use of the term "affect" by modern psychologists); a large number of them, covering the whole range of emotions, was recognized, and a particular composition or movement customarily adhered to one mood throughout its entire length. Many composers achieved the unity of mood required of them by introducing only one motive or theme in a piece,[1] thus shutting out the likelihood of musical contrast. This aspect of Baroque style was among the first to fall victim to the new "rational" urge.

For now, in place of the single-mood content made possible by unified phrases, groups of contrasting short phrases were introduced and were often repeated sequentially. The long line and the sense of inexorable movement which had characterized many typical Baroque melodies were abandoned; profuse ornamentation, analogous in function to "beauty patches" on a pretty face, adorned these new melodies. At their best, the latter became filled with a lyric content that made an immediate appeal to the senses; gracefulness

[1] See Schweitzer, *J. S. Bach*, from this point of view.

and external show became guiding principles in their construction
(see Example 7). At their worst, they became empty of emotional

EXAMPLE 7

FR. COUPERIN, Air

significance, shallow, or merely entertaining. The lightness and elegance of works written in this fashion justified the term *style galant;*
this term is generally adopted to distinguish compositions of the
Rococo period from those written in the strict style of the Baroque.

The death of Louis XIV thus marked a change from dignity to
lightheartedness. The change was reflected in the music of the courts
elsewhere in Europe. Dilletantism flourished, and musical amateurs
abounded. Noble lords and ladies took up the violin and the flute,
and played active parts in musical performances. This, too, hastened
the decline of the severe Baroque style, for the dilletantes were ill
equipped to cope with the ornaments which were indicated by abbreviation or symbol, with the figured-bass parts, and with the contrapuntal texture that was typical. Indeed, the formal, expressive
works of the Baroque were out of place in the new gay and frivolous
social atmosphere. Music became simpler in structure and easier to
perform; counterpoint was largely abandoned, and figured-bass
parts and ornaments were often written out completely.

The texture which resulted was almost entirely homophonic,
which is to say that a chordal accompaniment, with all its parts moving at essentially the same pace, was placed below the dominating
melody. Homophonic texture found its principal employment in
keyboard and chamber-music works; the few orchestral compositions that circulated in France played a decidedly minor role, and
only later did orchestral music in that country adopt *style galant* ele-

ments. But in other countries the new texture played an important part in all branches of composition.

For example, roughly contemporary with these developments in France, there was an extensive series of transformations in Italian music. They appeared first in the operas at Naples; we shall concern ourselves with them only insofar as they touch upon the overtures to those operas, for it is the overture that carried within it the seed of the future symphony.

Opera overtures in the seventeenth century had evolved, in general, from a few fanfarelike chords played before the opera proper. Various elements derived from the canzone and the sonata of the time influenced the overture to the point where it became a well-organized if brief piece of music. By the time when Venetian opera had assumed the dominant place on the Italian scene, roughly in the middle third of the century, the overture had become a one-part slow piece with chordal texture and dotted rhythms; we recognize here the prototype of the later French overture of Lully.

Perhaps the most significant step for the future occurred, however, when Alessandro Scarlatti (1659–1725) at Naples began to write three-movement overtures for his operas; the first of this type appeared in a revival of *Dal male i bene* in 1696. The overture in this form shows its relationship to the Baroque concerto in several respects: in its fast-slow-fast sequence of movements, in its stereotyped beginning with the tones of the tonic triad, and in its rather consistent adoption of continuo-homophony. This use of a homophonic texture, with the consequent virtual abandonment of counterpoint, is perhaps the most significant stylistic difference between the Neapolitan overture and its French rival. The overture was now often called *sinfonia;* that term, it will be remembered, was also applied to other instrumental movements which appeared within the operas and oratorios of the time.

The new *sinfonia* was adopted by Italians everywhere and became increasingly popular as the eighteenth century ran its course. Becoming larger and longer, it often became shallow and musically insignificant as well. Empty figurations, themes based upon broken chords, and sickly-sweet melodies characterized the form in its earliest decades. The structure of its individual movements remained largely two-part, as in the dance forms of the late seventeenth century, although an extended chord sequence occasionally took the place of a lyric slow movement.

The early eighteenth century witnessed a growing interest in providing the public with access to musical performances. Opera performances in Italy had been available since the middle of the previous century: the first public opera house had been opened in Venice in 1637. Series of nonoperatic concerts had been established in London by John Banister in 1672 and by Thomas Britton in 1678. Many "academies" devoted to public performances were established in Italy in the late 1660s. Thus, the common man had access to music in at least those countries.

In Germany, however, music had remained to a large extent in the hands of the aristocracy. Whereas the Italian opera had been democratic and the French had become national, German opera was held largely in courtly houses. Partly to combat their exclusion from such performances, amateur musicians and students at several German universities established playing and singing groups on the model of the Italian academies. Among the most important and long-lived of these *collegia musica*, as the groups were called, was one established by Telemann at Leipzig about 1705; we have seen that Bach himself served as conductor for Telemann's *collegium musicum* for a short time. They provided, through the early eighteenth century, almost the only opportunity a middle- or lower-class German had to hear and take part in concert music. Similar groups were established by guild musicians, and many smaller aristocrats established orchestras in their homes. When, in 1725, Anne Danican-Philidor founded the Concerts spirituels in Paris, public concert-going was well under way in the principal countries of Europe. There arose then the problem of enlarging the orchestra's repertoire.

Among the orchestral forms which were adapted to concert performance were the suite, the concerto, and the *sinfonia*. Developments in the suite have been discussed elsewhere; it remains to point out here that the form enjoyed more popularity in France and southern Germany than elsewhere, that it became virtually obsolete toward the 1750s, and that it was replaced by the divertimento to which it contributed many style elements. The concerto was longer-lived and more popular and was not confined to particular regions—except that in France the concerto, being an Italian form, found less favor. The emerging *sinfonia* attracted equal attention and became the most important form for the future. One bit of evidence of its growing popularity may be adduced from the fact that Reinhard Keiser's (1674–1739) opera, *Der Hochmütige . . . Croesus*, appeared first in 1711 with a French overture; but in 1730, when the opera was revived, Keiser felt impelled to cast out that overture and to compose a new one on the three-movement Neapolitan *sinfonia* model.[2]

Toward the 1740s the *sinfonia* was separated from the opera and became a full-fledged concert piece. But competition from the highly developed concerto was strong; it became desirable for the *sinfonia* to acquire a better-organized form and a deeper significance. Only in this way could it hope to compete with the concerto, the brilliant virtuoso appeal of which was an important factor in increasing the size of the listening audience. That change in the content and form of the *sinfonia* required forty years or more; not until the 1780s did the fully developed symphony take its important place on the concert stage.

The melodic aspect and the texture of the *sinfonia* underwent a development similar to that of the keyboard- and chamber-music forms in France. A light, ingratiating content became the rule. In the complete absence of counterpoint, imitative devices seemed inappropriate; in place of them came melodies constructed out of short phrases, with clearly defined tonality and with considerable rhythmic vigor. The trio sonatas of Giovanni Battista Pergolesi (1710–1736), published about 1731, are among the earliest examples of the new manner. (It must be emphasized that the division into separate fields

[2] Grout, *A Short History of Opera*, I, 163.

of orchestral and chamber music was a later development; no essential difference in style or texture between the two classes of works is apparent at this point.) Example 8, drawn from the fifth of the twelve sonatas, illustrates the new melodic type.

EXAMPLE 8

PERGOLESI, Trio Sonata No. 5

Changes in the construction of the first movement now became significant also, and contributed to the evolution of sonata-form. In a typical movement the groups of phrases became fixed largely in two contrasting tonalities: tonic and dominant (or tonic and relative major in minor-key movements) in the first part, and dominant and tonic in the second. The series of phrases in the tonic key were often so unified in style and contour that the single melody they create deserves the term "first theme." The corresponding group in the dominant key, however, seldom revealed a similar unity; the term "second theme" as applied to this group of phrases is seldom justified in the trio sonatas of Pergolesi, in the contemporary one-movement keyboard sonatas of Domenico Scarlatti (1685–1757), or in other works of the time.

But the group in the dominant key did exhibit elements which contrasted in contour, rhythm, and quality with the first theme. In the works of Pergolesi again, in the *sinfonie* of Giovanni Battista Sammartini (1701–1775), of Giuseppe Tartini (1692–1770), and of many others, the element of contrast became important. As a consequence, the unified, noncontrasting Baroque instrumental forms now had a formidable rival which would soon drive them into virtual oblivion.

Not only in a melodic sense did the first movement of the *sinfonia* develop, however; its overall formal pattern became more complex in the years after about 1730, and took a long step forward toward the sonata-form that was to remain its basic principle for a century or more. We have seen that the movement's two sets of melodic materials contrasted harmonically; the diagram given on page 12 may now be modified slightly to illustrate the usual formal plan in the years just before 1730:

THEME or GROUP:	‖: first–second	:‖: first–second	:‖
BASIC HARMONY:	tonic–dominant	dominant–tonic	

Pergolesi again stands in the forefront of this new formal development. The innovation consists of the insertion, in the second part after the dominant-key section, of the entire first theme again in the tonic key. Then followed the second group as usual, also in the tonic key. Simultaneously, the section after the double bar was transformed in content; it became a transition rather than a thematic statement, and often embraced key sequences which prepared the way for the new first-theme entrance in the tonic key. With these innovations, which appear in eight of the first movements of Pergolesi's twelve trio sonatas, the Classical sonata-form is present in miniature:

THEME or GROUP:	‖: first–second	:‖: transition–first–second	:‖
BASIC HARMONY:	tonic–dominant	dominant–tonic–tonic	

Patterns similar to the above are found in first movements, and occasionally in third movements, of many instrumental works in the period from c. 1740 to c. 1760—and not only among Italian composers. Germans and Austrians made liberal use of what had been essentially an Italian development, and the new form gradually gained international acceptance.

In texture also, the *sinfonia* was modified considerably. The tradition of the continuo was still strong; a single dominating melody and a supporting bass line constituted at first the principal elements of the texture. Inner voices were written only with regard for completing the harmonies. But now, in an attempt to raise the *sinfonia* to concert level, attention was devoted to the middle voices also; they became to some extent real melodic voices. They were invested with a certain amount of rhythmic movement, in that the sustained notes were broken up into repeated-note patterns; and they acquired a rudimentary melodic contour when broken chords, arpeggios, or melodic motives were entrusted to them. This having been achieved, the bass lost importance as a fundamental necessity and was freed to engage in thematic manipulation. The end of the *basso continuo* era was now close at hand; the relentless continuo-homophony was replaced (see Example 9).

Interestingly enough, the concerto now began to absorb elements from the *sinfonia*, although the former was the more mature form. The many alternations of tutti and soli, which had characterized the form as developed by Vivaldi, gradually disappeared. Its harmonic scheme most usually tended toward a three-part pattern: tonic-dominant, dominant-relative (major or minor), and relative-tonic. The importance of the internal tutti was lessened, especially in the middle section of the movement; in its place came a transition analogous in function to the transition in the *sinfonia*. The movement often began with a brief statement of the material with which the solo instrument would subsequently concern itself, and ended with a recapitulation of the same material. Thematic contrasts were usually better drawn in the concerto than in the *sinfonia*, and transitions, episodes, and development passages retained the brilliance and the striking virtuoso effects that had characterized the earlier concerto forms.

The enlargement of the orchestra was another of the factors which contributed to changes in the style, texture, and content of the *sinfonia* and its relative, the concerto. The Neapolitan opera orchestra for which the earliest of these three-movement *sinfonie* had been written consisted essentially of string instruments; an oboe and a bassoon were employed to double the string parts in appropriate passages, and sometimes a pair each of trumpets and tympani were introduced to add brilliance and pomp. Seldom were the wind instruments given independent solo passages; their function was

mainly to reinforce the strings where needed. The orchestra before 1740 scarcely ever exceeded this instrumentation.

EXAMPLE 9

In the following two decades, pairs of oboes and horns were added
to the orchestra, flutes were sometimes called for, and trumpets and
tympani were employed on festive occasions. In Mannheim and
Paris, a few years later, clarinets were often substituted for the oboes.

The presence of so large a wind group made it possible to turn over to it the responsibility of carrying the harmonies. Sustained chords scored for wind instruments became a feature of the *sinfonie* and concertos of the period. And now, with the inner string parts devoted to rhythmic manipulation of accompanying motives and with the harmonies provided by the wind instruments, there was no longer any need for the *basso continuo* nor for figured bass. Yet so firmly entrenched was the old practice that it remained alive for many years. Haydn is known to have accompanied his "London" symphonies at the harpsichord as late as 1793. And in a related field, namely church music accompanied by an orchestra, it lasted even longer: in 1823 Beethoven supplied his *Missa solemnis* with a figured-bass organ part, and Anton Bruckner did likewise about 1850.

The works of the decades under discussion reveal an essential similarity in form and style. Nevertheless, individual differences between composers existed. The minor German composers echoed, in general, the melodic innovations introduced by the Italians. The Viennese, however, stood in the shadow of the eminent contrapuntist and prolific composer, Johann Joseph Fux (1660–1741). Georg Matthias Monn (1717–1750), for example, retained conservative characteristics, kept aloof from national mannerisms, and wrote principally in a forthright, vigorous style that reveals traces of Baroque practices. Sequences and polyphonic writing abound in Monn's music. His inclusion of a minuet in his D-major *sinfonia* of 1740 must be mentioned here as perhaps the first attempt to create a four-movement set in that form.

Music composed by the Mannheim group illustrates yet another set of individual differences. The transfer of the courts of Heidelberg and Düsseldorf to Mannheim and the presence of the music-loving Elector Karl Theodor at the head of the court provided the external stimuli which led to the assembling of an orchestra renowned throughout Europe. Johann Stamitz (1717–1757), first as concertmaster and later as conductor of that orchestra, instituted a new style of orchestral performance. He developed an orchestral discipline and a conducting technique of such quality that he was able to demand from his orchestra the same flexibility of dynamics that solo performers customarily exhibited.

Dynamics in orchestra and chamber music up to about 1750 had seldom gone beyond alternations of loud and soft. Based on echo effects centuries old, used consistently in antiphonal choral works, and forming an important element in seventeenth-century trio sonatas, the tradition of loud-soft (the so-called "terrace dynamics") was characteristic of practically all Baroque ensemble music. Instrumental and vocal soloists, however, had employed intermediate tonal quantities, and had known the devices of increasing and diminishing the tone across long intervals. In a number of works dealing with violin instruction, published between 1730 and 1749, Francesco Geminiani had been among the first to specify a refined use of gradual dynamic changes, namely crescendo and diminuendo, in a solo context. It may well be that Stamitz, as an accomplished violinist, knew of Geminiani's work and received from it the impulse to apply the same standards to orchestral performance. At any rate, the Mannheim crescendo became famous throughout Europe, as did other refinements of performance. In Stamitz's *sinfonie*, changes in dynamic level—abrupt as well as gradual—became essential structural devices rather than arbitrary expressive ones.

Not only in the matter of dynamic contrasts, however, did Stamitz and his school contribute to the development of the *sinfonia*. The concept of thematic contrast, the principle whereby two groups of thematic material were constructed upon different harmonies and with different contents, had become well established in the larger instrumental forms by the 1740s. But now that concept was broadened to include contrasts across short time-intervals; extreme contrasts in adjoining phrases became typical of most German music. In this development, the works of the Mannheim school attracted more attention, possibly because of the precision with which they were performed. The following passage,[3] drawn from the fourth of Stamitz's *Orchestra Trios*, Opus 1, illustrates to perfection the new

[3] *D.T.B.*, Vol. III, Part 1.

manner in which contrast occurs within a narrow frame (see Example 10).

EXAMPLE 10   J. STAMITZ, Trio, Op. 1, No. 4

It must be said that Stamitz's contemporaries and successors at Mannheim remained largely within the framework of the *style galant* and did little to carry his innovations forward. Elsewhere in Europe, however, those innovations were eagerly exploited. Johann Schobert (c. 1720–1777), for example, was among the first to transfer the Mannheim "rocket" (a fast ascending arpeggio) and the

Mannheim "sigh" (an accented suspension or an appogiatura, found in Telemann and in Italian composers long before it became a Mannheim mannerism) to the piano. Schobert's music is characterized by an impulsiveness and a forceful quality that even Stamitz's lacked; in this regard it was of considerable interest to the Classical giants.

The music of Johann Christian Bach (1735–1782), the youngest son of the great Johann Sebastian, was of great influence upon English taste. It was among the first to bring the Italian, specifically the Milanese, light and sweet type of melody to the notice of the English. But that music has been all but forgotten. Very few of Bach's more than a hundred orchestral works are played to any extent today; the *Sinfonia in B flat* is one exception, and that work is an arrangement of the three-movement overture to his opera, *Lucio Silla*, of about 1776.

François-Joseph Gossec (1734–1829), in his capacity as director of the Concerts spirituels, did much to popularize the Mannheim style in Paris. But Gossec was also an important composer in his own right, perhaps the first significant French symphonist before Berlioz; and at the time of Mozart's second trip to Paris (1778), he was one of the most influential musicians in France.

To some extent Luigi Boccherini (1743–1805) incorporated Mannheim characteristics in his music. His compositions, great in number in the chamber-music field, are considerably fewer in the orchestral; twenty *sinfonie* and four cello concertos are its principal items. Ingratiating and elegant to the utmost degree, his works seldom reveal any great depth of feeling—an exception being the slow movement placed by Friedrich Grützmacher in his arrangement of the well-known B-flat cello concerto. Boccherini's consistent use of the most elaborate ornaments in his melodies was scarcely matched even by earlier French composers. Thick encrustations of trills and turns, arabesques, mordents, and other embellishments bring his music to a high level of graceful, well-mannered artificiality.

We have indicated that individual differences existed between composers and schools of the time. An even more important distinction between national styles gradually developed during the period also. In the time of the "enlightened absolutism" of Frederick the Great in Prussia and of Maria Theresa in Austria, the middle classes had been awakening steadily. As the *sinfonia* became popular and better-known in the German-speaking countries, it began to reflect a tendency toward a heavier sentimental style, especially in the works emanating from the Berlin school. By about 1750 the German version of the *galanter Stil* displayed elements that the French lacked. A nostalgic mood was present at times, along with a barely concealed tearfulness. Where French works remained rather mannered, frothy, and delicate, the German compositions displayed tender feeling and a sensitiveness to "atmosphere." The change, among the German composers, from *style galant* to something deeper is marked by the term *Empfindsamkeit*: feeling, sensitiveness, or expressiveness. Foremost among the exponents of this development was Karl Philipp Emanuel Bach (1714–1788), the second oldest of Johann Sebastian's surviving sons, known as the "Berlin Bach" to 1767, and thereafter as the "Hamburg Bach."

Bach and his colleagues, among whom Johann Joachim Quantz (1697–1773) and Franz Benda (1709–1786) were prominent, aimed principally at moving the feelings of their auditors. The purpose of their music was to convey emotional states from composer to listener; the feelings they wished to convey were quite necessarily more significant than the *galant* music usually aroused. Stereotyped affections such as sadness, happiness, and joy, each given a characteristic musical figure, were not suited to this ideal. In place of the mannered, formalized setting of short figures came a constant expressive contrast between dissimilar phrases and other musical elements (see Example 11).

Bach's version of the *empfindsamer Stil* emerged first in his three-movement piano sonatas; these are among the most important early examples in that field. The *sinfonie* appeared later; of the many ascribed to him, only ten or so were published during his lifetime, notably four in 1780. Bach remained the most important of the

North German composers in a stylistic sense. He went far beyond mere charm and pleasantry. His manner was flexible, and he revealed a quality of imagination far superior to that of his colleagues.

EXAMPLE 11

Cantabile   K. P. E. BACH, Sonata, F major

Widely ranging harmonies, bold strokes of modulation, and an undercurrent of passionate romanticism made his piano sonatas into powerful and significant works. Bach's orderly mind, trained in law and philosophy, constantly strove to give the new sonata-form a unified core and to relate primary to secondary material. He often derived a second theme from a first; equally striking is his occasional practice of dissecting and reassembling a theme in the development section, thereby giving to that section an expressive significance that throws reflected light upon his thematic materials. Later composers were outspoken in the debt they owed to Bach; the latter served as an important source of inspiration especially to Haydn and young Beethoven.

Out of these attempts to deepen the content of the music, the modern symphony emerged; we shall at this point discard the term *sinfonia* in favor of its modern counterpart. Many composers, of whom Sammartini was one, had introduced too many melodic fragments; the form suffered from diffuseness and tended to disintegrate. The successful symphonists, however, placed their greatest emphasis upon the principal theme or theme group. Bach's derivation of second theme from the first occurred most often in the keyboard sonatas, where the formal problems are similar to those of the symphony. Thus he insured a tight connection between the opposing thematic groups. Stamitz, roughly contemporary with Bach, had done likewise on many occasions. In the interest of unity the development section was expanded, in that considerable attention was centered upon manipulations of the first theme. This in turn made complete recapitulation after the development unnecessary; and often in works written about or shortly after 1760 the recapitulation is rudimentary.

The Austrian and South German composers were very much aware of the several opposing national and personal styles. In characteristic fashion they combined them and added significant elements of their own choosing. Vienna, at the crossroads of Europe and at the cultural center of the Austrian Empire, became the meeting ground of many foreign influences. Hungarian, Turkish, and other exotic strains appear in Austrian music; it was inevitable that German, French, and Italian elements should do likewise. Thus, it is not entirely accidental that Vienna should have become the spiritual home of the emerging Classical style.

Insofar as the preceding pages touched upon the years from 1755 to about 1770, they might well have contained references to Franz Joseph Haydn also; for Haydn was in most respects a younger contemporary of the minor composers discussed there. What has been said about the form, the orchestration, and the scanty emotional significance of the music of those men applies equally well to the earliest works of Haydn. Only in its melodic content did his music differ at first from that which surrounded it; a lusty, peasantlike tone pervades even the earliest of his works, and his healthy humor made mock of mere gallantry or refined *Empfindsamkeit*. Seldom has a great composer begun his creative activity with works so modest in scope and appeal; seldom has a great composer matured so slowly and developed mastery so late in life.

Haydn's contributions to the literature of the symphony are considerable. In the years 1759 to 1771 he composed about forty-two such works; between 1772 and 1781, about thirty; from 1782 to 1790, about twenty; and the twelve "London" symphonies were written between 1791 and 1795. This total of one hundred and four is the basis for the complete edition of his works, begun in 1907 and planned to include some eighty volumes. To date scarcely a dozen have appeared; a number of symphonies are still unpublished.[4] These facts necessarily make any discussion of Haydn's symphonic work rather general in tone; one can at best be approximate as to dates, groupings, and influences.

The account of Haydn's formative years scarcely needs retelling here. Let it suffice to say that after his summary dismissal from the choir of St. Stephen's in Vienna, late in 1749, in his seventeenth year, he was thrown upon his own resources. Composing and playing in divertimentos and serenades for Viennese patrons provided him with a small income, increased his competence as a composer, and enabled him to continue the studies which had been broken off so abruptly. Then followed a short term of employment at the home of Count von Fürnberg, about 1755, during which he wrote his first twelve string quartets. In this position Haydn gained some prestige and access to aristocratic circles, to such an extent that in 1759 he secured his first important position—that of musical director and composer for Count von Morzin. In the latter's employ was an orchestra of twelve to sixteen players; and for that group, then settled at the count's country home at Lukavec, Bohemia, Haydn wrote his first symphony and probably his second also.

In 1761 Count von Morzin was forced to reduce his expenditures for music; his orchestra was disbanded and Haydn was released. But the quality of Haydn's work, so unapparent today in the light of his later achievements, had impressed the wealthiest and most power-

---

[4] Some twenty-six, formerly attributed to Haydn, are now known to be by his contemporaries; thirty-six others are still in doubt.

ful of the Austrian Empire's princes: Paul Anton, the head of the
Esterházy family and a most lavish patron of the arts. Haydn was
immediately engaged as assistant conductor of the prince's choir
(the conductor, Gregory Werner, had served the princely house
since 1728) and was placed in charge of all matters concerning the
orchestra. At the age of twenty-nine, Haydn began his long association with the house of Esterházy: twenty-nine years in direct
control of the orchestra (Werner died in 1766, after which Haydn
was made responsible for all the music) and, from 1790, nineteen
years as a pensioner of the family until his own death in 1809.

During the first eleven years of his employment with the Esterházys he wrote thirty-nine symphonies, Nos. 3 to 42. The orchestra
for which he composed numbered about sixteen members; later
it was increased to about twenty-two. But it was of excellent quality;
Haydn himself supervised the employment of its members, and it
was in all respects competent to perform what he composed for it.
At Eisenstadt, the prince's main palace, and after 1766 at Esterháza,
a new palace which rivaled Versailles in magnificence, Haydn was
able to experiment and to develop toward the evolution of an individual style; secure in the knowledge that his works would be performed, and concerned only with pleasing his patron. Paul Anton
Esterházy had died in 1762 and was succeeded by his brother,
Nicholas. It speaks well for Nicholas's musical taste that Haydn's
ceaseless experimenting and his gradual progress toward a new style
were at all times acceptable to him.

The orchestra for which these symphonies were written was a
modest one: Haydn seldom specified more than two oboes, two
horns, and strings. In one notable case, two English horns replace
the oboes (see the chart of Haydn's symphonies, pp. 70–72), and
in several others four horns in addition to two oboes are required;
further, one work specifies a part for tympani. But these specifica-
tions give an incorrect picture of the orchestra of Haydn's time;
certain instruments were traditional in the orchestral ensemble,[5]
hence had no parts written out for them. For example, it was cus-

[5] Carse, *The Orchestra in the XVIIIth Century.*

tomary for the bassoon to add the weight of its tone to the bass part, quite in the old *basso continuo* manner; the strength of that tradition is seen also in the fact that cello and bass parts were rarely separated. In a document from 1768,[6] Haydn expressed himself concerning the first performance of his cantata, *Applausus,* at which he could not be present: the composer ". . . recommends the addition of a bassoon to the violoncello and double bass as this makes the bass of the composition more distinct than in a work that is scored only for string basses."

With trumpets, and to a lesser extent with tympani, a different practice prevailed. Traditionally, trumpets were associated with open-air performances or with theatrical and operatic works which were performed in large halls; they were less suited to the intimate halls in which symphonies were customarily played. Toward the 1770s, however, as the symphony increased in scope and the orchestra in size, it became customary to employ trumpets in certain loud or fast movements, but not always to specify them in the score. Mozart, for example, often wrote out parts for trumpets (and tympani) at the end of a score, or even on a separate sheet. Tympani served as the traditional bass instruments of the brass group; their parts were often improvised in a conventional manner. Further, in publishers' catalogues of the time, these parts were often marked "*ad libitum.*" Thus, the absence of trumpets and tympani in the scores of all but four of Haydn's symphonies up to No. 42 is by no means a guarantee that those instruments were not employed or that their use would have displeased the composer.

The flute entered the orchestra by a different route. Throughout much of the seventeenth and early eighteenth centuries, it had been considered a solo instrument. Flutes were employed in chamber music, took part in concertos and occasionally in *sinfonie;* but seldom were they limited to tutti passages as were the other wind instruments. The solo tradition for the flute entered into the orchestral thinking of later eighteenth-century composers also. And although a flute had been available in the Esterházy orchestra from 1762 at

[6] Summarized by Geiringer, *Haydn,* p. 220.

ORCHESTRA	EXCEPTIONS
I 2 winds and strings	a 2 fl. replace ob.
II 2 ob., 2 hr., and strings	b 1 bsn. specified
III 2 ob., 2 bsn., 2hr., and strings	c 2 fl. added
IV 1 fl., 2 ob., 1 or 2 bsn., 2 hr., and strings	d 2 trp. and tymp. added
V 1 or 2 fl., 2 ob., 2 bsn., 2 hr., 2 trp., tymp., and strings	e 2 Eng. hr. replace ob.
	f 1 fl. added
	g 4 hr. instead of 2
VI 2 fl., 2 ob., 2 cl., 2 bsn., 2 hr., 2 trp., tymp., and strings	h tymp. added
	i no bassoons
	j 1 fl.; percussion added
	k cl. not by Haydn

Note: The numbers given in column 2 are those listed in the complete edition published by Breitkopf & Härtel (Leipzig, 1908–). The dates in the last column indicate what is now thought to be the probable date of composition; the figures following the dates in parentheses represent the numbers supplied in the complete edition published by the Haydn Society (Boston, 1949–). The "old" numbers refer to an earlier Breitkopf & Härtel edition.

DATE	NO.	KEY	ORCHESTRA	
1759–1760	1	D	II^a	
	2	C	I (2 hr.)	
1761–1762	3	G	II	
	4	D	II	
	5	A	II	
	6	D	II^{bf}	("Le Matin")
	7	C	II^{be}	("Le Midi")
	8	G	II^{bf}	("Le Soir")
c. 1762–c. 1763	9	C	IIe	
	10	D	II	
	11	E flat	II	
	12	E	II	
	13	D	II^{fgh}	
	14	A	II	
	15	D	II	
c. 1764–c. 1765	16	B flat	I (2 ob.)	
	17	F	I (2 hr.)	
	18	G	II	
	19	D	II	
	20	C	II^d	
	21	A	II	
	22	E flat	IIe	("The Philosopher")

DATE	NO.	KEY	ORCHESTRA	
c. 1764–c. 1765	23	G	II	
	24	D	II^f	
	25	C	II^a	
	26	D minor	II	("Lamentation")
	27	G	I (2 ob.)	
	28	A	II	
	29	E	II	
	30	C	II^f	("Alleluia")
	31	D	II^{fg}	("Horn Signal")
c. 1766–c. 1769	32	C	II^d	
	33	C	II	
	34	D minor	II	
	35	B flat	II	
	36	E flat	II	
	37	C	II	
	38	C	II^d	
	39	G minor	II^g	
	40	F	II^b	c. 1763 (= 13a)
c. 1770–c. 1771	41	C	II^{df}	
	42	D	II	
c. 1772–c. 1773	43	E flat	II	("Mercury")
	44	E minor	II^f	("Mourning")
	45	F-sharp minor	II	("Farewell")
	46	B	II	
	47	G	II	
	48	C	II^d	("Maria Theresia")
	49	F minor	II	("La Passione") 1768 (= 35a)
c. 1774–c. 1777	50	C	II^d	
	51	B flat	II^f	
	52	C minor	III	
	53	D	IV	("Imperial")
	54	G	III^h	
	55	E flat	II^b	("Schoolmaster")
	56	C	III^d	
	57	D	II	
	58	F	II	
	59	A	II^b	("Fire")
	60	C	II^d	("Il Distrato")
	61	D	IV^h	
	62	D	III	
	63	C	IV	("Roxelane")
	64	A	III	
c. 1778–c. 1781	65	A	II	

DATE	NO.	KEY	ORCHESTRA		
c. 1778–c. 1781	66	B flat	III		
	67	F	III		
	68	B flat	III		
	69	C	III	("Laudon")	
	70	D	II^t		
	71	B flat	IV		
	72	D	IV		
	73	D	IV	("La Chasse")	
c. 1781–c. 1785	74	E flat	IV		
	75	D	V		
	76	E flat	IV		
	77	B flat	IV		
	78	C minor	IV		
	79	F	IV		
	80	D minor	IV		
	81	G	IV		
c. 1786	82	C	V	("L'Ours")	
	83	G minor	IV	("La Poule") c. 1785 (= 81a)	
	84	E flat	IV		
	85	B flat	IV	("La Reine")	Old No. 15
	86	D	V		Old No. 10
	87	A	V^1	c. 1785 (= 81b)	
c. 1786–c. 1790	88	G	IV		Old No. 13
	89	F	IV		
	90	C	IV		
	91	E flat	IV		
	92	G	V	("Oxford")	Old No. 16
1791–1793	93	D	V		Old No. 5
	94	G	V	("Surprise")	Old No. 6
	95	C minor	V		Old No. 9
	96	D	V	("Miracle")	Old No. 14
	97	C	V		Old No. 7
	98	B flat	V		Old No. 8
1793–1795	99	E flat	VI		Old No. 3
	100	G	VI^j	("Military")	Old No. 11
	101	D	VI^k	("Clock")	Old No. 4
	102	B flat	V		Old No. 12
	103	E flat	VI	("Drum Roll")	Old No. 1
	104	D	VI	("London")	Old No. 2

the latest, Haydn seldom included it in his symphonies. It appears in fewer than a dozen of the first forty-two, and is then given a solo or an obbligato part.

We return now to Haydn's early symphonies themselves. We may be sure that the composer was well acquainted with the form of the Italian *sinfonia;* indeed, his first two symphonies were based upon that form. But Haydn was not content to adhere to Italian models; the striving for originality which animated his entire creative career became evident in his works from about 1761. One problem to which he gave immediate attention was that of unifying thematic material; it is out of such attempts that his great innovation of the 1780s was evolved. Sometimes an entire movement is based upon a single melodic fragment; more often, when decided harmonic contrasts exist between theme groups, the second theme is derived from the first. Haydn seems not to have appreciated, in these early works, the importance that would later be attached to just the element he tried to expunge, namely, the element of thematic contrast or conflict. Even in his later works the contrasts were seldom as clearly established as in, say, the compositions of Mozart or early Beethoven. Thematic conflict is missing almost entirely in these symphonies, Nos. 3 to 42, and lyric second themes, such as occur in Mozart repeatedly, are equally rare. Usually the same bright, bustling mood that animates first-theme sections is carried over to the second as well.

Here and there in the symphonies of the 1760s, and to a greater degree in those of the following decade, a new subjective attitude took the place of objective writing-to-a-formula; the symphony became a personal expression of Haydn's aims, abilities, and emotional constitution. One evidence of this is provided by the *concertante* elements that are introduced in a few of these works.

Now, other composers of the period 1740 to about 1770 had occasionally introduced solo passages into symphonic movements; but in such cases the solo melodies were scarcely different from the tutti. In Haydn, on the other hand, a degree of intimacy and a sensitive expression characterize the solos. Haydn apparently became aware,

early in his career, of the essential differences between solo passages and those for large ensemble. After the 1780s, when he accomplished the separation of quartet style and symphony style, he
mixed them no longer; solo passages in his later symphonies hold
a decidedly minor place.

Prominent in these early symphonies is the healthy, somewhat
lusty spirit found in Austrian folk music. Haydn did comparatively
little, in the finales of those works, that other Austrian composers
had not done as well; a brilliant air, a fast tempo, and a sense of well-
being characterize the finales of most symphonies through the 1770s.
But in the other movements he provided a content that is far removed from the mannered, rather superficial content of his contemporaries' music. The latter's themes revealed their relationship to
the *opera buffa* and to the *galant* world; Haydn's are folklike, sometimes naïve, often humorous, and always unpretentious. But out of
those themes he created a kind of music the world had not heard before (see Example 12).

EXAMPLE 12

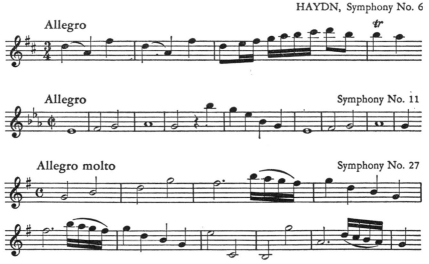

About thirty of Haydn's first forty-two symphonies include a
minuet as third movement; the dozen three-movement works are

scattered through the years to about 1764. Not until No. 20, written about that year, did the minuet find a regular place in his symphonies. And this was long after the Mannheimers, certain of the Parisian composers, and even Haydn's Austrian contemporaries had included the minuet as a matter of course.

The minuet remained singularly unaffected by the stylistic changes that took place elsewhere in Haydn's works. Even in the later symphonies it retained the folk spirit that it reveals in the earlier; and only on rare occasions do the learned elements of counterpoint and development appear. But the relationship of the minuet to its trio did change, even in the period to about 1771. In Nos. 3 to about 24, it was Haydn's usual practice to set minuet and trio in the same key, namely the basic key of the symphony itself. In these cases, contrast was provided only in melodic contour and perhaps in texture. From about 1765, however, the trio most usually appears in a contrasting key: tonic minor and subdominant are employed often, but subdominant minor and dominant keys occur also, with relative major and tonic major used when the minuet itself is in a minor key. Haydn rarely went beyond this rather conservative relationship, even in his later works. The minuet remained always the most stable movement of the symphony; in any case, far-flung harmonic contrasts would scarcely have agreed with its folk spirit. And scarcely ever, if at all, was the symphonic minuet quickened in tempo and labeled "scherzo"; in contrast, several minuets in the string quartets from Opus 33, of 1782, were so treated.

The years from 1772 to about 1781 constitute an experimental or tentative period in Haydn's symphonic composition that is even more productive of innovations than the first decade with the Esterházys. The period includes the symphonies No. 43 to about No. 73. It reveals, near its beginning, a new set of influences that altered considerably the content of his works; and near its end it gives rise to a new style of composition. In a sense, it represents the most important chapter in the evolution of Classical style, for that style stood fully revealed in the works written after 1782.

The symphonies of this group, insofar as they are available at present writing, reveal that shortly after 1772 Haydn began to seek a new type of expression, and greater strength and truth in his musical creations; and he became imbued with an outspokenly questioning attitude toward musical form.

In his string quartets of Opus 20 (1772), Haydn had discovered the melodic possibilities of viola and cello; he discarded the old concept of solo violin supported by group accompaniment and came face to face with a new medium that embraced four equal instruments. The logical consequence of this development was polyphony; fugal finales appeared in three of the six quartets of that set. But this marked only a return to Baroque learned practices, and Haydn was loath to regress. For almost ten years he wrote no quartets, but devoted himself to experiments in the form, texture, and content of the symphonies.

The symphonies of the preceding decade had been roughly balanced, as to length as well as to musical importance, in their exposition and development sections. Haydn's purpose there had been to achieve unity of expression within the confines of the traditional form. But, negatively, this made it inevitable that the development section could be no more imposing or significant than the exposition; and the nature of Haydn's themes being what it is, the sonata-form movement was circumscribed from the start. Now, in the symphonies dating from about 1772 to 1775 (roughly Nos. 43 to 52), Haydn often invented themes that were strikingly rhythmical, contained noteworthy contours, and in general were far removed from mere melodies. They often appeared in remote keys and provided a greater degree of contrast than heretofore (see Example 13).

But simultaneously the development sections became less significant. Haydn relied upon empty formulas, sequence repetitions, and in a sense returned to his practices of ten years before. Occasionally, as in No. 45, the "Farewell," a series of sequence repetitions is interrupted by a new melody which serves not even to enhance, much less to unify, what has gone before. The development section, upon which Haydn and his successors were later to lavish all their imagination and musical insight, became for a few years somewhat sterile and stereotyped. In the following decade Haydn was to reverse this lack of emphasis completely.

EXAMPLE 13

By 1775 his interest in subjective expression had lessened. He regained his customary smoothness of temper, avoided remote keys, and restored good proportions in the sonata-form movements by enhancing the significance of the development sections. But he also retained the interest in formal innovation that the subjective period had brought with it. To the end of his life he avoided rigid formulas and sought ways of bringing content and form into proper relationship. From about 1775, manipulation of thematic fragments began to play a greater part in his symphonies, and Haydn prepared the way for the great innovation of 1782. Wind instruments began to emerge from their long period of servitude to the common chord, and were employed in thematic contexts. And, finally, movements in variation form became more common than heretofore.

The winter of 1781–1782 was an important one in Haydn's development, for during that winter he became personally acquainted with Mozart. The latter had long admired Haydn from afar and had drawn from him the direct inspiration for many of his works. Now the influence was to become mutual and Haydn was to learn from Mozart. The stylistic evolution that Haydn's works reveal from about 1782 to 1795 can be appreciated fully only if it is based upon an understanding of Mozart's own style. For that reason, the present account of Haydn's symphonies will rest here. It becomes appropriate, in the following chapter, to examine the stylistic factors of Mozart's orchestral works to about 1782—the time when the two composers began mutually to affect one another.

IV

THE CLASSICAL PERIOD

WOLFGANG AMADEUS MOZART (1756–1791) grew up under the eye of his father, an experienced musician and teacher well qualified to recognize, foster—and exploit—his young son's enormous talent. Mozart was exploited; from his sixth year he was taken to visit neighboring cities and countries, thereby enjoying an unparalleled opportunity to hear music of all kinds.

Trips ranging in length from a few months to more than three years filled his life. Three separate visits to Italy, repeated journeys to Vienna and Munich, long stays in Mannheim, Paris, and London —these gave him a familiarity with the works of the greatest living composers and an insight into their styles. Always impressionable, gifted with a phenomenal memory and with impeccable taste, Mozart selected elements from the most diverse styles, refined them in the fires of his own musical genius, and made them his own. His teachers, in addition to his father, were in effect all the composers of the time; his textbooks, the whole body of music. Quite different from Haydn, Mozart became the great assimilator; his mature style is a direct result of his almost fourteen years of travel—fourteen years out of the twenty-nine between 1762, when the journeys began, and 1791, the year of his death.

It was characteristic of Mozart through much of his lifetime that he should write under the influence of whatever music he was hearing at the time, or had heard earlier and remembered. Several early symphonies recall Johann Christian Bach, with whom Mozart became acquainted about 1764. The four works of 1768 (see the chart

of Mozart's symphonies, below) introduce a powerful and dramatic
quality into his style; here one may see what effect Vienna made
upon the impressionable boy. And the nineteen symphonies—those
from K.81 (73l) to K.134, inclusive [1]—written between 1770 and
late 1772, partly on his Italian trips and partly in Salzburg, give evidence of Mozart's facility in imitating Italian models. The Austrian
symphonies usually include minuets; the Italian rarely do.

Here and there in the last few of these works, however, a deeper
and more searching expression replaces the mere tunefulness and
gaiety of his models. The thematic material of the first movements
is not only graceful: it becomes wide-spaced and occasionally powerful (see Example 14). A sense of proportion is felt also, along with

EXAMPLE 14   MOZART, Symphony, K. 124

contrasts that are drawn more firmly than in the Italian works. Slow
movements often exhibit a depth of feeling akin to the Mozart of
the 1780s. Mozart's subtle grasp of form becomes increasingly evident. His approach to recapitulations is made with greater skill and

[1] The conditions under which Mozart lived and composed, and the absence of a
continuous set of opus numbers in his works, required that a systematic ordering

THE SYMPHONIES OF MOZART

ORCHESTRA
I 2 ob., 2 hr., and strings
II 2 ob., 2 hr., 2 trp., tymp., and strings
III 2 fl., 2 ob., 2 bsn., 2 hr., and strings
IV 1 or 2 fl., 2 ob., 2 bsn., 2 hr., 2 trp., tymp., and strings
V 2 fl., 2 ob., 2 cl., 2 bsn., 2 hr., 2 trp., tymp., and strings

EXCEPTIONS
a fl. in 2d mvt. only
b 2 bsn. specified
c 2 fl. added
d 2 trp. added
e no flutes
f no tympani
g flutes replace oboes
h 4 hr.

DATE	PLACE	Old Koechel	Revised Koechel	B. & H. Complete Ed.	KEY	ORCHESTRA
1764	London	16	16	1	E flat	I
1765	London	19	19	4	D	I
1765	The Hague	22	22	5	B flat	I
1767	Vienna	76	42a	...	F	Ib
1767	Vienna	43	43	6	F	Ic
1768	Vienna	45	45	7	D	II
1768	Vienna	Suppl. 221	45a	...	G	I
1768	Vienna	Suppl. 214	45b	...	B flat	I
1768	Vienna	48	48	8	D	II
1770	Italy	81	73l	...	D	I
1770	Italy	97	73m	...	D	II
1770	Italy	95	73n	...	D	2 fl. or ob., 2 trp., str.
1770	Italy	84	73q	11	D	I
1770	Italy	74	74	10	G	I
1771	Salzburg	Suppl. 216	74g	...	B flat	I
1771	Salzburg	75	75	...	F	I
1771	Salzburg	73	75a	9	C	IIe
1771	Salzburg	110	75b	12	G	III
1771	Italy	96	111b	...	C	II

of those hundreds of works in chronological sequence be attempted. The *Verzeichniss* by Ludwig von Koechel (1800–1877) is the most complete and valuable of several such attempts. Reference to Mozart's works of necessity includes the Koechel index-number, usually abbreviated K. or K. V. A third edition of the *Verzeichniss*, prepared by Alfred Einstein in 1937, includes in its listings many corrections based upon newly discovered evidence of authenticity and proper chronology. In the following pages Einstein's revised number, whenever one exists, will appear in parentheses following the original Koechel number.

DATE	PLACE	NUMBER			KEY	ORCHESTRA
		Old Koechel	Revised Koechel	B. & H. Complete Ed.		
1771	Italy	112	112	13	F	I
1771	Salzburg	114	114	14	A	Ic
1772	Salzburg	124	124	15	G	I
1772	Salzburg	128	128	16	C	I
1772	Salzburg	129	129	17	G	I
1772	Salzburg	130	130	18	F	Igh
1772	Salzburg	132	132	19	E flat	Ih
1772	Salzburg	133	133	20	D	Id, 1 fl. obbl.
1772	Salzburg	134	134	21	A	Ig
1773	Salzburg	162	162	22	C	Id
1773	Salzburg	199	162a	27	G	Ig
1773	Salzburg	181	162b	23	D	Id
1773	Salzburg	184	166a	26	E flat	IIId
1773	Salzburg	182	166c	24	B flat	Ic
1773	Salzburg	200	173e	28	C	II
1773	Salzburg	183	183	25	G minor	Ibh
1774	Salzburg	201	186a	29	A	I
1774	Salzburg	202	186b	30	D	IIf
1778	Paris	297	300a	31	D	V ("Paris")
1779	Salzburg	318	318	32	G	IVh (one-mvt. overture)
1779	Salzburg	319	319	33	B flat	IIIe
1780	Salzburg	338	338	34	C	IVe
1782	Vienna	385	385	35	D	IVe, later made into V ("New Haffner")
1783	Linz	425	425	36	C	IVe ("Linz")
1783	Linz	444	425a	37	G	I (Introduction only; the symphony is by M. Haydn)
1786	Vienna	504	504	38	D	IV ("Prague")
1788	Vienna	543	543	39	E flat	V (1 fl., no ob.)
1788	Vienna	550	550	40	G minor	III (1 fl.; later, 2 cl. added)
1788	Vienna	551	551	41	C	IV ("Jupiter")

imagination than heretofore; codas, set off from the movement proper by double bars, make their appearance. In several cases, the finale becomes more important and tends to dominate the entire symphony. In all respects, the symphonies of 1772 are among the finest of Mozart's early works. Virtually every emotional effect and every technical device is carefully prepared; the listener comes to them with a feeling that they could not have been otherwise than they are.

We have seen how a succession of influences had left their marks on Mozart, and in each case how he had profited from them even as he grew beyond them. Now, in the summer of 1773, which Mozart spent in Vienna, another influence was to make itself felt. The benign figure of Haydn, which Mozart had known only at a distance, was to come closer, even though personal contact was to be denied the two composers for almost another decade. In Vienna Mozart became acquainted with Haydn's contrapuntal quartets of Opus 20 and with the symphonies which surround the well-known "Farewell," No. 45. He doubtless took pains to learn from them, just as he learned from every composition he saw or heard. An immediate result was his own set of six string quartets, K.168–173; here Mozart not only employed contrapuntal textures but unashamedly borrowed melodic patterns—irregular-length phrases, for example —and even themes themselves.

In the symphonic field, the Haydn influence was neither so direct nor so immediate. The three symphonies of the next group were written between November, 1773, and the following spring. The fact that each of them contains a minuet is merely an external matter by this time; what is new and significant is the content of the works: K.200 (173e), in C; K.183, in G minor; and K.201 (186a), in A major. Foreboding, passion, intensity, drama—such elements lift these works even above their immediate predecessors. The G-minor symphony brings to expression a subjective utterance that Mozart had not employed earlier and that hints at great inner suffering. The A-major symphony, contrasting greatly with its neighbor, brings the genial spirit of Haydn to direct expression. Its bustling finale, with flashing scale passages and an air of good humor, is like many movements in the older man's works. But elsewhere in the same work Mozart stands squarely upon his own feet. The first movement reveals traces of the chromaticism that is to dominate his later style; further, it is filled with a suave expression that none but he ever achieved. Taken as a whole, the three symphonies of 1773–1774 are among the works which reveal what his mature style will be based upon.

The concerto occupies an intermediate place in Mozart's instrumental works. It is not usually in the *galant* style that is appropriate to divertimentos; nor is it in the symphonic style, which is concerned as much with organization of materials as it is with the materials themselves. It is also far removed from being a display piece that exploits merely the technical dexterity of a soloist. The concerto in Mozart is likely to be a serious work with a definite series of changing relationships between the independent soloist and the equally independent orchestra. Thus, it bears similarities to the early eighteenth-century concerto with its contrasts of tutti and solo.

Mozart served, from 1770 onward, as concertmaster to the archbishop of Salzburg; presumably the five violin concertos he composed between April and December, 1775, had some connection with that office. All five are in the three-movement form that remained traditional for the concerto, and require a small orchestral accompaniment: oboes, horns, and strings are specified. The first two, K.207, in B flat, and K.211, in D, are minor works in conventional style and with a somewhat old-fashioned spirit; they have not remained in the repertoire. The others are, suddenly, masterworks in every sense, although only a few months separate them from their smaller companions. One, K.216, in G major, breathes a fresh spirit; brisk or poignant or humorous themes give it a glowing content. Another, K.218, in D major, is rich in sonority and intimate in its appeal; the violin comes close to the orchestra in spirit and inspires it to its own brand of eloquence. The last, K.219, in A major, discloses a Mozart who has virtually deserted tradition and written in a purely personal style. Free form, an improvisatory spirit, contrasting tempos within a movement, and a Turkish episode in the finale contribute to the great charm of this work.[2]

The majority of Mozart's twenty-one [3] concertos for piano and orchestra are among his great achievements. In most of them he accomplished what he had striven for in the last three violin concertos, namely a duality between solo and orchestra, but what of necessity had failed there because of the nature of that solo instrument. The piano is the only worthy competitor of the orchestra; and in Mozart's concertos it measures up to its new responsibility. Sheer virtuosity for its own sake still finds no place there; but the piano is given a role that allows it to reveal its inmost resources, which are equal to those of the orchestra. Mozart's piano concertos are so fluid that every shade of expression can find utterance; and every shade, from the lightest to the most somber, may be expected.

Mozart was one of the great pianists of his time, and the majority of his concertos were written for his own use. The influence of Johann Christian Bach, so apparent in the early symphonies, had been equally strong in Mozart's first essays in the concerto field; but that influence was quickly cast off. In 1777 he composed the concerto in E flat, K.271, for a young Frenchwoman, Mlle Jeunehomme; and the marks of the *style galant* are scarcely perceptible.

Here, in only his fourth solo-piano concerto, Mozart brought to pass the ideal of his concerto writing: real collaboration between its two opposing elements. The orchestral accompaniment rises to a new level of sensitivity, impelled thence by the majesty and richness

[2] Two other violin concertos are attributed to Mozart. One in D major, K.271a (271i), supposedly written in 1777, may be no more than a poor arrangement of Mozart's sketches. The other, K. Suppl. 294a, the so-called "Adelaide," is even more doubtful. Einstein says of it (in *Mozart*, p. 278) that it is, "to put it mildly, a piece of mystification à la Kreisler."

[3] The complete edition of Mozart's works includes twenty-eight concertos for piano (or pianos) and orchestra. The first four of these—K.37, K.39, K.40, and K.41—are transcriptions of sonata movements by various German and Austrian composers, however, and are thus disregarded in the tabular summary, pp. 86–87; and the last—K.382—is a rondo which Mozart substituted for the finale of K.175, his first piano concerto. The concerto for three pianos, K.242, and the work for two pianos, K.365 (316a), added to the above, account for seven of the twenty-eight concertos. The remainder, then, are the twenty-one spoken of here.

The Concertos of Mozart

ORCHESTRA	EXCEPTIONS
I 2 ob., 2 hr., and strings	a fl. in 2d mvt. only
II 2 ob., 2 hr., 2 trp., tymp., and strings	b 2 bsn. specified
	c 2 fl. added
III 2 fl., 2 ob., 2 bsn., 2 hr., and strings	d 2 trp. added
	e no flutes
IV 1 or 2 fl., 2 ob., 2 bsn., 2 hr., 2 trp., tymp., and strings	f no tympani
	g flutes replace oboes
V 2 fl., 2 ob., 2 cl., 2 bsn., 2 hr., 2 trp., tymp., and strings	h 4 hr.

DATE	PLACE	NUMBER		SOLO INSTRU-MENT	KEY	ORCHESTRA
		Old Koechel	*Revised Koechel*			
1773	Salzburg	190	166b	2 violins	C	I^d
1773	Salzburg	175	175	piano	D	II
1774	Salzburg	191	186e	bassoon	B flat	I
1775	Salzburg	207	207	violin	B flat	I
1775	Salzburg	211	211	violin	D	I
1775	Salzburg	216	216	violin	G	I^{ga}
1775	Salzburg	218	218	violin	D	I
1775	Salzburg	219	219	violin	A	I
1776	Salzburg	238	238	piano	B flat	I^{ga}
1776	Salzburg	242	242	3 pianos	F	I ("Lodron")
1776	Salzburg	246	246	piano	C	I
1777	Salzburg	271	271	piano	E flat	I ("Jeunehomme")
1777	Salzburg	271a	271i	violin	D	I (doubtful)
1778	Mannheim	313	285c	flute	G	I
1778	Mannheim	314	285d	flute	D	I
1778	Paris	K. Suppl. 9	297b	4 winds	E flat	I (*sinfonia concertante*)
1778	Paris	299	297c	fl. and harp	C	I
1779	Salzburg	365	316a	2 pianos	E flat	I^b, rev. to V^e, 1782
1779	Salzburg	364	320d	violin and viola	E flat	I (*sinfonia concertante*)
1778?	Salzburg	268	365b	violin	E flat	I^b (1 fl. added) (doubtful)
1782	Vienna	414	386a	piano	A	I, or str. quartet
1782	Vienna	412	386b	horn	D	2 ob., 2 bsn., str.
1782–83	Vienna	413	387a	piano	F	I^b, or str. quartet
1782–83	Vienna	415	387b	piano	C	II^b, or str. quartet
1783	Vienna	417	417	horn	E flat	I
1783	Vienna	447	447	horn	E flat	2 cl., 2 bsn., str.
1784	Vienna	449	449	piano	E flat	I, or str. quartet

DATE	PLACE	NUMBER		SOLO INSTRU- MENT	KEY	ORCHESTRA
		Old Koechel	*Revised Koechel*			
1784	Vienna	450	450	piano	B flat	III (1 fl.)
1784	Vienna	451	451	piano	D	IV
1784	Vienna	453	453	piano	G	I♭ (1 fl. added)
1784	Vienna	456	456	piano	B flat	I♭ (1 fl. added)
1784	Vienna	459	459	piano	F	III (1 fl.)
1785	Vienna	466	466	piano	D minor	IV
1785	Vienna	467	467	piano	C	IV
1785	Vienna	482	482	piano	E flat	V (no ob.; 1 fl.)
1786	Vienna	488	488	piano	A	1 fl., 2 ob., 2 bsn., 2 hr., str.
1786	Vienna	491	491	piano	C minor	V
1786	Vienna	495	495	horn	E flat	I
1786	Vienna	503	503	piano	C	IV
1788	Vienna	537	537	piano	D	IV ("Coronation")
1791	Vienna	595	595	piano	B flat	III
1791	Vienna	622	622	clarinet	A	2 fl., 2 bsn., 2 hr., str.

SINGLE MOVEMENTS

DATE	PLACE	NUMBER		SOLO INSTRU- MENT	KEY	ORCHESTRA
1781	Vienna	371	371	horn	E flat	I
1781	Vienna	373	373	violin	C	I
1782	Vienna	382	382	piano	D	II (1 fl. added)
1782	Vienna	386	386	piano	A	I

of the solo part. Great freedom of form is combined with eloquence of phrasing; and although this is a three-movement work as are all of Mozart's completed concertos, it contains, embedded within the fast finale, a set of variations on a minuet. Contrasts between this dignified minuet and the restless andante, between the brilliant sections of the finale and the noble first movement—these combine with the refined expression that permeates the whole to make the "Jeune-homme" concerto one of the most original and perfect of his works in any category.

We turn now to another group of Mozart's concertos: those which include more than one soloist. Prominent in this category, and written in Paris in 1778, was a *sinfonia concertante* for flute, oboe, bassoon, and horn. In that form the work has not been found. There is, however, an arrangement made by an unknown hand for oboe, clarinet, bassoon, and horn, K. Suppl. 9 (K.297b), in E flat. That version of the work has taken its place among Mozart's most delightful and gratifying compositions. It is distinctly characteristic of the Mannheim style; it is brilliant and provides each instrument with opportunities to display its good points.

An earlier multiple concerto, the *Concertone* for two solo violins and small orchestra, K.190 (166b) in C major, written in Salzburg five years earlier, had shown the direction Mozart would take in these concerted compositions. And another similar one, for flute and harp, K.299 (297c), also in C major, followed directly upon the concerto for wind quartet. These two C-major works differ widely from the wind concerto, however. The latter was written for outstanding virtuosi, and makes musical and technical demands even upon them; the former works remain largely in the *galant*, ingratiating style, and make small demands even upon those who listen to them.

One work in a different category may be mentioned here, for it was written within a year of the two Paris concertos and its content places it somewhere between the two: the concerto for two pianos, K.365 (316a), in E flat. Mozart's only work in this form, it was written for the joint concerts which he gave with his sister, the "Nannerl" who had shared in the triumphs of his early journeys. Although the concerto is brilliant, and its solo parts compete boisterously with the accompanying orchestra, it contains deeper moments also. But it cannot match another *sinfonia concertante* that was written a few months later and that marks Mozart's last excursion in the field of the multiple concerto.

That composition, K.364 (320d), is for violin and viola solos and was written in Salzburg in 1779. Here Mozart reached the peak of his writing for instruments other than the piano; and he came perilously close to overstepping the limits he had set for himself. For he had taken pains to distinguish between symphonic and *concertante* styles; solo passages had little place in the one and dominated in the other. In this case, the rich detail of the orchestral writing almost transforms the work into a symphony with *concertante* elements. Wind passages that are eloquent, brooding, and gay in turn; cantabile melodies in the strings which match in beauty and interest the phrases given to the two soloists; the quality of the whole accompaniment and its close relationship to the solos—such elements raise the E-flat *sinfonia concertante* to a high place among Mozart's orchestral works of whatever category.

However significant Mozart's activity in the composition of concertos during the symphony-free period of 1774–1778 may seem, it was by no means the only field in which he composed. Another important group of orchestral works is at hand in the divertimentos and serenades of these years. Mozart had written many divertimentos before 1774, both for orchestra and for smaller combinations. In the years 1774–1778 he returned to the divertimento repeatedly; almost two dozen such works for various combinations of instruments were written. Of these works, the "Haffner" serenade, K.250 (248b) is outstanding.

The Haffner family held a high position in Salzburg; the head of the family was burgomaster of the city. The immediate occasion for commissioning the serenade was Elizabeth Haffner's wedding in July, 1776; and Mozart delivered a work that amply displayed his talents. It contains no fewer than nine movements; and the march, K.249, designed to be played before and after the serenade itself, is one of its essential parts. Three minuets are included, one of them containing two contrasting trios; and virtually all the movements are considerably expanded in length. The serenade, being designed for diversion, scarcely admits of deep emotional expression; Mozart, consequently, revealed no great depth of feeling. But within the limits of permissible style, he achieved wonders in variety of mood and brilliance of effect. The *style galant* comes to life here, but in a way that gives eloquent testimony of Mozart's adroitness in making even triviality attractive. Several other divertimentos, written within a few months of the "Haffner" serenade, are brilliant and effective in their various ways, especially the *Notturno* for four orchestras,

K.286 (269a); but never again did Mozart spread his talent so lavishly in so restricted a field of expression as in the serenade for his burgomaster.

The long stay at Mannheim through the fall and winter of 1777–1778 brought Mozart in direct touch with the characteristics, performance standards, and mannerisms of the Mannheim symphonists —elements which had left their marks on virtually all parts of musical Europe. The advanced use of wind instruments in the orchestra, the virtuoso qualities exhibited by the string section, and the exploitation of the clarinet impressed him greatly. Later, at Paris, he assimilated the Mannheim influences, modified them to agree with French taste, and refined them in accord with his own requirements. Then at last he was ready to engage in the composition of a symphony; he had written none since 1774. The so-called "Paris" symphony, K.297 (300a), in D major, was written in the late spring of 1778. Written for the famous Concerts spirituels, in which all the wind instruments, including flutes and clarinets, were represented, the "Paris" requires the largest orchestra of all Mozart's symphonies.

On only one other occasion had Mozart used flutes and oboes in the same symphonic movement, namely in K.141a, an opera overture arranged as a *sinfonia;* whenever both these instruments are specified in the score (see the chart, page 81), one pair replaces the other in at least one movement. But now, for the first time throughout an entire symphony, and about fifteen years before Haydn (who used the same instrumentation in his No. 99, about 1793), Mozart wrote for the full "grand" orchestra: pairs of flutes, oboes, clarinets, bassoons, horns, trumpets, tympani, with a full string section. Only once again, in the "New Haffner" symphony, K.385, of 1782, was he to repeat that instrumentation. The many instruments are used independently; Mozart had learned much from the Mannheim virtuosos whom he had so lately heard and admired. In other respects also does the "Paris" symphony reflect Mannheim; repetition rather than development of themes, empty brilliance in the transitions, lack of deep feeling, and calculated long crescendos were all factors that entered into the design of the music. Only in the last of the three movements, with its excellent counterpoint and its striking modulations, is a measure of the true Mozart restored.

During the summer of 1779 Mozart finally returned to the path of the Viennese symphony with the symphony in B flat, K.319, in three movements and a minuet added later (perhaps in 1782). French taste and Mannheim mannerisms are gone, to be replaced by native melodiousness and charm. The orchestra is again reduced to modest dimensions: oboes, bassoons, horns, and strings. It is as though Mozart wished to purge himself of foreign influences and be himself again.

Again a year later, in August of 1780, another three-movement symphony was written: K.338, in C major, containing certain resemblances to its immediate predecessor.[4] Vigorous, forthright, and clear, it is again characterized by an absence or subordination of merely *galant* elements. The Mozart of the last years has come appreciably closer. Heroic qualities in a romantic frame, rich thematic material carefully proportioned, utmost simplicity combined with deep feeling—all are present. Technical innovations had characterized the last few symphonies; for example, the double bar marking the repeat of the exposition section had been done away with. But such innovations need concern us no longer; it is now the richness of content and mood that become important. The Classical style, built out of a variety of regional elements and types of expression, is near at hand in this C-major symphony.

Mozart's residence in Vienna began in the spring of 1781. Within a few months of that time he was freed from his archbishop's hated service and was forced to rely entirely upon himself. Probably during the following winter his ten-year-long personal association with Haydn began—and, simultaneously, his first acquaintance with the music of Johann Sebastian Bach and Handel. Having worked through all the influences that contemporary Europe had to offer, he was now faced with an influence from the past. The result was a foregone conclusion: contrapuntal writing and fugal textures play

---

[4] A minuet in C, K.409 (383f), was written to complete this symphony, Einstein believes, and should be performed in connection with it.

a more important part in his work from this point on, along with the simple, heartfelt expression he was to acquire from Haydn directly.

The first symphonic work written after Mozart's move to Vienna resulted from a request by the Haffner family at Salzburg, for whom he had written the serenade K.250 (248b). Again a work in D major appeared, K.385, and for essentially the same orchestra that the earlier "Haffner" serenade had required. Five movements including two minuets were written, and for the beginning and end Mozart wrote the march K.408 (385a). In that form, presumably, the serenade was performed in the summer of 1782. In the following spring, for one of his Vienna concerts, he cast out the march and one of the minuets; and to the first and fourth of the remaining four movements he added parts for flutes and clarinets. The resulting composition for full orchestra has become known as the "New Haffner" symphony, as distinguished from the "Haffner" serenade.

In its new form the symphony is deservedly famous. Its first movement is unique. Based on a single animated, angular, and abrupt theme, it pursues a course distinguished by far-reaching modulations and by contrapuntal textures which are filled with daring harmonic clashes. The second movement is a typical late-Mozart composition, deceptively simple in structure and content but marked by great depth of feeling artfully concealed. The finale is outstanding in its suppressed excitement and its swift flow. An added section of development near the end of the movement indicates that Mozart had adopted something of Haydn's practice: the device of adding a coda which is in effect a summarizing development of previous material.

In the fall of 1783 Mozart spent a few days in Linz on the way back to Vienna from Salzburg; there the C-major symphony, K.425, was written. One of his great works and one which gives a preview of the nobility and profundity which will characterize his last years, it is also a work that owes much to Haydn's inspiration. Three of Haydn's symphonies of about 1780–1783, namely Nos. 71, 73, and 75, begin with slow introductions; several of the earlier ones had done likewise. Mozart doubtlessly knew them; now, in the "Linz" symphony, he employed the same device for the first time—and he had written nearly forty symphonies before this.

But Mozart's slow introduction here is of a different type. Haydn had taken pains, in writing a symphonic introduction, to provide an imposing façade; the introductory adagios or graves, whenever they occur, are largely architectural features, sonorous and stately. Mozart's way in the "Linz" symphony, on the other hand, is to prepare a mood that contrasts with or enhances the following allegro. He was to use the same technique on several other occasions: in the great E-flat quintet for piano and winds, K.452; in the even greater C-major string quartet, K.465; and finally in the E-flat symphony, K.543. Elsewhere in the "Linz" symphony the spirit of Haydn is more direct, particularly in the finale, whose piquant flavor, pulsating figuration, and subtle structure are in the older composer's happiest vein. But even here, tinges of Mozartian chromaticism and anxiety remind us that the composer is not Haydn.

The "Linz" symphony is listed as No. 36 in the complete edition of Mozart's works. No. 37, in G major, K.444 (425a), begins with a similar slow introduction. But only that section is by Mozart; the rest of the symphony is by his old Salzburg friend, Michael Haydn (1737–1806), the younger brother of Franz Joseph. Evidently Mozart was pleased with the effect of beginning a symphony with an introduction; as a mark of homage he turned to a work which he had carried to Linz and supplied it with a similar introductory adagio.

Between February, 1784, and March, 1785, Mozart devoted himself chiefly to composing for the piano: besides four or five chamber-music works and a few sketches, he composed during that period three works for piano solo and no fewer than eight piano concertos. Then followed a few months given over to a variety of vocal and instrumental works; after which, between December, 1785, and December, 1786, four additional concertos were written. This round dozen of works for piano and orchestra, written during a thirty-five-month period that saw no symphonies composed, represents the peak of Mozart's concerto writing; some of his finest works in any category are included here.

The series begins with K.449, in E flat, an unusual piece that has enjoyed a place in the repertoire to the present day. Chromaticism employed to depict a restlessness of mood, refinement in the use of counterpoint, lavishness in thematic material—all presented in a simple and direct style—give this piece some of its concealed depth. It was followed quickly by a set of three which are major works in every respect, and which have only a few points in common: K.450, in B flat; K.451, in D; and K.453, in G.

The B-flat concerto is perhaps the most straightforward of the three, and the D-major concerto the most brilliant. Both require larger orchestras than any previous concertos; and in both richly varied textures and carefully worked-out orchestral details are characteristic, as they were in the "Jeunehomme" concerto of 1777. The orchestral parts are greatly enlivened; consequently, Mozart was forced to bring the solos to a higher level of effectiveness in order to retain the balance between the two opposing elements. The G-major concerto is a delicate and refined work in which external brilliance gives way to an infinite variety of tender and intimate expression. The competition between soloist and orchestra is here replaced by a cooperation between the opposing elements which sacrifices individual display for the sake of a higher unity.

Two more concertos were written in 1784, and two others early in 1785. One has become accustomed to seeing how greatly Mozart altered content and expressive idiom in works written close together; these four concertos, separated by only a few months, are perhaps the outstanding examples of his inexhaustible musical imagination.

The third of these four, K.466, in D minor, is perhaps the best-known of all Mozart's concertos. New elements make their appearance: passionate outcries, dramatic episodes, and a degree of pessimism, combined with intensified use of chromaticism, a lyric quality that is all but heartbreaking, and the most extreme use of contrasts. These are elements that were to distinguish Mozart's last works. Only at the very end of the work is a feeling of equanimity restored. The orchestra plays a different role in this concerto; no longer an equal partner, it follows a divergent path and opposes rather than complements the solo part. Within a few weeks of writing this work, in the C-major concerto, K.467, Mozart returned to the path of open, unclouded works. The C-major has none of the pathos and passion of its immediate predecessor; on the contrary, it is again a joyous and songful, even lighthearted piece. The march-like rhythms of its first movement, the soaring melodies of the andante, and the piquant chromatic harmonies of the finale combine here to create one of Mozart's happiest inspirations.

The four remaining concertos of the dozen written between the "Linz" and the "Prague" symphonies constitute a rising series and culminate in Mozart's greatest work in this species. The beginning is modest enough, for the E-flat concerto, K.482, contains melodies that are reminiscent of those written ten years earlier, and betrays what might be termed an element of fatigue. Only in its colorful writing for the orchestra's wind instruments does it reveal the mastery to which Mozart had attained. The A-major, K.488, is a prime example of those works which, apparently simple and naïve, are yet profound and highly organized. Clear textures and perfect proportions are everywhere at hand and serve to conceal a growing intensity of emotion that culminates in the bright, vivacious finale.

The rising level is continued in the C-minor concerto, K.491. Now the intensity concealed in the A-major comes to open expression; the emotional effect of this work is heightened tenfold by the richness of an accompaniment that all but dominates the solo part. The dramatic moments and the gloomy tone of the first movement are revealed in their full grandeur by contrast with the sublime slow movement, a contrast which the agitated finale does nothing to dispel. Finally, at the end of 1786, the twelfth of this great set of concertos was written—K.503, in C major. The deep passion and the anguished outbursts that had marked the two previous works are transcended. Containing something of the straightforwardness of K.450 and K.467, but marked by a more objective, almost remote attitude, the C-major concerto depicts a world which is problem-free only because the problems have been surmounted.

Only twice more was he to return to the composition of piano concertos: in 1788, when he wrote the D-major or "Coronation" concerto, and in 1791, when he produced his last work in the field, K.595, in B flat. The D-major concerto was a most happy choice for the festivities which accompanied the coronation of Leopold II in 1790, for it is brilliant and effective and makes no unusual demands upon its listeners.[5] The B-flat concerto, more intimate and sensitive than the works of 1784–1786, is appealing in quite another way. The tumult and the outcries engendered by those works have passed away, along with the gloom and passionate resentment some of them revealed. There remains only the spiritualized essence of those subjective emotions; and that essence provides the last of Mozart's piano concertos with its content.

It is noteworthy that Mozart had little to learn from Haydn in the field of the concerto. Indeed, from late 1786, in the period of Mozart's great examples of that form, the influence of the older man upon the younger was scarcely perceptible in any branch of composition. Whatever stylistic devices or formal innovations Mozart had gleaned from any source were, by the end of that year, completely assimilated. No longer may one speak of elements as having been derived from this or that school or composer. One may only recognize their origin even as one marvels at how thoroughly the details are embedded in the whole. Having been exposed to all the musical influences that his time had to offer him, Mozart emerged supreme: obligated to all, but beholden to none. Rather is the indebtedness now, as it has been since about 1783, on the other side: it is Haydn who stands in Mozart's shadow. We shall therefore return to the account of Haydn's works about 1782, to observe the manner of Mozart's influence upon the man from whom he had learned so much.

[5] The existing version of the "Coronation" concerto is merely an arrangement of Mozart's sketches that leaves much to be desired. Even his other concertos have not come down to us exactly as he played them: only a few are provided with cadenzas, and Mozart also elaborated additional ornaments during his own performances (cf. Einstein, *Mozart*, pp. 313–14).

A notable difference between Haydn and Mozart comes to light in their respective attitudes toward the concerto. We have seen that the piano concerto occupied Mozart throughout the greater part of his maturity. It was personally as necessary for him to perform as it was to compose. Haydn, on the other hand, showed little interest in the concerto either as a form or as a means for self-expression. His performing ability on the violin or the piano did not remotely approach Mozart's; he never became an outstanding performer on either instrument. Possessing no virtuoso qualities and having no incentive to write for his own use, he produced relatively few concertos—scarcely two dozen.

Three of those works have remained in the repertoire. One, for cello and orchestra, is in D major and was written in 1783; the D-major piano concerto is dated about 1784; and a *sinfonia concertante* for violin, oboe, cello, and bassoon plus full orchestra was written about 1792, at the time of the first London trip. The cello concerto, one of the monuments of that instrument's restricted repertoire, is a brilliant work without being a display piece. Its ingratiating melodies and its idiomatic figurations exploit the full range of the cello's expressive possibilities; its slow movement gives us Haydn at his lyric best.[6] The piano concerto is effective, brilliant, and thoughtful; but this is faint praise. In spite of its forceful, impassioned slow movement and its final *Rondo alla ongarese*, it remains one of Haydn's better occasional pieces and cannot compare with Mozart's late concertos. Similarly, the *concertante* of 1792; in his attempt to combine symphonic development techniques with the requirements of instrumental idioms, Haydn succeeded only in writing an interesting piece in a rather uninteresting style. Individual differences between instruments seldom come to expression, and a degree of monotony is inevitable. Only in the symphonies of the late years is Haydn's real stature to be measured.

[6] The popular supposition that this work is not authentic rests upon incomplete knowledge of the facts. No less reliable an authority than Koechel saw the manuscript (since lost) with its date of 1783; and the concerto is listed in Haydn's own thematic catalogue. See Geiringer, *Haydn*, p. 258.

In the years between 1782 and about 1786 he composed fourteen symphonies, Nos. 74 to 87. These works give further evidence of a characteristic that had marked Haydn's slow growth to artistic maturity: as that maturity approached he substituted quality for quantity. The symphonies of this period are longer and become individual works of art rather than representatives of a group style-tendency. Most importantly, they embody a radically new technique of composition.

When, in 1782, Haydn published six quartets, Opus 33, he proudly announced them as having been "written in an entirely new manner." The almost ten-year pause in his quartet writing between Opus 20 and Opus 33 had borne fruit: he had composed these quartets under the full influence of the principle of thematic development; that principle is perhaps his greatest technical contribution to music. The dilemma between homophonic and polyphonic textures, resolved once before by Bach in the early eighteenth century, was now resolved again by Haydn near the century's end—and in an entirely different way. The "new manner" required the use of a new type of thematic material, a type which had gradually emerged in the symphonies of the 1770s.

The vast bulk of Haydn's music before the mid-1770s is melodically unified to a considerable extent. Its themes are usually based either upon tones of the common chord, upon consecutive scale steps, or upon combinations of these. Such a theme has much in common with other themes constructed similarly; one broken-chord melody sounds much like another, for example. As a consequence, great variety of expression in any two stylistically similar movements was not always apparent. Indeed, one of the outstanding characteristics (even flaws) of large numbers of mid-eighteenth-century compositions is their sameness. Thematic materials being conventionally prescribed by *galant* or *Empfindsamkeit* taste standards, and manipulation of those materials following definite patterns of repetition, modulation, and imitation, the sameness could scarcely be avoided.

One may well believe that Haydn had grown weary of that sameness of expression after more than twenty years. The constant search for new effects and the constant transformation of forms that are evident in his writing—no matter how little change actually resulted —give eloquent testimony of his desire to find newer or deeper means of expression.

About 1782, with the "new manner," he formulated another principle of melodic construction. The chord patterns and scale lines were subordinated to a variety of distinctive intervals and a more diverse rhythmic scheme. The intervals and mixed rhythmic patterns were more loosely held together, and in fact constituted many short motives. Themes such as those quoted (see Example 15) are seen to contain a number of separate melodic factors, each

EXAMPLE 15   HAYDN, Symphony No. 78

of which is distinctive enough to be remembered, to be manipulated, and to be transformed. In the manipulation and transformation of such melodic factors, or motives, into yet other melodic fragments, under the influence of contrapuntal techniques—there lies the crux of Haydn's new principle. He discovered a way of combining polyphonic textures and homophonic melodies—that is, melodies which are entities in themselves and require no contrapuntal associates to complete their significance.

There are some who hear only the open, ingenious tone of Haydn's themes, and think of him as being like his themes. In so doing they give evidence of having overlooked completely the relationship between the theme and its subsequent treatment. The pretentious or portentous is not suited to his method; nor is, at least in sonata-form movements, the lovely lyric melody. Neither is boundless inspiration, which can create new melodies at a moment's notice, of great use to him; in this respect Beethoven was like Haydn. The latter requires a theme of striking contour or rhythm, a theme made up of elements each of which has musical character. The great art of Haydn lies in his manner of manipulating those elements and, out of their recombination, constructing significant transitions and developments. Kretzschmar compares Haydn's method to that of a great poet who creates a universally appealing tragedy or comedy out of the most common—and hence most universal—materials; in such a poet, the content of the poetic theme is less important than the use made of it.[7]

It is this new principle of thematic development that separates Haydn's post-1782 instrumental works from those which lie before that date. From the standpoint of texture and content, of balance and proportion as applied to all the elements of composition, the years about 1782 mark the beginning of the Classical period. And although Haydn was now in possession of a new technique of composition and was the bearer of a new style—which he did not as yet share with anyone—the influence of Mozart upon him grew stronger.

The Mozart influence is not always tangible. It is revealed first in an enhanced lyric quality. The fourteen Haydn symphonies of the period 1782–1786 show a broader contrast between the dynamic first theme and the lyric, cantabile second; this is seen in the symphonies Nos. 74, 80, and 81. Slow movements take on a nobler, more song-like content as they approach Mozart, lose some of their good nature, and become more thoughtful. The wind instruments play a greater part in thematic manipulation, with a consequent beneficial effect upon the color and the texture of the music.

The last six symphonies of the period under discussion were written in response to an invitation Haydn had received from a musical

[7] *Führer durch den Concertsaal*, I, 55.

society in Paris in 1784, namely the Concerts de la Loge Olympique; these are the so-called "Paris" symphonies, Nos. 82 to 87. The set contains great variety in emotional content, and ranges from the light and almost superficial No. 87 to the rather heavy and somber No. 83.⁸ The new development principle, which had gradually become less tentative in Nos. 74 to 81 and had begun to supersede sequence repetitions, imitations, and the like, now was employed confidently and consistently. No. 82, nicknamed "The Bear" because of its drone-basses in the finale, contains extensive thematic developments even in its first movement's transitional passages. Likewise, the first allegro of No. 84 is based almost entirely upon developments of a single theme.

The "Paris" symphonies bring to the fore a characteristic that had played a small part only in Haydn's earlier music. One may leaf through hundreds of pages of his symphonies before about 1784 and scarcely ever find a melodic fragment based on the chromatic scale. Haydn's melodies up to that point were consistently diatonic in all but a few instances. But from about No. 82, of 1786, the chromatic melody-fragment became an important factor in deepening the melodic aspects of the music. Passages such as those in Example 16 contribute an air of poignancy and provide a degree of concentrated emotion that Haydn had seldom revealed. Nos. 85 and 92 are full of similar passages; and the main theme of No. 91 is formed largely out of the chromatic scale.

Now, Haydn's acquaintance with Mozart had begun about 1782; in 1785 the latter completed a set of six quartets which he dedicated to the older man. And chromatic lines of the kind depicted above play an important part in those quartets, as they had done in many of Mozart's earlier works, and as they were to do to the end of his life. As early as K.43 Mozart had employed short chromatic fragments; in K.297, in the finale of K.385, in the "Linz" symphony's

<hr>

⁸ According to Geiringer, *Haydn*, p. 199, those two symphonies are numbered incorrectly in the complete edition; they were the first two of the Paris set to be written, hence should be inserted between Nos. 81 and 82. Geiringer suggests No. 81a for 83, and No. 81b for 87.

last movement, in the serenade K.320, and in countless larger or smaller works such fragments contribute a poignant, resigned mood.

EXAMPLE 16

The mournful air so characteristic of late Mozart is caused in no small measure by the chromatic lines. Earlier composers, such as Purcell in *Dido and Aeneas* and Bach in the B-minor Mass, had turned to chromatic lines to depict intensities of emotion not easily achieved through the diatonic scale; some of their most pathetic utterances are set amid chromatic melodies. Mozart's intensity was not linked only to pathos, however; he arrived at a concentration of emotion in allegros and even in minuets, and supplied such movements with a drive and a significance that diatonic melodies alone could not have provided.

That particular aspect of Mozart's style had not found a place in Haydn's music. But virtually from his first encounter with Mozart, Haydn realized its importance. The series of symphonies mentioned above and the string quartets of the period 1785–1790 reveal how earnestly he applied the device to his own music. Haydn's nature was not as intense or pensive as Mozart's, however; such concentration and moodiness as the chromatic fragments carried with them were foreign to his direct, open-hearted style. When, therefore, Haydn traveled to London late in 1790 and was removed from direct personal contact with Mozart, he reverted gradually to his innate style. Chromatic lines become much less evident in the symphonies of 1791–1793; No. 94 still contains a passage or two with chromatic idioms. And in the last set of symphonies, from 1793 to 1795 (Nos. 99 to 104), they are missing almost completely.

To return to the "Paris" symphonies: "The Bear" is not alone among them in carrying a nickname; No. 83 is "The Cock," and No. 85 "The Queen." These and many other nicknames call attention to a sense for program music that existed during the late eighteenth century. Kretzschmar points out that the poetic "naming" of instrumental compositions extends well back into the seventeenth century.[9] Biblical sonatas; *sinfonie* written to describe the nine muses, or the twelve months, or characters in literature and legend —these and similar manifestations of the program-music instinct were still current in Haydn's day. Haydn himself, with his three program symphonies, Nos. 6, 7, and 8, had contributed to this literature. It is Kretzschmar's point that the public, especially the French portion of it, leaned toward program or poetic content in instrumental works. Hence the nicknames in addition to those mentioned: No. 22, "The Philosopher"; No. 43, "Mercury"; No. 44, "Mourning"; No. 55, "The Schoolmaster," and many more. In other cases

[9] *Führer durch den Concertsaal*, I, 58.

a technical detail was singled out and unduly emphasized: No. 31, "The Horn Signal"; No. 94, "The Surprise"; No. 101, "The Clock"; No. 103, "The Drum Roll," and again many more.

It is revealing that only one of Mozart's symphonies bears a nickname that even remotely touches upon its content: the "Jupiter." A few others, true, are tagged with names or place names: thus the "Paris," the "New Haffner," the "Linz," and the "Prague." But Mozart's work seems never to have touched the familiar chord in peoples' hearts; whether it be aristocratic dignity or profound appeal that keeps listeners at a slight distance, so to say, the fact remains that the music of Mozart has not acquired the easy acceptance that goes with nicknames. One may say that Haydn was one with his listeners, and wrote to them and for them directly. Mozart, on the other hand, stood aloof; and although his music is for all the world's people, he did not personally identify himself with them.

The "Prague" symphony mentioned above was written in December, 1786, in Vienna, probably with Mozart's forthcoming trip to Prague in mind; it is K.504, in D major. Again a slow introduction is provided, but the customary third-movement minuet is not. This is pure Mozart; Haydn casts not the slightest shadow over the work. None but a Mozart could have composed the introductory adagio, stately and formal without being pompous; its solemnity and scope point toward the nineteenth century. Only Mozart could have combined nervous excitement with audacity and restraint, only he could have concealed rich contrapuntal writing in so open a texture, as he did in the first movement. The andante's pathetic strain, which grows out of his employment of chromatic phrases and cantabile expression, owes nothing to anyone. Here is the real Mozart again; the "Prague" is one of his great monuments. As if these two movements were not enough, he provides a finale whose mixture of joy and pathos prepares one for the pathetic tone of the works of 1788.

The three great symphonies, and Mozart's last, K.543, K.550, and K.551, were written in the summer of 1788. Dated respectively

June 26, July 25, and August 10, they would appear to have been written in the space of about two months. But a number of other works are also dated in or about that period. The masterful E-major piano trio is dated June 22; the well-known C-major piano sonata and two smaller chamber-music works, presumably written only a short time before, all bear the date June 26. A sonatina for violin and piano, the C-major piano trio, and a canzonetta lie between July 10 and July 16. Thus not three, but ten works, half of them among Mozart's greatest, were composed within two or three months of each other.

The first of the three symphonies, in E flat, begins, like the "Linz" and the "Prague," with a slow introduction that is broad and solemn; it provides a striking contrast to the romantic, melodious first allegro. The andante, in the romantic key of A flat and with a stirring if brief middle section in F minor, is in general filled with calm and repose. The minuet, universally known and serving almost as a popular model of Mozart's style, is dignified and affable in turn. The finale is an economically written movement: one figure serves as both first and second themes with but slight modification. But the modulatory freedom of the movement is enormous. One senses Mozart's wish to overcome the blandness of the basic key of E flat before leaving it for the last time. In fact, rich harmonies and bold modulations characterize the entire symphony.

This symphony includes clarinets but omits oboes. This fact is explained by the nature of the clarinet's entry into the orchestra. Although the instrument was developed early in the eighteenth century, it found slow acceptance. For several decades it was employed occasionally in the church and the theater. Not until the 1770s, and then only in such larger orchestras as those of Mannheim, Milan, and Paris, did the clarinet find regular employment. Oboists seem to have been among the first to play the instrument; opera and symphony scores of the time sometimes called for "oboes or clarinets" or "clarinets ad libitum." London had apparently seen clarinets earlier; in 1764 Mozart had copied out the symphony by Abel (long attributed to Mozart as his third symphony, K.18) for a small orchestra which included two clarinets. From 1778 to his death in 1791 he employed the clarinet in only four of the ten symphonies he wrote in that interval, and in two of those cases they were added subsequently (see the chart on page 82). Haydn came to the clarinet even later; for only from 1793, in his symphony No. 99 and thereafter, did the instrument find a relatively permanent place in his orchestra.

With bassoons specified after about 1780, with flutes becoming more frequent about 1772 and required after 1780, with clarinets legitimized about 1788, and with trumpets and tympani occurring regularly after about 1790, the so-called "Classical orchestra" is a late entrant into the eighteenth century. Scarcely half a dozen symphonies by the two great masters of the period require the orchestra which is popularly supposed to be standard equipment for playing their works. This slow evolution of the orchestra is paralleled by the equally slow evolution of the concept of orchestration. The emergence of individual wind instruments from the mass of the wind tutti, which is perhaps the principal element in that concept, is to a large extent the contribution of Mozart's last years.

The great G-minor symphony, K.550, unlike its predecessor, originally contained parts for oboes but not for clarinets; the latter were added at a later time by Mozart, at which time the oboes parts were modified. The first movement opens directly, without an introduction; an apprehensive, nervous mood is felt from the start. Restless and with an undercurrent of pessimism, the entire movement is concentrated. The second movement, an expressive piece, contrasts greatly with the first; but even its lyric tone is colored by chromatically twisted, grief-laden passages. The minuet, with its square and solid rhythms, conceals a strongly-felt passion which is resolved by the quiet, transparent trio. The finale discloses the full extent of Mozart's fury and anguish. Wild, almost brutal at times, and relentless in its driving pace, it runs without relief. Throughout the symphony, chromatic elements and polyphonic textures are prominent; they bring about moods of unrest, poignant feeling, and veiled passion. Distant harmonies contribute to the dark colors and the general melancholy air that pervade the G-minor symphony.

The C-major, nicknamed the "Jupiter" symphony by an unknown admirer, represents in many ways the culmination of Mozart's symphonic writing. True, the orchestra employed here is smaller than it had been in the E-flat, in the "Paris," and in the "New Haffner" symphonies; and the dark moods that he seldom shook off in his last years are largely missing. But in general content, in quality of workmanship, in attention to detail and proportion, and in emotional significance, the "Jupiter" symphony is unsurpassed. Here Mozart fully overcomes the dualism between *galant* expression and thoughtful, serious polyphony. The finale, with its fugal episodes in the midst of a sonata-form movement, is perhaps Mozart's greatest technical achievement. Yet it runs its course effortlessly, with a divine abandon that makes light of the most intricate chordal combinations. If ever Mozart illustrated the "art that conceals art," it is here.

A unique blend of formality and personal expression pervades the "Jupiter" symphony. The series of stereotyped rhythmic figures that animate large sections of the various movements might, in an earlier period, have resulted in another Italian *buffo* work; here, combined as they are with the most meaningful and attractive melodic bits, they bring an air of freshness into the symphony that even Mozart had not always achieved. In the "Jupiter" he has come to terms with himself and the world. Neither resigned nor pessimistic, neither hysterical nor morbid, the "Jupiter" is the perfect work of art. It marks a fitting close to Mozart's career as a composer of symphonies.

In the years after 1786, Haydn too revealed himself as one of the eternal masters. The influence of Mozart upon him worked as beneficially in those years as its opposite had worked upon the younger composer in the previous decade. Haydn's symphonies of 1786–1788 (Nos. 88 to 92), reveal how he profited from the mutual friendship.

We may be sure that he knew Mozart's "Linz" symphony of 1783 and had become acquainted with the newly composed "Prague" symphony of 1786; in those works Mozart had introduced the new content in the preparatory adagios. We may gather how greatly Haydn was impressed by that achievement from the fact that from this time (1786) he virtually abandoned the façade-type of introduction and adopted the contrasting-mood type of Mozart's. With only one or two exceptions, the seventeen symphonies which Haydn was yet to write begin with introductions akin to the type that Mozart had employed in the "Linz" symphony. Here is a beautiful revelation of the reciprocal relationship that existed between the two composers. Mozart had learned from Haydn that a symphonic introduction could be impressive; but the content of that section was modified to reflect his own musical needs. Haydn, in turn, realized fully that it had now become significant as well as impressive; subsequently he adopted the new content.

In the symphony No. 88, his approach is still tentative; the impressive chords are there, but the pompousness has been taken from them. The same holds for No. 90, whose introduction is short and somewhat architectural. But in No. 91, and even more in No. 92, the full influence of Mozart is felt. Tender and yearning melodies, veiled harmonies, and a mood that contrasts widely with what is to come—these characterize the new type. Haydn has learned well from the examples offered by Mozart; the symphonies of the London years will reveal how consistently he applied the lesson.

In other respects, the symphonies of this group are uneven in quality. The first and last of the five have enjoyed a place in the repertoire to the present day. No. 88 reveals how far Haydn had traveled toward providing contrast within unity; one motive serves a variety of purposes: as an accompaniment to the first theme, as transitional material leading toward the second, and as an important idea in the development. Nos. 89 to 91 are not among Haydn's masterpieces, even though his imagination in matters of musical form had never been keener, and his use of chromatic fragments never more subtle. No. 92, on the other hand, is one of the great

works of Haydn's maturity. Its nickname, the "Oxford" symphony, rests upon the fact that it was performed upon the occasion
of Haydn's receiving the doctor's degree at Oxford University.

The qualities that set the "Oxford" apart, qualities which it shares
with the twelve "London" symphonies of 1791–1795, contradict
the general understanding of the term "Classical sonata-form." Several decades of development by scores of composers had contributed,
toward the late 1770s, to a rather standardized formal pattern: two
contrasting theme-groups were presented in the exposition, were
manipulated in the development, and were repeated with appropriate modulations in the recapitulation. Minor composers had adhered to this plan somewhat rigidly, for example, Dittersdorf, Van-
hall, Gossec, Boccherini, and many others; so rigidly, in fact, that
the form became dominant over the content. The form became so
obvious that it even entered into the purview of textbook writers
in later generations, and was considered a thing in itself. It is this
adherence to the *form* of the Classical sonata that eventually brought
the Classical style into disrepute in the nineteenth century.

The masters of that style, however (and here one can refer only
to Mozart and Haydn), were not so narrow. They treated the
sonata as a living, flowing organism. They adhered to the essential
elements of thematic manipulation, harmonic contrasts, and symmetrical and proportioned forms—and beyond that, exercised the
greatest possible freedom. We have seen how often Haydn, in his
symphonies of 1770–1790, paid little attention to thematic contrasts; often a second theme is rudimentary or derived from the
first. We can examine dozens of Mozart's works and find new lyric
themes in place of development sections. But harmonic contrasts
and beautiful proportions are always present; conflict between tonic
and dominant theme groups was the important element in the
sonata-form movements of these composers.

Similar freedom prevails in their employment of the development
principle. The masters by no means confined their developments
to the middle section of the form. In Haydn, the development often
begins after the first phrases of the theme have been announced; that

procedure is followed in the very works that introduced the "new manner" in 1782. Transitions between theme groups are often developments of what has gone before. And in large codas, which became increasingly significant after the 1780s, development is continued; the coda in Haydn becomes in effect a second large development section.

In their view of symmetry, too, the masters interpreted broadly. The symmetry in sonata-form movements occurs, of course, in that the theme groups heard in the exposition are repeated in the recapitulation; but whereas the harmonies of the exposition had been contrasting (usually on tonic and dominant), they were alike (tonic and tonic) in the recapitulation. The return of the second theme on the tonic in the latter section carried a problem with it; adherence to the parallel musical effect in the exposition required that the theme sound as though it were again on the dominant (so that, in the recapitulation, the contrast between tonic and dominant could be implied). The problem was a fascinating one, especially for Mozart. Seldom can the course of the recapitulation be predicted in his works; the most amazing variety of devices is employed by him to give the *effect* of contrasting harmonies. It is in this respect, finally, that the Haydn of the "London" symphonies profited so greatly by Mozart's example.

The determining factor in the sonata-form of the works after about 1782 is the balance between form and content. Whereas the minor composers of the day adhered rather rigidly to the external framework and forced their thematic material into that preconceived form, and whereas later (Romantic) composers were often to give thematic material free scope without regard to formal considerations, the great masters provided a perfect balance between the two. That is the essence of Classicism. In this sense the three last symphonies of Mozart achieve their Classical perfection; and in this sense Haydn's "Oxford" symphony of 1788 is a fitting prelude to the twelve great "London" symphonies.

Nicholas Esterházy died in 1790. His heir, another Paul Anton, had little interest in music and immediately disbanded the orchestra over which Haydn had presided for twenty-nine years. Haydn, with a handsome pension, returned to Vienna. Almost at once he accepted the invitation of Johann Salomon (1745–1815), an enterprising violinist and concert manager, to go to London. He was to compose an opera, six symphonies, and a number of other works; the fee promised him was considerable. Late in 1790, at the age of fifty-eight, Haydn set out on the most extensive trip of his lifetime. The visit was successful in every respect, and lasted almost two years. In 1794 he returned to London for a second time, and remained some eighteen months with similar success. The so-called "London" or "Salomon" symphonies, twelve in number, were written for those visits: Nos. 93 to 98 for the first trip, 1791–1793; No. 99 in the interval between the trips; and Nos. 100 to 104 in 1794 and 1795.

These are the works upon which Haydn's fame rests largely today. Several of them have become universally familiar under their various nicknames (see the chart on pp. 70–72); and their qualities are such that they have completely overshadowed all but a few of the ninety-two symphonies Haydn wrote before 1791. They, with half a dozen of Mozart's, stand as virtually the only surviving representatives of the Classical period's symphonic efforts before Beethoven. And they reveal a composer whose skill, imagination, and artistry were at their highest point. Increasing age had not adversely affected the quality of Haydn's writing nor had long service to the art of composition dulled his versatility, energy, or humor.

Scarcely a work of Haydn's has been without its delicious manifestation of his effervescent spirit and his quick-wittedness. Now such elements come to the fore and increasingly animate the fast movements and often the minuets. Unexpected thematic entrances, false recapitulations, pauses, sudden chords, and the like are among the more obvious of Haydn's humorous effects. But he also reveals subtle touches that are sometimes lost in the sheer joy of hearing the music. Irregular phrases and abrupt modulations, sly bits of imitation and irrelevant turns of phrase, brief moments of apparent confusion and sudden mock-serious passages—such devices call forth

many an appreciative chuckle. The "London" symphonies are particularly rich in humor, and repay the most attentive listening.

Nowhere else in his symphonies did Haydn reveal greater freedom and mastery of form problems. New combinations of phrases
emerge in unending stream; everything is alive, flowing, and captivating. Formal effects which he had embraced tentatively in earlier
years are now employed with self-confidence. Rondo and sonata-
form are combined, as in the finale of No. 93 and the andante of No.
101; episodes in the rondos are often full developments. Masterful
use is made, in the set of variations of No. 103, of a double theme
whose parts are respectively in minor and major. On several occasions Haydn looks toward the nineteenth century by concerning
himself more with developments of the second theme than of the
first, as in Nos. 99 and 102; this had seldom happened in earlier
works. The slow introductions—and all but No. 95 begin with an
adagio or a largo—take on new dimensions and embrace a greater
emotional range. Mysterious tonal realms are explored as daring
modulations increase the scope of these slow sections. And the free
forms always carry perfect proportion with them.

No marshalling of the facts about Haydn's and Mozart's music
can hope to give any sense of its emotional variety, its technical
perfection, its purity, or its charm. One cannot recapture verbally
the essence of what Haydn and Mozart accomplished; one can but
show relationships, or at the most reveal historical connections. The
music lives and speaks its own message. That message is as vital today as it was when it came from the minds and hearts of its composers.

V

LUDWIG VAN BEETHOVEN

O NE OF THE MOST noteworthy social facts about the early 1800s
is the gradual change in the individual's position toward his society.
Through much of the eighteenth century he had been bound by
tradition, by religious and civil authority, and by class. His lifework
was marked out for him, almost preordained, in fact; and the freedom with which he could move within that lifework was strongly
circumscribed. The musician in that society existed only through the
grace of a patron; he was supported by and beholden to his patron
almost entirely. Haydn provides a perfect example; for throughout
his nearly thirty years of service to the Esterházys, he was in effect
a high-class servant, and his mode of life would have been unthinkable
outside that service.

During the course of the century social attitudes changed. Writ-
ings of the philosophers of rationalism, the works of Rousseau and
Voltaire, the American and French revolutions, the emergence of
the democracies—these had all been steps on the path toward eman-
cipating the individual. And while Haydn was content to remain
within the framework of the old system, Mozart struggled against
it even while he vainly sought its advantages. Mozart's life, as opposed to Haydn's, is an equally good example of an individual caught
in a transitional period: content to accept the security offered by the
system, but too independent to conform to its requirements.

It remained for Ludwig van Beethoven (1770–1827) successfully
to complete the struggle against patronage. True, he did have patrons occasionally; but he scorned them even as he made use of

them. He was subservient only to his art, and he cleared his own path
—perhaps the first important musician (Handel excepted) to do so.
Beethoven became a symbol of the nineteenth century's free individual.

As a principal feature of the old system, works were commissioned or written for specific occasions. Haydn and Mozart were
men of their own time, wrote for their contemporaries, and considered carefully the technical levels of those to whom the works
were addressed. Only rarely did they exceed those levels.

Now, Beethoven too accepted commissions and wrote to order;
but in him a new attitude is apparent. For the content and technical
quality as well as the musical stature of many of the commissioned
works far transcend the occasion. And in works which were not
occasional pieces or commissioned—of which types, incidentally
earlier composers knew little—the new attitude is still more marked.
In them, Beethoven wrote not for his public but according to the
dictates of his musical spirit. His imagination and his sense of fitness
determined the shape and content of his music. He rarely attempted
to be merely entertaining or to meet the social and cultural needs
of his contemporaries; he forced his public to rise to the new world
he created—or revealed. The enormous increase in the technical
difficulty, the sheer size, and the power of his works is but external
evidence of this heightened purpose. It is with the emotional content, the *kinds* of emotions affected, that Beethoven brought a new
impulse to music. A composition deserved to be written—even
more, had to be written—simply because Beethoven willed it so;
whether a practical possibility existed of having it performed or
understood immediately interested him not at all.

The orchestral works of Beethoven were composed within the
period extending from 1794 or 1795, when he had been in Vienna
a few years, to 1823, four years before his death. They include
symphonies, concertos, overtures, and a few lesser works. In discussing the works of Haydn and Mozart, it was possible to proceed
more or less in chronological order. With Beethoven, easy chronology does not exist; for there is little exact relationship between time

of writing, opus number, and date of publication. It was Beethoven's habit to work at themes for months or years before setting a work on paper—the many sketchbooks give evidence. Often several compositions were worked on simultaneously, were subject to drastic revision, and were published (with higher opus numbers than their place warranted) years after later works had been introduced to the public. Thus, any account which is based on the apparent chronology of Beethoven's works must at best be approximate. In the following pages a combination of chronological and groupwise discussion will be attempted, the better to disclose relationships between works of the same category.

Among Beethoven's first orchestral compositions are two piano concertos: Opus 19, in B flat, written about 1794–1795; and Opus 15, in C major, about 1797–1798. The B-flat concerto is a graceful work; ornamental figurations fill out the melodic line of the solo part, purely symphonic factors are kept to a minimum, and a delightful play between solo and orchestra results. But Beethoven's dissatisfaction with this early work (written about the time of his Opus 1) may be seen in that the solo part was considerably revised about 1800, a year before its publication. Even in its present form the work gives little promise of what Beethoven was later to achieve.

The C-major concerto, on the other hand, is a larger work in all ways. The influence of Mozart is to be seen in many details; but in most respects the work is purely Beethoven's. It is significant that the solo instrument nowhere concerns itself with the orchestra's first theme (except in the three separate cadenzas which Beethoven wrote for the first movement), but introduces thematic fragments of its own. Further, the second theme, which is in E flat in the orchestral tutti, appears in G major in the piano part. This, in turn, prepares for and justifies a large section in the middle of the movement, where the solo instrument presents a dreamy and magical development of that theme—now in E flat.

The slow movement is a romantic and charming piece in A-flat major; the final rondo is brilliant throughout. In all three movements, considerable symphonic development of themes and theme fragments takes place. What Beethoven is later to accomplish in the direction of a real symphonic partnership between piano and orchestra is revealed here in miniature. The C-major concerto is one of the important works of his first period; it was published in 1801 (earlier than the B-flat concerto, which is known today as No. 2).

About a year before that date Beethoven wrote a third concerto. Publication of this work, in C minor, was delayed until 1804, however; then it was called Opus 37. The short time-interval between the C-major and the C-minor concertos scarcely prepares one for the great differences between them. For the latter presents the impassioned, impulsive Beethoven to a far greater degree than does any other work of the time. The first movement is fiery and dark, with relentless drive, forceful accents, and sharp contrasts of mood. Development of thematic fragments here reaches symphonic proportions. The solo part, in spite of its brilliance, provides essentially a rich background upon which the striking themes are developed.

Beethoven's choice of E major for the slow movement gives strong evidence of his interest in expanding key relationships. Even in his first years in Vienna (from 1792) his use of mediant and submediant keys (E flat and A flat in a C-minor context) had been demonstrated with skill and subtlety. Now the use of the major mediant in a minor context illustrates an expansion of that interest; and in this case, with profound effect. The contrast of mood which the E-major tonality brings with it is in itself noteworthy; but even more significant is the way in which this remote key returns in the finale. For there, in a brief passage, the apparently wide gap between the keys is closed, a modulation of striking beauty is achieved, and the basic key of C minor is seen in a new light. Elsewhere in the finale, the pungent themes and driving rhythms carry the movement forward to great climaxes.

Sketches for Beethoven's first symphony, in C major, date from about 1794, but the work was not completed until about 1800. The spirit of Haydn had inspired it; be it out of veneration or the desire to imitate that spirit, it was stylistically not as advanced as works written years earlier. Not until the "Eroica" symphony and the quartets of Opus 59 was Beethoven to give his ensemble works the type of expression that his piano sonatas had contained since about 1797. The symphony was published in 1801 as Opus 21.

The first movement is preceded by a slow introduction; and although the latter resembles introductions by Haydn and Mozart, it has a different function, for it is no more than a greatly enlarged perfect cadence which leads toward the C major of the first allegro. A firm sense of tonality and an amazingly fertile imagination which is directed toward making his harmonic intentions clear—these characterized Beethoven's entire creative career. Here is one early bit of evidence of this regard for establishing a key without ambiguity. Along with harmonic clarity, however, is a strong feeling for harmonic boldness. The first movement, alive and humorous, contains many daring touches. For example, the development begins suddenly on a fortissimo in A major, and touches D, G, and C minor in its first few measures; later sections are in B flat, E flat, and A minor. Beethoven's harmonic palette is immediately seen to be richer than his predecessors' and contemporaries'.

His ability to derive new melodies from isolated thematic fragments taken out of context is strikingly revealed in the slow movement. There Beethoven employs melodic scraps or motives as source material for his development sections and derives an *ostinato* figure from a rhythmic pattern first heard in the main theme of the movement.

The scherzo in Beethoven's symphonies is a new form. This is no longer the fast, transformed minuet which Haydn had introduced in his quartets of Opus 33 (1782) but a large, powerful, often humorous, sometimes profound movement which has only its triple meter and its three-part form in common with the minuet. The scherzo in the first symphony, which Beethoven still calls "Menuetto," foreshadows those later developments. Fast tempo, driving rhythms, sudden contrasts of mood and texture, and sections in which thematic fragments are briefly developed—these constitute the first part. The trio provides great contrast, and presents a series of repeated chords over a running figure in the violins. The effect is enchanting, and the movement is all too short.

The finale begins with a slow introduction which has a twofold purpose: to provide the theme of the allegro with a springboard from which to take off; and to introduce a mock-serious moment which enhances the humor of that allegro. The latter is in sonata-form, with a lilting set of themes that are well proportioned and skillfully manipulated.

The C-major symphony, on the whole, sparkles and is full of fun. There are no problems here, and Beethoven is completely the master of his material. As a technical accomplishment it ranks high among his early works. But it has negative qualities also. Beethoven departed here from the refined expression Haydn and Mozart had brought to perfection; in its place comes a rough vigor which is no longer in the spirit of aristocratic grace. This new spirit clashes to some extent with the form he had inherited from the Classical giants. He took great pains to establish cadences somewhat formally and to provide musical breathing places. The result, in certain passages, is a motion which can be described only by the term "jerky." The long line which will characterize his works after the "Eroica" is not yet present.

Brief mention may be made here of the so-called "Jena" symphony. Discovered at Jena in 1909, it is alleged to be an authentic work because one or two of the parts are inscribed: "par Louis van Beethoven." It reveals stylistic elements which would place it well before 1800—if indeed Beethoven was its composer.

One has but to read the "Heiligenstadt Will" of 1802, in which Beethoven bemoans his deafness, hints at suicide, and discloses himself as the unhappiest of men, to realize how great a gap exists between his personal life and his music. In the midst of the first anguished realization that his deafness was incurable, Beethoven composed his second symphony, in D major, published in 1804 as Opus 36. Powerful, limpid, boisterous, and probably the largest symphony written up to that time, it gives no hint of the morbidity and melancholy which encompassed him.

Its slow introduction inclines toward the late style of Haydn in its melodiousness and modified architectural character. Only in its last few measures does the introduction reveal its true purpose: to enhance the lyric breadth of the first movement proper and to provide contrasts which allow the long lines of that movement to be perceived fully. For the allegro is a massive movement. Each of its three themes contains two parts; and transitions are almost thematic in style. The short development is offset by a large coda which, in effect, completes the manipulation of the themes. Rhythmic vitality and a certain formal air are characteristic, and the movement contains little of the humor that the first symphony had revealed.

Some thirteen minutes of lyric beauty, slowly unfolding with stately grace, are contained within the larghetto. Refined themes as well as vigorous ones contribute to a feeling of spaciousness. Beethoven's ability to sustain a single mood across a long time interval is shown here for virtually the first time. The scherzo is brief and contains little more than a number of incisive rhythmic fragments which are manipulated in concentrated and brisk fashion.

The finale is a rondo of tremendous power. Themes appear in a luxuriant texture and a broad framework; the normal statements and expected contrasts culminate in a final return which rises to a great series of climaxes, and which constitutes more than one third of the movement. Beethoven's technical skill, his mastery of harmony and rhythm, and his tremendous drive are here disclosed in full measure. This movement prepares one for the great size and emotional power Beethoven's later works will reveal. With one stroke he has broken the bonds of the symphony, enlarged its scope, and made it into a medium for the expression of gripping emotions and the display of superhuman energy. The second symphony bridges the gap which separates all previous symphonies from the enormous works of subsequent years.

From the late symphonies of Haydn one receives the impression that energy and elegance are beautifully balanced; from Beethoven's second, that energy overpowers the grace and elegance inherent in the style. Occasionally, in the finale of the second, one is reminded of the purposeless energy of an adolescent: the control and poise one may expect of a mature adult are not always present. The influence of Haydn, noticeable in most of Beethoven's early works, has here diminished greatly; and this is the last major work in which one may trace the hampering effect of that influence.

Beethoven's third symphony is in E flat; written about 1803–1804, it was published in 1806 as Opus 55. If ever a composition deserved the name "Eroica," it is that symphony. For this work is heroic in every sense: in size, in the scope of the emotional states it reflects, in the extent of the conflicts and dramatic passages it contains, in the revealed mastery over its components. There is little need to lean upon the familiar anecdote about Beethoven's admiration for Napoleon, his eventual disillusionment, and his subsequent altering of the symphony's dedication; even without that anecdote, it is an heroic work.

The expansion of form shown in the second symphony is here transcended. For in the "Eroica's" first movement are at least ten sets of thematic fragments, motives, or theme groups. This large amount of thematic material enables Beethoven to lay out a movement of gigantic proportions. Yet for all its size it is terse, concentrated, and intelligible. An air of suppressed excitement, coupled with moments of dramatic power and restrained sentiment, dominates the movement. Fierce, pounding rhythms are set opposite lyric passages; relentless motion contrasts with relaxed beauty; and the strong developments culminate in an overpowering climax. In no other work, probably, is the organic growth process of music so clearly revealed.

The second movement, a broad and sustained funeral march, is of a rare type; for its content may affect one in opposite ways at different times. One may see in it only gloom, agony, and a reflection of the dissolution caused by death; or one may lift up the elements of courage and hope which it contains and see it as a monument to Beethoven's optimism and warm humanity. For emotional depth and intensity of mood it is unsurpassed. In a formal sense, the movement is related both to the rondo and to sonata-form, containing a number of phrases in C minor, a contrasting section in C major, a fugal development, and an extended coda. The last few measures of the coda are filled with a degree of poignancy and pathos that is heartbreaking; for there, after the restrained closing section, after the funeral march has ended and feelings of anguish have been laid to rest, the opening phrase returns, hesitant and fitful, and is rhythmically transformed, broken down, and dissolved (see Example 17). Here is a musical counterpart of the processes which accompany death.

EXAMPLE 17

BEETHOVEN, "Eroica" Symphony

The tension and emotional intensity of the first two movements are completely relaxed in the scherzo, for that movement has an air of good nature about it. Two or three short theme-fragments and a bit of chromatic melody are presented, developed, and recapitulated; a long step has been taken toward the sonata-form which later scherzos will reveal. The trio, in decided contrast to the restless motion of the scherzo, is concerned largely with fanfarelike passages given to three horns; these are set opposite twisted phrases for full orchestra. A noteworthy feature of the movement is that the *da capo* is written out and differs slightly in rhythmical aspects from the first part.

The finale is a highly original movement which brings to expression Beethoven's characteristic manner of resolving thematic conflicts. In formal plan it consists of a set of ten variations on a theme, interspersed with development passages and supplied with an introduction and a coda. The theme is one which Beethoven had used in three earlier compositions—in a contredanse for orchestra, as the finale of the ballet, *The Creations of Prometheus*, and in a set of variations with fugue, Opus 35, for piano—all written about 1800–1802. But only in the "Eroica" did he reveal its essential duality and give expression both to the conflict between the two elements and to the ultimate victory of one of them. The elements are, respectively, the bass and the melody of the theme (see Example 18).

A short, powerful introduction prepares directly for the first ap-

EXAMPLE 18

BEETHOVEN, "Eroica" Symphony, *Finale*

pearance of the bass alone, which is presented as the main theme of the movement. This is followed by two contrapuntal variations. Over the third variation of the bass phrase the melody is introduced. Now four free variations, concerned alternately with the bass and the melody and set in a variety of keys, lead to an extensive fugal development (this serves as the eighth variation) of the bass phrase. The latter is virtually developed out of existence even while it animates a rousing, massive climax for full orchestra. Thereupon, as the sound dies away, the winds present the melody in an idealized form and in a slower tempo; the passage is among the most moving and beautiful in all of Beethoven's works. The tenth variation is again concerned with the melody; but now the latter is shouted out by the full orchestra, is seen to have emerged victorious from its conflict with the original bass phrase, and is now melody and bass at once. The coda begins quietly with yet further development of the melody, and ends with a massive climax.

In many other works did Beethoven treat a conflict of elements as he did here. We shall see, in the G-major piano concerto, how one delicate phrase neutralizes a domineering one; we can find, in the *Grosse Fuge* for string quartet, Opus 133, that a quiet theme, though beaten to earth by a boisterous, energetic one, can yet emerge successfully from the conflict and fulfill its destiny. It is that type of conflict which is presented in a personal, idealized fashion in the third symphony. The content of the Prometheus legend, and the relationship of the "Eroica's" melody to that legend, need not be discussed here.[1] Yet it cannot be without significance that the same melody comes at the climax of the *Prometheus* ballet; and Prometheus symbolizes the victory of human intelligence and freedom over the tyranny of the gods.

No previous work could have prepared the first audience for what the "Eroica" revealed to them; the most dramatic or forceful work by any composer then known could not have given them a handhold to this massive composition. Tension, mounting climax, great length, extreme emotional states, tragedy and joy in close

[1] See Scott, *Beethoven*, pp. 152–56.

juxtaposition—with such elements the work was revolutionary. The audience for which Beethoven wrote did not yet exist; it had to come into, or be shocked into, being. And one of his great accomplishments was to raise the concert audience of his day to the level he demanded of it.

Shortly after completing the "Eroica" symphony, Beethoven turned to the composition of a triple concerto for violin, cello, piano, and orchestra. The work was published in 1807 as Opus 56. It has become popular to minimize the worth of this unique concerto largely because it cannot compare, in intensity or profundity, with the works which surround it. True, it contains little concentrated emotion, wild abandon, or even great drama. But it has melodious themes, fine proportions, richly contrasting harmonies, and stirring climaxes. The three movements are laid out spaciously, with leisurely transitions and with repetition rather than development of themes; routine figurations and passage-work dominate the texture. In an overall view of Beethoven's creative activity, one comes to realize that contrast between consecutive works plays as great a role as does contrast of movements within a single work, or even sections within a movement. The triple concerto represents one of those moments of lesser intensity which may be expected between the concentrated, profound periods. It is works such as this which allow one to measure the greatness of Beethoven's accomplishments elsewhere.

We turn now to an account of his concert overtures. In quality, function, form, and historical place, the eleven works of this type have little in common. Yet one element serves to unite them to some extent, for they represent a totally new type of concert music which was to be of great influence upon later composers. One senses in them a tenuous relationship between dramatic program and absolute music; it is almost as though the concept of the symphonic poem began here.

The overture to the ballet, *The Creations* (or *Creatures*) *of Prometheus*, was written in 1802, about a year after the first symphony was completed, and was published as Opus 43 in 1804. The short, incisive chords with which the slow introduction begins serve to establish the C-major tonality firmly; but they also give warning of the forcefulness which is to come. The allegro proper is in expanded sonata-form; for at the normal end of the overture the development is repeated almost note for note, after which comes a stirring, vigorous coda. The relationship of the overture to the Prometheus legend as modified by Salvatore Vigano, the choreographer of the work, is not apparent. This work represents the first of Beethoven's many attempts to bring sonata-form and dramatic truth into an harmonious unity.

The four overtures to Beethoven's opera, *Fidelio*, reflect the revisions to which that work was subjected. The text of the opera, based upon a contemporary libretto, had been set to music by Gaveaux in French and by Paer in Italian; those versions were called *Leonore*, after the heroine. To avoid confusion, Beethoven's setting (written about 1805) was given the name *Fidelio*—the name assumed by Leonore when, in men's garb, she visits her husband Florestan in his dungeon. Beethoven protested against the change of name, but was overruled by the producer. Nevertheless, he called the overtures *Leonore* when they were published separately from the opera score.

When first performed, late in 1805, at which time the overture now known as *Leonore No. 2* was played, the opera was a failure. Beethoven revised it for an 1806 performance and reworked the overture also: *Leonore No. 3* resulted. These versions carry the number Opus 72a. A revival in 1814 brought forth further revisions, introduced an entirely new overture—*Fidelio*, Opus 72b—and resulted in the present form of the work.

After Beethoven's death in 1827, yet another overture to the opera was discovered: the so-called *Leonore No. 1*, published in 1832 as Opus 138. The status of this work is still in doubt; the most acceptable theory is that it was composed for the first performance, was felt by Beethoven to be lacking, and was withdrawn in favor of *Leonore No. 2*. It is a lengthy piece, and gives the impression of formlessness. Seldom does it reveal the sense of direction one expects from Beethoven, and it scarcely provides a suitable introduction to the beauty and drama contained in the opera itself.

A completely different work is at hand in *Leonore No. 2;* the material is largely new. The slow introduction presents the melody of Florestan's great second-act aria and continues with a long, suspense-laden passage which leads to the allegro. In the latter the element of dramatic excitement is uppermost; an extended development culminates in the famous trumpet calls. At this point, a complete recapitulation would have been false to the dramatic action. Beethoven chose to return to the Florestan melody, which is followed by a spectacular coda.

The revision of 1806 took the form of a drastic shortening. The three acts were combined into two, several numbers were omitted, and a general tightening of the structure took place. But the revised overture, *Leonore No. 3,* is not at all shorter; its revision led to a different emphasis, to a complete change of intention. *Leonore No. 2* had pointed toward the opera itself and had induced an air of excitement; *No. 3,* on the other hand, leads to the trumpet calls which, in the opera, provide the climactic point; and it presents a rounded, symphonic form. For here the introduction and second theme are related (both are concerned with Florestan's aria), the development is shorter and keeps in mind the dramatic effect of the trumpet calls. The latter are followed by a full recapitulation of the thematic material, and a brief coda further develops the first theme. The contrasts, the suspense, and the climax of the opera are here presented in a unified composition which does not require stage action for its completion. Thus, *Leonore No. 3* is the opera itself, or rather a condensed summary of its dramatic purpose. As such, it has taken a high place as one of Beethoven's most venerated compositions. The connection between it and the later symphonic poem is not difficult to find.

By 1814, in time for the second revision, Beethoven may have sensed that a large, dramatic overture was not suited to what is essentially a lyric opera. Indeed, there was some danger that the summary of the opera's dramatic import, as contained in *Leonore No. 3*, would work against the complete realization of the staged work. Consequently, the overture written for this revision is an operatic curtain-raiser in every respect. *Fidelio* is in E major and has none of the characteristics of the two great overtures of 1805 and 1806. Bright in key and mood, it reveals little thematic connection with the opera and is concerned largely with developments of a single theme. It merely prepares for the opening scene and in no wise presents a résumé of the opera's dramatic action.

About a year after the 1806 revision of *Fidelio* Beethoven turned again to the theater—this time to compose an overture for a play, *Coriolanus*, written by an obscure contemporary named Heinrich von Collin. Completed in 1807, the overture to *Coriolanus* was published in 1808 as Opus 62. The tragic figure of Coriolanus was known to Beethoven from several sources, Plutarch and Shakespeare among them; and the dilemma in which the proud, imperious Roman general is placed when his wife and his mother beg him to disperse his army and give up his planned revolt appealed strongly to Beethoven's dramatic sense. This dilemma is reflected in the overture.

The themes are brusque and pleading in turn, and suggest respectively the character of Coriolanus and the entreaty which undermines his resolve. Again a conflict of themes results; the forceful first theme, in the course of a long development and especially in the coda, is modified, broken down, and finally gives way to the appeal of the second. Beethoven's feeling for dramatic truth is strikingly revealed here; for although the overture is in sonata-form, the recapitulation is entirely free. One senses in the development the moral struggle to which Coriolanus is subjected; his character has been transformed. Consequently it would be false to bring back the first theme unchanged. Thus, the recapitulation begins in F minor (the work itself is in C minor), contains only fragments of the theme, and proceeds quickly to the second theme. The coda then completes the transformation and dissolution of the first theme.

A concentrated, psychologically true drama is enacted here, one which in effect reviews the entire course of this episode in the career of Coriolanus.

Beethoven's only violin concerto, written in 1806, was preceded by two single movements for violin and orchestra, both written about 1802–1803. They are called "romances"; the first, in G major, was published as Opus 40 in 1803; the second, in F major, was delayed until 1805, when it appeared as Opus 50. These pieces present no problems to the listener. They represent a Beethoven without strong compulsions, without a driving need to write, and yet animated by the highest standards. As they stand, they are merely pleasant, melodious works.

Quite otherwise is the violin concerto, Opus 61, in D major, published in 1809. Few works are so placid in general mood, so clear and economical in form, and so unfailingly melodious. And few works, even of Beethoven's, are more profoundly moving; the simplest of materials are used with far-reaching effect. Exquisite turns of phrase, subtle modulations, an air of understatement, and an absence of external brilliance—these constitute the first movement. A rhythmic motive—four quarter-notes on the same tone—is employed throughout; its constant reiteration (one commentator notes some seventy returns of the motive) unifies and concentrates the movement. Yet the melodies and their variants move on in an unclouded, serene fashion.

The slow movement is among the most restrained and economical of works. Its profound appeal is not to be found by mentioning technical details or by taking refuge in ideas about a poetic content. This is pure music, simple music, and must be heard to be appreciated. Only in the finale does a jaunty air enter the concerto. Lighthearted almost to the point of frivolity, the movement provides a perfect foil for the qualities so beautifully exhibited in the adagio. Brilliant passage work and a number of charming melodies allow the solo violin to display all its capabilities. Yet the basic relationship of solo to orchestra is never lost sight of. The D-major violin concerto is one of Beethoven's great achievements.

The fourth piano concerto, Opus 58, in G major, was written about 1805–1806. That period was above all a time of powerful works; further, it marked the time of Beethoven's greatest control over the most elemental of emotional states as well as the most refined. And as a representative of his most refined writing, the concerto, published in 1808, takes a high place.

Here, for the first time in his concertos, the piano is revealed as an equal partner of the orchestra. Instead of the usual long tutti in which the orchestra announces themes and establishes moods, the piano itself, in a shy and diffident way, begins a theme. True, the exposition and commentary are immediately carried forward by the orchestra; but the mood of cooperation has been established and the relationship between solo and orchestra tightened. The entire first movement is pervaded by an air of nobility and restraint; the dignity of its themes would make any brilliant display seem tawdry.

The slow movement is unique; for here, in a small frame requiring no more than seventy-two measures, Beethoven reveals the heart of his musical philosophy. The movement presents the gradual transformation of a hard, forceful, and apparently unyielding phrase. Under the influence of the piano's tender supplication (see Example 19), the orchestra's phrase is modified, broken, and com-

EXAMPLE 19   BEETHOVEN, G-major Concerto

pletely changed in character. Beethoven's manner of employing one mood as a catalyst for another has been seen elsewhere; but nowhere is the process carried forward with greater refinement, delicacy, and simplicity than here. The movement is a magical piece of writing.

The robust, incisive character of the final rondo comes as something of a shock after the tenderness of the andante. And that is probably what Beethoven intended. On many occasions he is reputed to have ended a series of profound improvisations with a loud chord or a raucous laugh. A finale which contrasts abruptly with the previous mood, in order to preserve balance and bring the listener down to earth again, is the written equivalent of that device. In the G-major concerto the contrast is not as extreme as, for example, in the "Archduke" trio, Opus 97, or in the quartet, Opus 135; yet this finale does restore that element of sane balance which is never missing in Beethoven's works.

After a lapse of over three years, Beethoven turned to the concerto form for the last time: the E-flat piano concerto, Opus 73, was written in 1809 and published two years later. Symphonic size and content are here combined with majesty and brilliant virtuosic effects in so masterful a fashion that the nickname "Emperor" is more justified than most nicknames. For this is a work of imperial stature. Its imposing introductory flourishes—on E flat, A flat, and B flat—establish the basic key with a solidity that brooks no opposition; its broad themes and even broader developments bring a feeling of rich spaciousness. The fiery passage-work of the solo part is concerned so largely with thematic materials that one senses the movement's great concentration in spite of its length. The cadenza, written into the score by Beethoven himself, leads to a flashing coda; the latter's regal display and perfect proportion are essential to the shape and character of the movement.

Where the first movement is rich and imposing, the B-major adagio is noble; no other term adequately describes its restraint and warm-heartedness. With no attempt to be "effective," with no concern but to write simply, Beethoven here created a movement which is profound and moving out of all proportion to its materials. The most ordinary harmony and figurations are used; yet one would seek far to find another example of emotional warmth achieved so simply.

In the finale the symphonic texture of the first movement returns, along with greater animation and even more brilliance. The respective roles of piano and orchestra have changed subtly during the course of the concerto. For in the first movement the piano is an important member of the ensemble, contributing the weight of its tone and the flexibility of its expression to the development of the material; in the adagio it is an equal partner and subordinates itself to the special requirements of the movement. But in the finale it is a soloist and carries the orchestra along in its imperious stride. The result is a work of infinite variety, great power, and profound beauty—truly, an "emperor" among concertos.

We return to the years 1805–1806, to the time of the first *Fidelio* revision and the inception of the fourth and fifth symphonies. The fourth was completed about 1806 and was published in 1809 as Opus 60; it is in B flat. In texture and content it marks a return to the style of Haydn; but no longer did the manner of that composer hamper Beethoven. The entire symphony reflects a deliberate turn away from the confusion and tension of the year 1805. Even the orchestra is relaxed in size; one flute is required instead of the usual two, and only two horns (the "Eroica" had required three).

The slow introduction has little in common with earlier types. Mysterious and portentous, it hints at remote keys—B-flat minor, G-flat major and minor. It suggests distant brooding, and its veiled harmonies bring an air of suspense. Only in its last few measures does the mood brighten; then it builds up a great momentum with which it leads directly into the vital, clear, and rhythmically powerful first movement. Here, more than ever before, Beethoven employs wind instruments for thematic statements; a transparent, colorful quality characterizes the entire movement. The slow movement is unique in Beethoven; it is pure melody set above a pulsating accompaniment. More florid than usual, its themes progress in an almost unbroken line from beginning to end. The movement presents no thematic conflicts; free of tension, it contains a wealth of imaginative and wonderfully proportioned detail.

The scherzo offers an abrupt contrast. Two phrases, one angular and the other smooth, vie for supremacy in a movement which is vigorous and characterized by great freedom of rhythmic accent. The trio consists of short phrases set for winds and strings alternately. The form of the whole is enlarged by two thirds, for in place of one *da capo* return of the scherzo come two. A five-part form emerges: scherzo-trio-scherzo-trio-scherzo. The rhythmic drive of the movement is greatly increased by this innovation. The finale is a large piece in sonata-form; a relentless sixteenth-note figure is employed to suggest a kind of perpetual motion. Moments of comparative relaxation are provided by the somewhat quieter second theme; but in the main the movement goes by with great animation and Haydnesque humor. The fourth symphony as a whole is among the merriest and most approachable of Beethoven's major works. Overshadowed in size by the other symphonies, supplied with a content that eschews dark emotion and deep conflict, it reveals the composer's happiest side.

The completion of the fifth symphony, in C minor, was delayed until 1807. Published in 1809 as Opus 67, the fifth is one of the most concentrated works in the entire repertoire. Its overall length is no greater than that of many a symphony by Haydn or Mozart; yet it covers a range of emotion and explores psychological areas which the Classical giants had not often presented in musical form. Its instrumental resources are greater, also; for here Beethoven borrows a piccolo, three trombones, and a contrabassoon from the opera orchestra and incorporates them into the symphony's finale.

The first movement is based almost entirely upon a four-note motive which is too well known to require quotation. And although all its themes contain this common element, each one develops a nature of its own. The utmost conciseness and economy of motion characterize the entire movement; only in a brief lyric phrase for solo oboe is the concentration relaxed momentarily.

The slow movement is cast in the form of a set of variations on a double theme. But Beethoven treated the variation form freely, for the second member of the theme appears only twice. Thus, the latter serves to introduce a contrasting tonality (C major) and to enhance the suave quality of the basic A-flat major. Graceful and melodious passages dominate, and the terrible passion displayed by the first movement finds no place. And yet the organization of the andante's details to create a unified whole is no less masterful than that of the opening allegro.

The third movement presents a radically new content. Tempo, meter, and form of a scherzo are here; but the lively good nature which had elsewhere characterized the form are not. In their place come mysterious, disconcerting, and unearthly qualities. The trio, concerned with a short and truly ugly phrase, is filled with mutterings and discontent which the shortened *da capo* repetition of the first part does nothing to dispel. But then, in a long and tense transition which leads directly into the finale, the disconcerting quality of this movement gradually recedes and is replaced by the triumphant energy of the final allegro.

Beethoven is said to have remarked, in connection with the motive of the first movement, "Thus Fate knocks at the door." Many commentators see the whole fifth symphony as representing Beethoven's struggle with and victory over his own fate; from this point of view, the outbursts of joy with which the finale begins may be said to symbolize that victory. In clear, sparkling harmony and with strong, forthright rhythms the first theme breaks forth jubilantly. Unusually long for a Beethoven theme (about forty-five measures), it carries everything before it with elemental power. Not even the somewhat twisted second theme can stand against it; only the self-confident third can halt its drive. The short development ends triumphantly and is succeeded not by the expected recapitulation but by a portion of the third movement. Here is a masterstroke of the highest quality. So that the jubilation may not be too great, so that the feeling of victory may not overwhelm, Beethoven reminds himself and his listeners that the disconcerting, mysterious forces are only being held in abeyance.

When, finally, the recapitulation is heard, the effect is all the greater because of the interruption. Now no doubt about the final victory can arise. And the coda, which is almost twice as long as any previous part of the movement and which constitutes in effect a terminal development, compounds the jubilation. Its sections present the movement's themes again, but virtually in reverse order—the opening phrase of the first theme being heard last of all. The final fifty-odd measures constitute an example of reiteration unmatched in the literature; the tonic chord, reinforced by an occasional dominant, is repeated over and over with the greatest possible emphasis. It is as though Beethoven were sealing his victory by stamping out, with triumphant C-major chords, the last shreds of opposition to his will.

The great concentration and rhythmic drive which characterize the fifth symphony are absent in the sixth, in F major, which was begun in 1807, about the time the other was completed. During 1807–1808 Beethoven's desire for success in the field of opera became almost an obsession. He studied plots and librettos in an unending stream; he read translations of Shakespeare's plays, and in the spring of 1808 gave serious thought to *Macbeth*. The gloomy phase passed, however; and in the mood of relief which the abandonment of the operatic project brought with it he returned to and completed the symphony. Nicknamed the "Pastoral" by Beethoven himself, it was published in 1809 as Opus 68. Piccolo and two trombones are added to the standard orchestra in the fourth and fifth movements, respectively.

This is a leisurely work which represents the composer's response to the idyllic countryside, and is in his own words, "more the expression of feelings than painting." For the only time in Beethoven's symphonies the movements bear explanatory titles. "Awakening of Cheerful Impressions upon Arrival in the Country"—thus the first movement. Bright little tunes redolent of fresh air, simple developments, and romantic and colorful key contrasts are included in that movement. Nowhere does Beethoven depart from the mood imposed by the descriptive heading.

The second movement is a "Scene at the Brook." An air of calm repose is achieved by the use of many melodic fragments over an undulating, all-pervading string accompaniment. Only in the coda is the smooth, rhythmic flow of the movement interrupted; for there a trio of birds appear: nightingale, thrush, and cuckoo (flute, oboe, and clarinet, respectively). This little descriptive passage fits well into the scene and saves it from the danger of monotony.

The last three movements are connected. In a scherzo labeled "Merry-making of the Peasants," we are taken to a country festival complete with village band. Tunes which vaguely suggest pastoral melodies are heard against deliberately heavy, rustic strains. The trio, a wild and impetuous dance movement, brings an important innovation, for it is in duple meter, in contrast to the prevailing triple. And, as in the fourth symphony, two *da capos* are indicated.

The fourth movement, called "The Storm," is one of Beethoven's few attempts at musical realism. All the natural phenomena occur: distant thunder; pattering raindrops; the storm itself, with near thunder, flashes of lightning (and in Beethoven's meteorology the thunder comes before the lightning), and whistling wind; and the quick passing of the storm, with distant thunder again. The fifth movement's content is given by its heading: "The Shepherd's Song. Feeling of Thanksgiving after the Storm." The clearing of the air is beautifully represented by a short introduction in which dominant and tonic chords overlap. The themes again have a pastoral quality about them; leisurely motion and absence of conflict are characteristic, along with short and subdued climaxes.

Beethoven was at his best in dealing with large, subjective, and essentially human problems. When he concerned himself, as he did here, with simple and unsophisticated matters, his work assumed another character. Incisiveness, psychological insight, and complete mastery over the forces he unleashes—such elements animate his great works and raise him to his high place among the greatest composers. And such elements are largely missing from the "Pastoral" symphony; their absence is felt keenly. The subject matter is not entirely worthy of symphonic handling; either it is presented too elaborately or it does not utilize the full resources of the medium. Thus, the "Pastoral" becomes, in this author's opinion, one of the few works of Beethoven in which the relationship between content and treatment is less than satisfactory.

The sixth symphony was first performed late in 1808 at a concert of Beethoven's works; the program was to include also the fifth symphony, the G-major piano concerto with Beethoven as soloist, and portions of the C-major mass, Opus 86. A desire to combine the forces available there led to the writing of the Choral Fantasy, for piano, chorus, and orchestra. The work was rushed to completion, performed at the close of that concert, and subsequently published as Opus 80 in 1811.

It begins with a brilliant movement for piano alone. Forceful virtuosic passages over widely ranging harmonies establish an air of expectancy. A section labeled "finale," for piano and orchestra, serves to introduce the main allegro. The latter presents an undistinguished theme (which Beethoven had used fifteen years earlier in a song) and a series of figural variations; long developments and elaborate solo-piano passages enter into remote keys and contrasting tempos. After the introductory material returns, the chorus proceeds with the variation theme on the text of a poem, "Gegenliebe," by G. A. Bürger; successive stanzas are set in contrasting styles, to which the orchestra provides a thin accompaniment and the piano a running commentary. The piece ends with a rousing climax.

One can find little aesthetic justification for this strange combination of forces; there is only thematic connection between its various parts, and that connection is somewhat mechanically made. And yet, with all its weakness and its badly proportioned form, there are prophetic moments in the work. Certain choral effects, subtle turns of phrase, an occasional modulation, and the general atmosphere of the ninth symphony's finale are heard here in embryonic state. As a study for that enormous movement, the Choral Fantasy deserved to be written.

The summer of 1809 found Napoleon's troops in Vienna. Full of concern over inflated costs and depreciated currency, Beethoven rose above his unhappy, confused state to conceive and compose the "Emperor" concerto. He also worked on sketches for the seventh and eighth symphonies during this time, but these he laid aside when he was commissioned to write an overture and incidental music for Goethe's drama, *Egmont*. That work was completed in 1810 and was published in 1811 as Opus 84.

The drama is concerned with the tyranny of the duke of Alba over the citizens of Brussels and with the place of Egmont as a symbol of liberty and courage. In the overture the essential character of the hero, the emotional currents of the drama, and a final "symphony of victory" are represented. *Egmont* is thus similar to *Coriolanus* and *Leonore No. 3* in its type of content. A somber beginning, a tremendously intense middle part, and a triumphant closing section—these form a work that gives every indication of being based upon a program even though none is specifically given.

A year later Beethoven composed incidental music for two plays by August Kotzebue, which were to be given at the opening of a new theater in Pesth in 1812: *The Ruins of Athens* and *King Stephen*. Each set consists of an overture and of several choruses, marches, arias, and the like. The overtures contain little that is at all noteworthy. Slow introductions, marchlike allegros, superficial developments, and noisy climaxes characterize both. Fortunately, they have all but disappeared from the repertoire. The overture to *The Ruins of Athens* was published in 1823 as Opus 113; that to *King Stephen* in 1826 as Opus 117.

The quality of the *Nameday* overture, Opus 115, is somewhat similar. Written in 1814 for the nameday of the Austrian emperor, it is an occasional piece of only routine worth; its publication was delayed until 1825. The dignified rhythms of its slow introduction, along with the fast section which contains a few contrapuntal passages, suggest that Beethoven modeled the work on the Handel overture-type (even though it is in full sonata-form). Little poetic content shines through, and dramatic intensity is lacking in the overture. It, too, has been virtually forgotten.

Quite different is Beethoven's last overture, written in 1822 for the opening of the Josephstadt Theater. A paraphrase of *The Ruins of Athens*, now called *The Consecration of the House* was made for that occasion. Beethoven altered the music of 1811 to fit the new text, cast out the old overture, and wrote the work known in German as *Die Weihe des Hauses*. It was published in 1825 as Opus 124. The new overture is dignified, passionate, and strong. A series of broad and noble melodies in the majestic introduction give way to a fast and forceful movement in quasi-concerto style. One motive supplies virtually all the thematic material, and the work becomes in effect a long development section with powerful climaxes and great rhythmic drive. Yet it also contains profound and tender passages which suggest that it was written in close proximity to the ninth symphony. It is an unduly neglected composition which deserves many more performances than it receives.

We return now to an account of Beethoven's symphonies. The sixth, as we have seen, had been completed in 1808; sketches for the seventh and eighth date from about 1809, the works themselves were completed in 1812, and both were published in 1816. The seventh, Opus 92, is in A major; the eighth, Opus 93, in F.

The long introduction of the seventh symphony is broadly conceived with chromatic bass lines, quiet melodic fragments, and a smooth transition—one of the most masterful in Beethoven. Seldom has a basic tonality been so carefully established on so broad a scale as here. And seldom had even Beethoven achieved the rhythmic drive present in the vivace which follows. A single rhythmic motive animates that movement's themes; Example 20 shows the close relationship that exists between them. The resulting concentration, high degree of unity, and energy engendered here are enormous. Brilliant orchestration and overwhelming exuberance characterize this most optimistic of movements.

Beethoven's free use of the variation form has been spoken of earlier. But rarely has his ingenuity been more strikingly revealed or has it led to a happier result than in the second movement. The well-known melancholy theme, which is not so much a melody as an harmonic progression built upon a rhythmic motive, is followed

EXAMPLE 20
Allegro   BEETHOVEN, Seventh Symphony

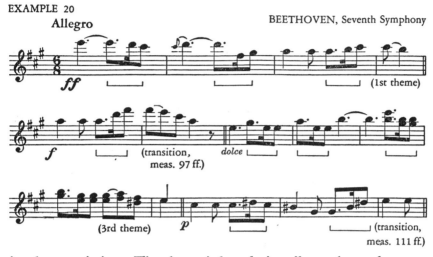

by three variations. The theme is heard virtually unchanged except in instrumental dress; but each new variation adds one new element to the texture (see Example 21), even while the previous elements are retained. With a change to A major comes a new lyric theme; but the rhythmic motive of the A-minor variations is still present. After a brief transition the variations are resumed, with developments and a fugato interspersed. The A-major theme is recapitulated, and a coda is added. The movement ends as it began, with a two-measure A-minor chord played softly by the woodwinds.

A bright and vital scherzo, even longer and more vigorous than the great scherzo of the "Eroica," is the third movement. All the elements of sonata-form are present: contrasting themes, conflicting harmonies (F and A major), a short development, and a recapitulation. In the quieter D-major trio, with its slower tempo and its song-like quality, the tremendous rhythmic vitality is momentarily relaxed. Again, as in the fourth and sixth symphonies, a five-part form emerges.

All the energy and drive of the first and third movements are as nothing when the finale is reached. Here Beethoven has written an impulsive movement whose joy and animation are unequaled in the literature; sheer rhythmic vitality and boisterousness are depicted.

EXAMPLE 21

BEETHOVEN, Seventh Symphony

But again Beethoven reveals his perfect control of mood and proportion; for the form is quite clear and reserves its greatest climax for the coda—which is again a terminal development and is longer and even more concentrated than the earlier development. And as an example of the fury to which the climax ascends, it may be pointed out that here, for the first time in a symphony, Beethoven employs the dynamic level *fff* (measures 428 and 444). Not even in the passionate conflicts of the "Eroica" or in the triumphant coda of the fifth symphony had he required so large a tonal volume. When

that dynamic level is employed by later composers, it often represents coarse bravado or brutality. In the seventh symphony, however, it is a symbol of the highest point yet attained in sustained vigor
and climactic intensity.

Beethoven often revealed great contrasts in consecutive works;
his "twins" are rarely identical. Differences between the fifth and
sixth symphonies have been noted; similar contrasts exist between
the two piano trios of Opus 70 and elsewhere. Usually the first work
of a pair is intense, passionate, and dramatic, while the second is
leisurely and expansive. The same type of contrast is found between
the nearly consecutive seventh and eighth symphonies. For in place
of the size, concentration, and overwhelming force of the seventh,
the eighth has humor, clarity, and lyricism as its outstanding qualities. Beethoven himself recognized the difference between these
works, for he called the eighth "my little one."

And yet the idea, often expressed, that the eighth is a less important work than his others is completely false. Beethoven has been
identified so strongly with heroic or triumphant or abandoned
moods (witness the three "favorite" symphonies, the third, fifth,
and seventh) that one forgets his was an all-embracing personality.
Humor and joy are important elements in that personality, too; and
those elements come to expression in the eighth symphony. Indeed,
humor is present in Beethoven to a greater degree than is usually
recognized. One need mention only the finale of the "Eroica," the
finale of the quartet, Opus 59, No. 2, the scherzo of the quartet,
Opus 131—and these are among his most profound works—to realize that humor was an essential ingredient in Beethoven's emotional
life. Good-natured moments in the eighth, far from being evidence
of that symphony's triviality, disclose how well-rounded and complete Beethoven's music is.

But much more than humor is present in this work. Abrupt contrasts give its first movement an impulsive air; a concentrated development of a single measure of the principal theme leads to powerful
climaxes—so powerful that Beethoven is again impelled to employ
the dynamic level of *fff* at the entrance of the recapitulation and on

a striking dissonance in the coda. The humor of the piece is nowhere as clearly shown as in the last few measures of that coda, where series of chords alternately in strings and winds prepare for the final flourish of the first motive.

The second movement, an allegretto scherzando in B flat, is associated with Johann Maelzel, of metronome fame. A mechanical quality about this movement gives the effect of a good-natured caricature. One rhythmic pulse is present throughout the piece, along with a delightful absence of sentimental expression. The unique conception of the whole sets it apart from the normal Beethoven symphonic movement.

In the absence of a true slow movement, a third-movement scherzo would have raised the basic tempo of the symphony too greatly. Consequently, Beethoven writes a minuet; but no longer a minuet in the style of Haydn, rather a rhythmically transformed one full of strong accents and contrasting moods. The trio is a leisurely piece which makes much of the melodic possibilities of the horn. Courtly grace is gone, to be replaced by bucolic directness and warm sentiment in turn.

The greatest explosion of energy is reserved for the last movement. A first theme in F, more the embodiment of rhythm than melody, ends with an ambiguous final note, C sharp; the latter's function is not immediately made clear (see Example 22). A lyric

EXAMPLE 22

second theme in A flat completes the ninety-measure exposition. The development and the recapitulation are unusually short also—about seventy measures in the one and about one hundred in the other. And in the latter the ambiguous C sharp is still unexplained. But then in a massive coda which constitutes almost half of the entire movement, and which contains at once a second development and a second recapitulation, the harmonic puzzle of the opening phrase is solved. At the end of that quasi development the C sharp is briefly seen to be actually a D flat (the minor submediant), but immediately returns to its C-sharp function, namely to serve as the dominant of F-sharp minor. And the quasi-recapitulation begins not in F major, but a half-step higher. In a passage full of the greatest intensity the E sharp of the dominant chord is suddenly made into the equivalent of F natural; the return "modulation" from F-sharp minor to F major takes place during the confusion. From here on, all is as expected; the movement ends with a strong and continual pounding away at the original tonality of F major.

The entire symphony is characterized by a struggle between F and non-F. The first movement's restlessly modulating second theme (which hints at D major and C major, with a half-cadence on G), followed by a diminished chord, gives the earliest evidence of far-reaching harmonic motion. Long sections in A major and D-flat major in the development, many sequences, and the like—these throw a revealing light upon F major; when that key is reestablished at the recapitulation, it is done so with the greatest possible intensity (witness the *fff* at that point). The allegretto illuminates the basic tonality from the subdominant side; it is in B flat. And the minuet, both parts of which are in F, acts as a stabilizing movement and to confirm the key once more before the enormous finale with its harmonic ambiguities can contribute the climax. If evidence were needed that the eighth symphony is one of Beethoven's masterworks, it is supplied by these daring, overwhelming, yet simple harmonic conflicts.

About a year after the symphony was completed Beethoven wrote a "battle symphony" called *Wellington's Victory, or the Battle of Vitoria*, Opus 91. This work represents one of the strangest aberrations of judgment committed by any major composer. It was written for the "Panharmonion," a mechanical instrument invented by Maelzel, and to celebrate the victory of the Duke of Wellington over the forces of Napoleon at Vitoria (1813). Beethoven later arranged the work for full orchestra including rattles, many percussion instruments, and cannons "fired on the English side" and "on the French side."

It is a hodge-podge of trumpet fanfares, battle scenes, and noisy chord progressions; it includes two marches: "Rule, Britannia" and "Malbrouck" (better known as "We Won't Get Home Until Morning"). Further, "God Save the King" appears both in hymn-tune style and as the subject of a long fugue in fast tempo. A dozen or more unrelated sections arranged into two large movements; great freedom of key structure; and, except in the fugal part, virtual absence of counterpoint—these characterize the piece. A brilliant work it may be; but Beethoven's reputation will not suffer if it is forgotten entirely.

Probably no work of his was as slow in taking final shape as the ninth symphony. Sketches for the first three movements date back to 1812; active work was begun in 1817, and the symphony was completed about 1823 and published in 1826. But the concept of the finale existed as early as 1793, in which year Beethoven had expressed his intention of setting Schiller's "Ode to Joy" to music; thirty years later the concept was realized. His instrumental needs grew as his purposes expanded; piccolo, contrabassoon, two extra horns, three trombones, and a variety of percussion instruments are employed in various movements to create a larger orchestra than Beethoven requires elsewhere.

The content of Schiller's ode, with its appeal for universal joy and for a brotherhood of all humanity, is the central fact of the symphony, and is the impelling force which shapes the first three instrumental movements. But rather than presenting a cumulative rise to the climax of this sentiment, Beethoven characteristically reveals its opposite or negative aspects first. And strangely enough, this was not planned from the outset, for his first plan had been to write an instrumental finale (on a theme which was later used in the A-minor quartet, Opus 132).

A joyless state is suggested by the first movement. Dark, demoniac, and full of unresolved strife, it embodies the loneliest of moods. Sharply contrasting tonalities—which appear even in the two versions of the first theme, in D minor and B flat, respectively—and a subtle avoidance of dominant-tonic cadences give an air of inexorable progress to the music. The large amount of thematic material is driven forward under the impulse of a restless harmony; and this sense of motion gives to the entire movement an unremitting, elemental force which is like nothing else in the literature.

The scherzo is placed second instead of third. As in the fifth symphony, the element of humor is lacking; the divine joy that will be expressed in the finale has not come appreciably closer here. It is the largest of all Beethoven scherzos; three contrasting themes, key conflicts, full development, and recapitulation create a complete sonata-form. The technical mastery achieved here is tremendous; for the scherzo is confined largely to a one-measure motive and to fragments of diatonic scales. Two fugatos, in which the same theme is cast into three- and four-measure phrases, respectively, provide contrasts in texture without impeding the rhythmic drive for a moment. The trio, a fast-moving section in D major and in duple meter, provides relaxation from the emotional tension engendered by the scherzo. For here a phrase with the simplest melodic contour is repeated a dozen times on different scale steps and in different instruments, and is provided with extensions and brief interludes—nothing more. How much, then, are the organization and intensity of the scherzo felt when they return in the *da capo*. The trio is exactly right in its simple form, its unvarying content, and its air of pleasantry.

Having depicted a strong yet joyless and lonely condition in the first movement, and a revealing picture of driving self-will in the scherzo, Beethoven now approaches his subject from the other side. The third movement, an adagio, transcends the joyous state toward which he is striving, and suggests its spiritualized aspects. Melodic beauty, an air of serenity, and a divine spaciousness characterize the movement. It is a set of variations on a double theme, as in the fifth symphony. And while the second member of the theme appears only twice, its presence is felt throughout the movement, and its subtle animation vitalizes the quiet detachment of the whole. The last word has been said here about the attractiveness and rewards of divine joy. It remains only to achieve that state itself; that is done in the finale.

The difficulty with which Beethoven made the transition to the chorale finale has been adequately described elsewhere.[2] We need be concerned only with the end result. After a striking orchestral introduction in recitative style, fragments of the previous movements pass in review, along with a tentative first version of the finale's theme. Thereupon Beethoven introduces the D-major theme which, in contour, degrees of tension and relaxation, clarity, and appeal, is perfectly adapted to the uses he will make of it (see Example 23).

EXAMPLE 23

BEETHOVEN, Ninth Symphony

Allegro assai

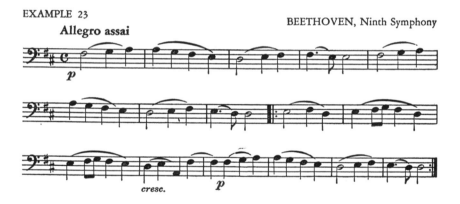

This is presented in four versions, each of which acquires a new countermelody or a figuration; the section is developed vigorously and rises to a sonorous climax. Then comes a return of the introductory recitative, now given to the baritone soloist and concerned with Beethoven's own words: "Not these tones; rather let us sound more pleasant and joy-filled ones."

The choral section, in D major, begins at this point; and for its

[2] See Riezler, *Beethoven*, pp. 208ff.; and Thayer, *The Life of Ludwig van Beethoven*, III, 144–51.

text Beethoven made free use of Schiller's "Ode to Joy" (written about 1785–1787). Schiller's poem contains eight eight-line stanzas, each of which is followed by its own four-line refrain. Beethoven employed only the first three stanzas and the refrains to the first, third, and fourth. The first and third refrains, however, are lifted out of their proper order, are given themes of their own, and become the culmination of the movement.

Each of the three stanzas is set as a variation on the theme: solo or soloists sing the entire stanza, after which the chorus repeats the last half. A transition then leads through a rousing climax to a change of meter and key; the orchestra plays, in B-flat major, a variation in march style, and the chorus follows with the fourth refrain. The text of that refrain, in Edward Bulwer-Lytton's translation,

> March, brothers, on your path,
> Joyful as victorious knights,

suggests a reason for the march style. Then follows a large and serious orchestral fugue; it is as though the foregoing textual sentiments were being meditated upon. And after the fugue and a transition, in a passage of imposing weight (again in D major), this section is concluded with a stirring return of the entire first stanza, now given to full chorus and orchestra, and again on the main theme of the movement.

Schiller's first refrain is introduced in the section which follows:

> Embrace, ye millions; let this kiss,
> Brothers, embrace the earth below!
> Yon starry worlds which shine on this,
> One common Father know!

The new theme given to this sentiment is in itself vigorous; but it is developed in an atmosphere of divine repose and spiritual ecstasy (see Example 24). (It is more than significant that the figuration which surrounds this sentiment suggests the mood of the slow movement of the later A-minor quartet, Opus 132, which is entitled, "Holy Song of Thanksgiving to the Divinity. . . .")

EXAMPLE 24

With a sudden change of key and tempo, and after an orchestral interlude, the chorus introduces the third refrain—the other principal sentiment of the poem:

> Why bow ye down—why down, ye millions?
> O world, thy Maker's throne to see,
> Look upward: search the star pavillions—
> There must His mansion be!

The hymnlike theme of this section suggests an even greater mood of reverence (see Example 25).

EXAMPLE 25

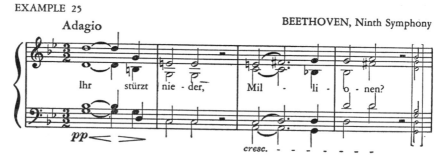

With a return of the faster tempo the chorus presents, in D major and in fugue style, the first stanza and first refrain simultaneously; the themes of Examples 23 and 24 appear in double counterpoint. And suddenly, in a mysterious, halting passage the text of the third refrain returns: "Why bow ye down? . . . look upward. . . ."

Now the text of the first stanza is reintroduced, again in the meter of the first choral section. This is no repetition, however, but a free extension and development of the thought; the latter is carried to the utmost intensity in a sublime B-major passage for the solo quartet. And finally, in prestissimo tempo, the chorus and orchestra repeat the first refrain, "Embrace, ye millions . . . ," on a greatly compressed version of the theme of Example 24. The intensity grows; and here, at the highest point of the entire movement, the first two lines of the poem, which stress the joy that is a "spark from the fires that gods have fed," bring the symphony to an end on a majestic and triumphant note.

When "man in man but hails a brother," and when the world "shall look upward . . . [for] there must His mansion be"—then shall joy be found; that is the prophetic vision Beethoven reveals in the ninth symphony. All discussion about the vocal difficulty, the impracticability of the form employed, the looseness of the form itself—these fall into insignificance beside the grandeur of the conception here set to music. Beethoven wrote not for his time, nor yet for ours; but for a far-distant future.

VI

THE EARLY ROMANTICISTS

THE WORKS OF Beethoven constitute one of the most important cultural heritages of the first quarter of the nineteenth century. Any discussion of that period's music must necessarily dwell on the content and significance of those masterpieces. But exactly contemporary with them are the works of another composer—Franz Schubert (1797–1828). And although Schubert's major orchestral works are less numerous than Beethoven's and reflect a completely different personality, they are sufficient to raise him, too, to a position among the very greatest masters.

Schubert was born in Vienna and remained, except for a few brief trips to neighboring regions, a resident of that city during all of his short life. His career was spent in obscurity for the most part, and his genius was recognized by only a few friends—and by Beethoven, when that composer lay on his deathbed. During his formative years the works of Haydn and Mozart were his daily companions; the unique nature of his musical gifts led him to stress elements other than those revealed by each new work of Beethoven. Thus it is understandable that the two greatest exponents of eighteenth-century Classicism should have provided him with a point of departure.

Schubert's first orchestral works were four overtures, one of them written for a comedy, *Der Teufel als Hydraulicus*, and all of them probably written before 1812, at which time Schubert was still a pupil at the Imperial Choir School; the first is in B flat, the others are in D. While these works are written in the transparent manner of the time, they also contain elements which point toward his future style.

Schubert's first three symphonies were written in 1813, 1814, and 1815, respectively, probably for the amateur orchestra which was an outgrowth of the Schubert family quartet. Attempts to link introduction and first movement thematically may be seen in the first and third symphonies. Those works are strongly reminiscent of Haydn in thematic outlines, adherence on occasion to elaborations of a single theme, and in general buoyance.

The fourth symphony, in C minor, was written in 1816. Here is a radically new content, for a dark and restless mood prevails throughout. Schubert himself supplied a nickname—the "Tragic." And it is filled with the same thematic conflicts which animate many of Beethoven's C-minor works, the *Coriolanus* overture and the fifth symphony, for example. Indeed, its first movement bears a striking resemblance to Beethoven's C-minor string quartet, Opus 18, No. 4. Pulsating figures in the accompaniment, diminished-seventh chords, and the like give the movement a gloomy air which the closing C-major section does little to dispel. And yet there are brighter moments in the symphony also, particularly those which modulate into the mediant and submediant tonalities.

The fifth symphony, in B flat, was also written in 1816; but here Schubert returned to the earlier type of content. For not only is the orchestra reduced in size—clarinets, trumpets, and tympani are omitted and one flute is called for instead of two—but the slow introduction is eliminated also. Further, the dimensions of the work are smaller than any previous symphony of Schubert's, and its scope and content are those of early Mozart. Melodious themes, tight transitions, and a development section which is terse and to the point —such elements constitute the first movement. Yet Schubert's handiwork is seen in that sections in D-flat major and E-flat minor add their characteristic colors. Again in the slow movement does a perfect blend of Mozart and Schubert appear: a suave, graceful lyric theme in E flat—and a contrasting second part in C-flat major and G minor. The movement is in an open, chamber-music style; its length does not lessen its appeal. The minuet recalls the spirit of Haydn in its rough vigor; that of Mozart in its minor key and chromatic inflections—but the trio is pure Schubert in its melodic serenity. And in the finale Haydn appears again; the movement might well have been modeled upon the 1770 style of that master.

With the sixth symphony, in C major and written in 1817, Schubert returned to a large framework; but the content remains small. For this work is similar in style to the first three and the fifth symphonies. The slow introduction is leisurely and terse in alternate sections; broad chords and melodic fragments in a variety of keys lead to a charming first movement. But the dimensions of that movement require more than a charming content; piquant themes of a ballet-music type scarcely permit of symphonic development. Schubert therefore has recourse to constant and delightful repetitions of fragments in colorful harmonies and colorful instrumental groupings. The fact that the first phrase is given to woodwinds alone establishes the mood of the entire movement. The andante contains a similar mood in spite of its slow tempo; graceful in the manner of a folk song, it presents short rhythmic motives (triplets) and running figures in animated fashion. A great amount of busy-work, heard alternately in strings and winds, gives an impression of contrapuntal devices; this in the midst of a marchlike style.

The majority of Schubert's third movements had been fast minuets. Now, in the sixth symphony, he composed a true scherzo on Beethoven's model. Its first part is in miniature sonata-form; but in spite of its fast triple meter, it deals with fragments of melody and its harmonic scheme is wide: D, G, and A flat are touched upon. The trio, in E major, is a strangely halting and fitful section with sharp chords and running passages combined in various ways. The finale is a weak movement, for it embodies so many different stylistic elements that unity of expression becomes impossible. In general a dancelike piece, it contains fanfares, running figures, coarse rhythmic effects, and a wider harmonic range than is usual even in Schubert. Its brilliance does not conceal the fact that it is essentially a potpourri of several melodic ideas, nor does its charm hide its diffuseness of form.

Three overtures also date from 1817, the year of the sixth symphony. The first of these, in D major, represents a formal experiment on Schubert's part; for the slow introduction, containing two contrasting tempos, is recapitulated in part at the end of the main movement, and portions of the introduction's themes appear in the development. The second, also in D, was later (in 1820) transposed to C major and expanded, and thereupon became the overture to the play, *Die Zauberharfe*. Still later (in 1828) Schubert arranged that C-major version for piano duet and called it *Rosamunde*.[1] In the *Rosamunde* (or more correctly, the *Zauberharfe*) version, the one which is most frequently performed today, a songful introduction in C minor proceeds in a variety of keys, E flat and G flat among them, to a lilting and altogether charming allegro in conservative sonata-form. Sweet melodiousness coupled with vigor and straightforwardness rise to new heights here. Finally, the third of the 1817 overtures is "in the Italian style"; Italian style in this case means the style of Rossini. The brilliance, noise, and characteristic crescendos of that style are well reflected in Schubert's overture. A variety of themes appear in a variety of keys, are orchestrated with taste and effectiveness, and are loosely recapitulated. It is a delightful work without serious intent or great importance.

The E-minor overture of 1819 is Schubert's last work in this form. Italian elements are here replaced by a quality which again points toward his later style. Rhythmic intensity marks large portions of the work, along with the constant play of harmonic color. Theme repetition (instead of theme development) had long since become characteristic of much—but by no means of all nor of the best—of Schubert's production. Here all sense of proportion is lost, for the repetitions are carried on at great length. But the charm of the

[1] But at the performance of the play *Rosamunde* in 1823 a different overture, one intended for the opera *Alfonso and Estrella*, was played. See Abraham, ed., *The Music of Schubert*, pp. 33, 214, and 270n.

melodies, the delightful woodwind effects, and the colorful modulations overcome to a large extent its formal lacks; the overture is still worthy of performance.

About 1821 Schubert began a symphony in E minor; the usual slow introduction and four movements were planned. The manuscript contains ruled pages, tempo indications, names of instruments —in short, it was fully prepared to receive on its pages the notes themselves. About one hundred measures were completed in full score, after which Schubert merely sketched out the rest. Themes, accompanying figures, dynamics—all the essentials—are present; only details are missing.[2] The work was completed, on the basis of these sketches, by Felix Weingartner in 1934, and has even been published and performed. Had Schubert himself finished the symphony it would have taken its high place as a transitional work between the six rather derivative symphonies of 1813–1817 and the mature, individualized B-minor and C-major symphonies of 1822 and 1828, respectively.

A vast distance separates the B-minor—the so-called "Unfinished" —symphony from earlier works. Written in 1822, the two movements of this famous composition reveal the perfect fusion of Schubert's lyric expression and the framework of Classical sonata-form. Lyric themes had been present in the earlier period, of course; but usually they served as foils to more dramatic or characteristic contrasting themes. It is in depicting the conflict or contrast between themes of two types that the essential nature of sonata-form is found. Now a symphony emerges in which *all* is lyric feeling. And therein lies the unique nature of Schubert's B-minor symphony. It is ironic that the one instrumental work which leads directly toward the future and which contains no trace of derivative influence should have remained unknown until 1865, thirty-seven years after its composer's death.

Schubert's desire thematically to unite introduction and first movement here takes a new form. For the first phrase of the move-

[2] See Grove, "Schubert," in *Grove's Dictionary*, 4th ed., IV, 598; and a fuller account in Abraham, ed., *The Music of Schubert*, pp. 60–63.

ment, while it does serve to prepare the mood of the work, is employed thematically and illuminates almost the entire development section and coda. Nowhere in the composer's symphonies is a closer integration of thematic material encountered than here. This beautifully symmetrical movement, containing some of the most touching melodies Schubert ever wrote, also contains an undercurrent of pessimism. That feeling grows as the development, which is as tightly knit as any in his works, presents in dramatic and wild fashion a thematic conflict between the introductory phrase and descending arpeggios drawn from the transitional material in the exposition.

The second movement, a large, free rondo with extended themes and considerable development of thematic material, forms the perfect complement to the first movement. For a mood of resignation, carried by exquisite melodies, is the most striking feature of this andante. Large sections in C-sharp minor and A minor, in contrast to the basic tonality of E major, provide rich harmonies and a wide range of color. The instrumental combinations employed here also add to the beauty and variety of the movement.

It becomes obvious from any performance of this symphony that sustained lyricism has, for the first time in an instrumental work, become an essential stylistic ingredient. And the lyric melodies are of a new type: they are things in themselves. No longer do they have "meaning," or do they require analysis or reflection to make them understandable. Schubert's melodies in general, and in this symphony in particular, are objects of rare beauty which need only be admired, not studied. The melodies appear in instrumental combinations which reveal the beauty of pure sound. Schubert's use of wind instruments, especially oboe, clarinet, and trombone, contributes greatly to the color of his works.

The vexing question of Schubert's reason for not finishing the B-minor symphony has not been answered to everyone's satisfaction. A sketch for a third movement in scherzo form, written out in piano score as far as the second part of the trio and including nine measures fully orchestrated, exists. Among the various explanations offered are that, the scherzo not going well, Schubert abandoned the project and lost interest in the work; that two other movements were indeed written, but were subsequently lost.[3] But even the proponents of these theories must admit to the complete effectiveness and the complementary nature of the two existing movements. The first stresses pessimism and a rather somber mood; the second is a movement of resignation. What more could Schubert have done in this direction? Two aspects of a single mood are depicted in two unlike yet mutually dependent movements; the symphony was complete. Schubert, realizing this in time, broke off work on the scherzo and never again returned to the composition. And the unusual fact that a symphony may contain only two movements and yet be complete has escaped those for whom the term "Unfinished Symphony" has romantic and sentimental connotations.

The Schubert literature contains references to a symphony supposedly written at Gastein in 1825. Here again one may take one's choice of speculations: the work was sent to the Gesellschaft der Musikfreunde and was subsequently lost; or it is but a reworking of the sixth symphony; or it is contained in unorchestrated form in the Grand Duo for piano (four hands). The fact remains that no score of the "Gastein" symphony has yet been found; the field is wide open for further surmises about this, perhaps the greatest mystery in Schubert's career.

A discussion of his last orchestral work may be prefaced by the following. His letters often referred to his desire to write a "grand symphony"; in 1824 he declared that chamber music had become a means of developing a larger style in preparation for full-scale symphonic writing. Indeed, the Octet of that year gives evidence of his preoccupation with expanded orchestral forms. As early as 1817 he had given the title "grand" to his sixth symphony, but later dropped it as being inappropriate. Not until his last year of life, in 1828, did he complete a work to which that term may properly be applied: the C-major symphony is such a work.

A word must be said here about the numbering of Schubert's last symphonies. At a time when the B-minor of 1822 was unknown and

[3] See Abraham, ed., *The Music of Schubert*, pp. 63–64.

the E-minor sketch of 1821 was disregarded, the C-major of 1828 became his seventh; after 1865, the newly-discovered B-minor became the eighth. A later attempt to correct the faulty chronology took into account the E-minor sketch, which is actually his seventh, and thus the C-major became known as the ninth (the B-minor retaining its eighth place). But there are those whose faith in the existence of the "Gastein" symphony of 1825 impels them to include it as the ninth; whereupon the C-major becomes the tenth. Thus, in various editions, recordings, and programs Schubert's last symphony has been referred to as the seventh, the ninth, or the tenth.

The outstanding facts about that C-major symphony concern its size, its rhythmic concentration, and its intense emotional expression —the latter carried as much by driving motion as by the extent of its climaxes. Even more than in other works of Schubert, the slow introduction contains the melodic germ not only of the first movement but of the entire symphony. Many of its themes and rhythmic motives are based upon the rising or falling interval of a third (see Example 26); this element is present in the very first measures of the introduction and animates the greater part of the work. The first

EXAMPLE 26

SCHUBERT, C-major Symphony

movement proper contains three contrasting themes; an enormous development which includes fragments of the introduction, passages in which theme fragments are masterfully recombined, and others in which magical use is made of the trombones (on a phrase derived from the second measure of the introduction); a complete recapitulation; and an extended coda which contains further development of thematic material as well as an imposing statement of the introductory phrase. The movement develops enormous rhythmic vitality and rises to great climaxes.

Nostalgia of the most touching kind fills the second movement, a rondo in A minor. A piquant theme over a light accompaniment alternates with a quiet diatonic section (Example 26, c and d, respectively). Considerable manipulation of two fragments of the former (marked x and y in Example 26c) gives the movement a high degree of expressive unity. The whole is one of Schubert's most profound inspirations; particularly noble is a transitional passage in which a duet between oboe and cellos eloquently disproves the statement that he could not write counterpoint.

The scherzo is probably the largest of its kind in Schubert's works. Without altering the absolute speed of the movement he gains immeasurably in nervous excitement by filling alternate measures of the theme with six eighth-notes instead of three quarters (see Example 26e). Short-breathed soft-loud contrasts and fully developed sonata-form in the first part testify to Schubert's adoption of Beethoven's scherzo content. The type of contrast which the trio brings is, however, purely Schubert's own. For where the first had been rugged and dainty in turn, the trio is mysterious and remote. The whole is a powerful movement.

The finale, one of the most massive symphonic movements written up to its time, contains not themes as much as rhythmic motives and scale passages. It puts even the first movement to shame with its tremendous drive and power. Long developments, particularly of the first four measures of Example 26g, are intense and rise to great climaxes; here, as also in the other movements, Schubert's sure harmonic touch is much in evidence. Magical modulations, notably one from G to B major (measure 202), add considerable color to the movement; and the free harmonic scheme of the recapitulation, which begins in E flat and moves to F major, carries the rich color through to the great coda. The latter is essentially a further development of the rhythmic motives upon which the entire movement is based.

The C-major symphony exhibits a strong mixture of Classical elements and those—later to be called Romantic—which were to lead to the future. But it contains a Classicism that is expanded beyond all previous dimensions, Beethoven's ninth symphony excepted. Schubert did not reveal, in his symphony, the organizing genius and self-critical judgment of the older composer, it is true. But in the place of those characteristics he utilized his tremendous gift for melodic invention to overcome the work's diffuse structure. The rhythmic compulsion of the C-major symphony is overwhelming; its melodies and harmonies are ravishing in their pure beauty. The symphony's appeal is direct and immediate. It is found not in a tightly organized and economical form, but in a succession of moments full of isolated beauty and utmost sincerity and in an atmosphere of unpretentious but intense feeling.

Pretentiousness was foreign to Schubert; and though his music contains many passionate and dramatic passages, the emotions he reveals are those of a normal human being. There is little of superhuman stature about him, as there is about Beethoven. Schubert's music reflects all the emotions common to humanity and seldom transcends them, as Beethoven's does; seldom does he rise above his essential nature and fail to be unassuming and modest. Schubert appeals not through complexity but through pure beauty.

The symphonic repertoire, insofar as the period from about 1782 to 1828 is concerned, confines itself largely to the works of Haydn, Mozart, Beethoven, and Schubert. The manner in which those composers have been discussed in the present book in itself reflects that fact. A few dozen works by those masters have, in the long interval since their creation, proved themselves and demonstrated their right

to enjoy long life. But in that very fact lies a danger: the casual
listener receives the impression that the major composers wrote in a
vacuum, as it were, and that no other works were written during the
years these giants roamed the earth. With that danger comes another:
one cannot properly appreciate how greatly they tower over the
minor composers. The latter seldom revealed individual traits of
style, it is true; yet many of them, writing in a vein similar to that
of the masters, produced compositions that are worthy of occasional
performance today.

Among the contemporaries of Haydn, Karl Ditters von Dittersdorf (1739–1799) may be singled out. Dittersdorf, an excellent
violinist, was also a prolific composer in many fields. One hundred or
more symphonies and some three dozen concertos for various instruments are among his orchestral compositions. Twelve of the symphonies, written about 1785, are unique early examples of program
music for orchestra; they are based upon selections from Ovid's
Metamorphoses and are descriptive to a high degree. Dittersdorf
found himself at his best in combining elements of two styles; a considerable amount of Haydnesque humor and lightness characterizes
his work, along with a suave, cantabile melodic turn strongly reminiscent of late Mozart.

Michael Haydn (1737–1806), with some thirty symphonies, in-
clined more to the style of Mozart than to that of his illustrious elder
brother. We have seen (page 93) that one of his symphonies, copied
out in admiration by Mozart, was long attributed to the younger
master as K.444 (425a). Great competence in technical matters, wit
and imagination in thematic invention, fine proportions and clear
forms—these characterize the works of the younger Haydn. Only
in emotional significance, in quality of mood and depth of insight
does he fall below his friend. Among French composers, Étienne-
Nicholas Méhul (1763–1817) may be mentioned. Here is a more
pretentious version of Haydn's style. The two symphonies by Méhul
that have been preserved reveal him bound by traditional formal
patterns and unwilling or unable to develop thematic material along
the lines suggested by Haydn.

A number of composers contemporary with Mozart lived on well into the nineteenth century and thus became contemporaries of Beethoven as well. Muzio Clementi (1752–1832), piano virtuoso, composer, and business man; Ignaz Pleyel (1757–1831), pupil of Haydn, composer, and manufacturer of pianos; Johann Nepomuk Hummel (1778–1837), pupil of Mozart, brilliant pianist and improviser, and prolific composer; Luigi Cherubini (1760–1842), famed composer of operas and sacred music—these were among the minor masters of the time.

Clementi, Pleyel, and Hummel seldom advanced beyond the principles of late Mozart without, of course, even approaching the latter's content. Available works of these composers reveal, in general, a thematic similarity to Mozart's and the same moods of clarity, transparence, and grace. Clementi favored a somewhat affected style; an arbitrary mixture of normal harmonic procedures and unrelated chords give the impression that he consciously desired to be more "original" than Mozart.[4] Hummel's piano concertos are brilliant and superficial, but also contain graceful and elegant passages in the best Classical tradition. Cherubini's single symphony, written in 1815, reveals a contrapuntal quality which virtually none of the works by minor composers of the time contain. Sonorous textures, intricate detail, and much canonic writing alternate with poetic passages of rare melodic beauty.

Cherubini occasionally succeeded, in his opera overtures and particularly in the overture to *Les Deux Journées* (produced in England as *The Water Carrier*) of 1800, in hinting at dramatic conflicts to come and briefly summarizing them. Thus he may well have been of influence upon Beethoven in this respect. But a reversal of this influence was not apparent: none of the composers mentioned here showed any understanding of the new impulses Beethoven was bringing to music, nor were they stimulated in any degree by the content, scope, and grandeur of that composer's works.

Likewise, the instrumental works of Ludwig Spohr (1792–1859) are devoid of any perceptible relationship to the styles of Beethoven.

[4] Kretzschmar, *Führer durch den Concertsaal*, I, 208.

A refined, sweet melodiousness characterizes Spohr's nine symphonies; the strong, masculine aspect of Classical style, which in Haydn and Mozart is so well blended with refinement, is largely missing. His interest in descriptive music may be inferred from their titles: for example, *The Consecration of Tones, Historical Symphony in the Styles of Three Ages, Mundane and Divine in Human Life,* and *The Seasons.* But Spohr seldom allowed that interest to conflict with the requirements of strict Classical form as he understood it. Only in the more than a dozen violin concertos does one encounter elements which justify placing Spohr on the fringe of the Romantic movement. One, in G minor, contains a rondo based on Spanish themes; another, the well-known *Gesangszene,* introduced the accompanied recitative into the concerto form. (See page 171 in this connection.)

About a dozen of the forty-odd overtures of Gioacchino Rossini (1792–1868) have enjoyed a place in the repertoire to the present day. Between *La scala di seta (The Silken Ladder)* of 1812 and *William Tell* of 1829, Rossini wrote a great variety of humorous, dramatic, and unfailingly melodious works. His method in the overtures was not to present dramatic contrasts which foreshadowed later stage actions, but to bring to expression a selection of tunes from the operas. Ostensibly in a kind of sonata-form, the overtures are little more than potpourris of charming, brilliant melodies. The range of Rossini's humor was great: subtle, sly, and ironic; but also broad and coarse. Carried by his fabulous gift for melodic invention and set in sparkling orchestral contexts, the humorous qualities shine through abundantly. The overtures are seldom marred by dull or dry moments; they reflect the mood of *opera buffa* (or grand opera in the case of *William Tell*) at its best.

The freedom of form found in Schubert's works and his interest in the pure sound of music (as illustrated by his search for, and use made of, new instrumental groupings) were shared by other composers of the time, notably by Carl Maria von Weber (1786–1828). Weber composed two symphonies, a number of brilliant concertos for piano (these will be discussed below; see page 171) and some for solo wind instruments, and a variety of other instrumental works. But he is remembered today, insofar as the symphonic repertoire is concerned, largely for the overtures to three of his late operas: *Der Freischütz* (1820), *Euryanthe* (1823), and *Oberon* (1826). These overtures reflect a compromise between the dramatic unfolding of the opera's conflicts, as revealed in Beethoven's dramatic overtures, and Rossini's principle of presenting merely a medley of operatic melodies. Ostensibly in sonata-form, they delay the *dénouement* of the conflict until the coda; the largest climax is reserved for the end.

The instrumental color of Weber's overtures, however, represents a new element in orchestral writing. His use of extreme instrumental ranges, his imagination in devising new combinations, his subtlety in contrasting dynamics and unusual instrumental effects—these and many more factors contribute to the new sound of his music. The interest in orchestration as an art may be said to have begun in Weber's time; principles revealed in his works were employed and expanded by Berlioz, Wagner, and a long line of orchestral masters who succeeded them. The end result was the huge, colorful, modern orchestra and the flexible, imaginative orchestration which called that orchestra into being; but credit for the original stimulus undoubtedly belongs to Weber.

The new subject matters to which Weber turned in the first decades of the nineteenth century were among the first evidences of the changes in thought, in artistic outlook, and in aesthetic philosophy which were to dominate the entire century and were to be summarized in the term "Romantic period." Dissatisfaction with the stylized, form-dominated Classicism of the minor composers, the influence of the "Storm and Stress" movement of German writers and poets—these and many other cultural phenomena contributed to a reaction directed against the musical practices of the previous century.[5] It became necessary to find new subject matters; oriental

[5] See Lang, *Music in Western Civilization*, pp. 734–50 and 801–9, for a fuller account of those phenomena.

tales, supernatural stories, the whole corpus of mythology, the fertile field of folklore—such matters inspired both dramatic and instrumental composers. A search for new musical effects led to modification of the older structural principles on the part of many composers; miniatures as well as grossly inflated musical forms appeared. A desire to combine the arts, to find musical stimulation from a literary work, in a word, to "tell stories" in music, became dominant. The new orchestration revealed in Weber's works provided composers with means to implement such new thoughts; the period progressed in the direction of more and more instrumental color, extreme experiments in musical form, and a subjective, self-revealing kind of musical expression.

The Romantic movement, so rich in enthusiasm and interests, could not keep within bounds. Indeed, it recognized no bounds. Enthusiasm became fanaticism; musicians and laymen alike took sides eagerly in this or that development. Friendship became undying love; the feeling of brotherhood, among the typical and less-restrained Romanticists, grew to great proportions. Sentiment became sentimentality, and the latter permeated other circles than musical ones. The Romanticists, no matter how varied their individual attitudes toward the world, shared a common avidity for intense emotional experience and a lively interest in their environment. Out of that feeling grew the intense subjectivity which is the outstanding characteristic of Romanticism. Out of the all-embracing love for the world grew the lyric expressiveness, the tender emotion, and the impulsiveness which are its musical counterparts.

"It is the addition of strangeness to beauty that constitutes the romantic character in art; and the desire of beauty being a fixed element in every artistic organization, it is the addition of curiosity to this desire of beauty that constitutes the romantic temper. When one's curiosity is deficient . . . one is liable to value mere academical proprieties too highly . . . and when one's curiosity is in excess, when it overbalances the desire of beauty, then one is liable to value in works of art what is inartistic in them." [6] And insofar as strange-

6 Walter Pater, *Appreciations*, V, 246.

ness may be taken to include exotic or new elements, and curiosity taken to imply a conscious search for new effects, Pater's observation characterizes the music of the nineteenth century's first half excellently well.

Not all composers were equally drawn to the new movement, of course; nor did all its elements come into being on a particular date. Indeed, one Romantic characteristic may be seen as far back as the 1780s: the use of an introduction to prepare for a forthcoming mood. We have seen such introductions in certain of Haydn's and Mozart's symphonies; and we have seen, in Beethoven's ninth and Schubert's B-minor and C-major symphonies, how the introductory material could become an integral part of the composition. Other Romantic elements gradually took hold of musical expression during the first decades of the nineteenth century, notably the new art of orchestration and the stimulus derived from extramusical experiences.

Many of the first generation of Romantic composers worked most typically in the operatic field, and then as disciples of Weber; Heinrich Marschner (1795–1861) is prominent in this group. But an equally large number were especially drawn to instrumental music; among German composers of the time, Mendelssohn and Schumann were outstanding. Each in his own way contributed to the complex Romantic idiom and firmly established a style which a later generation embraced enthusiastically.

Felix Mendelssohn [7] (1809–1847), the son of cultured and wealthy parents, enjoyed every advantage in education and environment. The Mendelssohn home in Berlin was a center of musical life; small orchestra concerts were a feature of that life, and many of his early compositions, which began in his twelfth year, were written for those concerts. He had every opportunity to hear them and to profit from the expert criticism made by the eminent musicians who considered it a privilege to attend the performances. His maturity

---

[7] The surname Mendelssohn-Bartholdy was adopted by the family when they renounced the Jewish faith and entered the Protestant church.

as a composer dates from about his sixteenth year; for the overture to *A Midsummer Night's Dream*, the Octet for strings, and similar works in which virtually all of his later style traits are revealed were written within a year or two of 1825. From about that time his style underwent little significant change. Secure in his mastery of form, confirmed in his espousal of a sweet lyricism, and true to his conflict-free temperament, he composed steadily and fluently for virtually all musical media. Five symphonies, six works for soloist with or-chestra, and about a dozen overtures and miscellaneous compositions represent his contributions to the orchestral literature.

Among Mendelssohn's early works are about a dozen symphonies for string instruments, on the level of student work and presumably written for the concerts in his home; they have not been published. The symphony which is called the first, however, was written in 1824: Opus 11, in C minor. It contains the traditional four move-ments and requires only the traditional Classical orchestra—the usual pairs of woodwinds, brass, and tympani, and strings. This is a modest work, regular as to form and undistinguished in its melodic lines. It gives little evidence of the rich imagination and melodic subtlety which will characterize the later works.

Three symphonies were begun about 1830–1831, a time in which Mendelssohn traveled extensively; Italy and Scotland were among the countries visited. The three were completed at widely different times, however, were published not even in the order of their com-pletion, and were numbered in accord with neither scheme. Thus, the first to be completed (in 1832) was the D-minor, the so-called "Reformation" symphony; this was published posthumously as Opus 107 and became the fifth symphony. Then followed the A-major, nicknamed the "Italian," symphony, completed in 1833 but known as the fourth symphony, Opus 90. Finally, the A-minor, called the "Scotch," symphony, labeled Opus 56, was finished in 1842 and numbered third among the five. And to add further con-fusion, the work known as Mendelssohn's second symphony is a vocal composition, *Hymn of Praise*, written in 1840 and published as Opus 52.

The "Reformation" symphony, written for a celebration commemorating Martin Luther's church reforms and for an orchestra which is enlarged by three trombones, exhibits characteristics which are in keeping with its purpose. The slow introduction which precedes the first movement includes a quotation of the "Dresden Amen." A rather archaic tone pervades the first movement; it suggests to Kretzschmar [8] the quarrelsome nature and the strong religious faith of the early sixteenth century. After the second movement, which is a scherzo with minuet overtones, comes a short andante written in the manner of a recitative, again suggestive of earlier times. The finale is prefaced by a short movement which is built entirely upon the chorale, "A Mighty Fortress is our God." The finale itself is an allegro quite in the manner of a chorale-prelude: single lines of the chorale are heard as counterpoints above elaborate chordal figurations. Then, with a turn to allegro maestoso, the chorale is developed in a texture which includes imposing fanfares and vigorous unison passages. The work as a whole is a mixture of melodious sections and others in contrapuntal style. It pays comparatively little attention to fine internal detail, and the careful craftsmanship which distinguishes so many of Mendelssohn's other works is largely missing.

The "Italian" symphony, in A major, is in an entirely different category; it represents Mendelssohn in his best and happiest mood. More than almost any other work, it brings his unique qualities as a composer to full expression. Although the symphony reflects his memories of the pleasant trip to Italy and was in fact largely composed during that visit, it was written for the Philharmonic Society in London and performed there in 1833. It contains the usual four movements and is written for the standard orchestra of the time (without trombones).

A combination of brilliance and reflectiveness, also of honest feeling and sentimentality, characterize the first movement. Beginning impulsively and in a mood of sheer excitement, it contains solid and vigorous elements as well. This is not the fairy-tale style we shall

[8] *Führer durch den Concertsaal*, I, 247.

see elsewhere in Mendelssohn, but a fast, bright, and masculine manner that was new to orchestral music. And seldom did he write so captivating a movement as the andante which follows. Having the character of a long narrative, it is concerned with two themes, somber and light-hearted respectively. The prevailing tone is moody, but moodiness in Mendelssohn does not lead to black despair. No emotion deeper than minor annoyance is touched upon here, and the narrative flow of the piece is nowhere impeded.

A third movement in the style of a German *Ländler* takes the place of the traditional scherzo. Comfortable, elegant, and unfailingly melodious, it contains a magical middle part which recalls Mendelssohn's youthful enthusiasm for Weber; for its series of mysterious chords for horns and bassoons suggest the remote realms and supernatural forest glens in which that composer's operas abound. Only in the finale may one speak directly of Italian influences; the movement is a saltarello, a fast and violent dance then popular in Italy. In expanded sonata-form, it contains several contrasting themes all of which contribute to restless, fleet motion and rousing climaxes. The "Italian" symphony is one of Mendelssohn's great works. Detailed working-out of charming or powerful ideas, an unfailing grasp of fine proportion and proper form, a boundless imagination in matters of instrumental color, a minimum of the cloying sentiment that sometimes mars his pages—these are among the elements which raise it to the honored place it enjoys in the repertoire.

The work which is usually referred to as Mendelssohn's second symphony is a hybrid. It was written for a celebration of the four-hundredth anniversary of the invention of printing and accompanied the unveiling of a statue of Gutenberg in Leipzig in 1840. Its full title is as follows: "Hymn of Praise, a symphony cantata on texts from the Holy Scriptures. Opus 52." Opening with a three-movement *sinfonia*, which constitutes about one quarter of the work, it continues with nine vocal numbers set in great variety but basically in B-flat major: several full choruses, duets, solos, and the chorale, "Now Thank We All Our God." The principal sentiment of the text is found in the words of the first chorus: "All that has life and breath, sing to the Lord."

The "Scotch" symphony, Opus 56, in A minor, was not completed until 1842. Like its "Italian" predecessor, it is a reflection of Mendelssohn's travel impressions; this time the impressions gained from a visit to Holyrood Castle in Edinburgh, the seat of the unfortunate Mary Stuart. A restrained, somewhat gloomy mood prevails throughout large parts of the symphony. True, three of its movements are fast, it contains many ingratiating and even warmly sentimental melodies, and the composer's fiery temperament comes to full expression. Yet in spite of this the work reveals little of the cheerful impulsiveness, the sheer creative joy which is typical of Mendelssohn at his best. Phrases follow one another at expected intervals, and great regularity—almost heaviness—of structure is apparent.

In a formal sense, the work contains several innovations. Perhaps of greatest importance is the composer's direction to connect the four movements in performance. The "Scotch" symphony in this respect may be said to mark another step toward the later nineteenth-century developments which led to the creation of the symphonic poem. Further evidence is given in the construction of its first movement; for here a slow introduction precedes the main movement, the latter is thematically connected with the former, and the material of the introduction appears in the form of an epilogue. Later composers continued that process by connecting all movements with the first: cyclical form resulted, and with it the symphonic poem.

Again in this symphony, the internal fast movement is given a new content. For here, and as second movement instead of third, Mendelssohn wrote a wild, reckless dance in duple meter, a dance said to be based on a Scottish folk song. Gone is all trace of the traditional scherzo–trio–scherzo *da capo;* triple meter has disappeared also, along with the scherzo's humorous content and abrupt dynamic and emotional contrasts. The internal fast movement proved to be the least stable of all symphonic movements. Changes in Beethoven's examples of the form have been pointed out; one can find similar changes in Schubert's, but primarily in his chamber music. Now, in Mendelssohn, almost every work brings its own modifications. We may note the use of a larger metrical group in his first symphony, the somewhat archaic combination of scherzo and minuet moods in the "Reformation," the *Ländler* in the "Italian," and now the duple-meter dance in the "Scotch." We may mention the equally great variety in the string quartets of Opus 12 and Opus 44 and in the two piano trios; and finally, the completely new style of scherzo in the *Midsummer Night's Dream* music.

The solo concerto in the early nineteenth century, and here we include Mendelssohn's version of that form, exhibits enough new elements to justify its discussion in this place, out of exact chronology and by way of introduction to that composer's concertos. For to a greater extent than in the eighteenth century it became a display piece. One may indeed say that much of the century's instrumental music in all forms became increasingly concerned with virtuosic display, and that the concerto was simply a more exposed victim of this tendency.

While public concerts had increased in number during the eighteenth century, they did not yet dominate the musical scene. Aristocratic establishments, private salons, and the like continued to restrain the democratization of music. Not until the French Revolution weakened the hold of the old aristocracy on music did public concerts as an institution become the largest single force in European music-making. And along with this development, possibly as a corollary to it, came a renewed interest in virtuosity for its own sake; but parallel to this again was the emergence of the symphony as the dominant musical form and a corresponding decline in the importance of the concerto. This, in turn, affected the attitude of composers.

To a great extent, eighteenth-century composers had also been leading performers (Haydn being perhaps the outstanding exception); and solo concertos had been composed largely to meet the needs of those who wrote them. Virtuosity as an ideal scarcely interested the major composers of the time; but even those composers were fully aware of the technical levels to which the virtuosi had attained, and could not but invest their works with a brilliance to match. Thus, the concertos by the masters of the period 1800 to about 1850 exhibited a technical quality which measured up to the abilities of the new performers.

The major composers, by and large, were also affected by Romantic attitudes toward musical form. Among the problems to which they turned their attention were the traditional double exposition of themes (for orchestra and solo instrument, respectively) and the matter of connections between movements. Now, Beethoven himself had indicated what might be done in both regards, for neither of his last two piano concertos remains bound to the double-exposition tradition; and in his last piano concerto a transitional passage connects the second and third movements.

One concerto of Ludwig Spohr, spoken of earlier, represents an early attempt to solve the second of those problems: the *Gesang-szene*, for violin and orchestra, written in 1816. For while that work contains the traditional three movements, it is designed to be played without interruption; each movement runs into the next, and in effect a one-movement form emerges. Spohr's avowed purpose was to produce, for an Italian trip, an instrumental piece analogous in content and form to the operatic aria favored by the Italians; hence the piece in the form of an operatic scene, complete with recitative.

The process is somewhat similar in Weber's *Konzertstück* for piano and orchestra, written in 1821. Here, four movements or sections are connected and continuity of playing is essential. But in another respect Weber's concerto is unique in its decade, for it is based upon a program: the lovers are separated by wars, she has visions of his death, he returns unharmed, and they are united in love (with a triumphant conclusion). To this program Weber applied the full sweep of his great imagination and his enormous command of the piano. Technical devices, some of them foreshadowed by Beethoven, here find rich development; an effective, brilliant piece results, and one which remains faithful to its program. Its musical qualities are a different matter.

The two concertos for piano by Frederic Chopin (1810–1849) reveal a temporary halting of the tendency. One, in F minor, was written in 1829; another, in E minor, a year later. When published, however, this order was reversed: the E-minor became Opus 11, the F-minor Opus 21. Both of them reveal Chopin's unwillingness (or inability) to depart from Classical formal models. Each begins with the old double exposition, and each contains the usual three movements, well separated. The composer ignored or misunderstood the traditional relationship between solo and orchestra. Here the piano dominates; the orchestra is reduced to giving the mildest kind of harmonic support, or emerges stiffly to do duty in old-fashioned ritornello interludes. The result, in virtually every movement of the two works, is a charming set of miniatures in contrasting moods. Fiery, passionate, or lyric in turn, such sections are dominated by the air of melancholy which hangs over considerable portions of the nineteenth century's music. Chopin's piano writing here is brilliant without effort; there is in it little virtuosic display for its own sake, but rather a type of expression in which freedom of improvisation is not bound by technical limitations. In general, the concertos tend to disintegrate; they exhibit little of the long line and cumulative effect which distinguish both earlier and later works in this form.

In Nicolo Paganini (1782–1840) concert audiences beheld a violin virtuoso whose technical feats have remained unsurpassed to the present day—if the accounts of contemporaries are to be believed. From about 1808 up and down the length of Italy, and after 1828 in western Europe, Paganini dazzled all who heard him. He specialized in performing music of his own composition; in it he introduced a number of new technical devices—complex double stops, increased use of overtones, left-hand pizzicati, and the like. Yet his skill was exhibited primarily in improvisation; his works are scarcely more than frameworks within which his brilliant fireworks were displayed. Among his posthumously published compositions are two concertos, in D major and B minor respectively; these

works give but a pale reflection of the noble style, passionate expression, and technical wizardry that his generation attributed to
him. Traditional forms and procedures characterize his works; it is
only in content that they contributed so greatly to the growth of
virtuosity. Paganini's sensational accomplishments inspired many
pianists, Liszt and Schumann among them, to do likewise on their
instrument; and his influence on other composers was equally great.

It was neither Chopin nor Paganini who carried forward the evolution of form in which Spohr and Weber had interested themselves,
but Mendelssohn. The latter's first piano concerto, in G minor,
Opus 25, written about 1831, presented at once a solution of both
of the concerto's formal problems. The double exposition is done
away with, for the piano and the orchestra share equally in a single
statement of the themes. And the parts of the concerto are connected
by means of a fanfarelike passage which appears between first and
second as well as between second and third movements. Each movement, however, retains its integrity and contributes to the forward
motion of the whole. The second piano concerto, in D minor, Opus
40 from 1837, contains a similar telescoping of themes in the exposition, but does without the transitional fanfare between movements.
The latter are connected harmonically, however, and proceed without pause between. A few years later Mendelssohn was to treat the
"Scotch" symphony in like manner.

Mendelssohn's only violin concerto, in E minor, Opus 64, written
in 1844, is constructed similarly. But in that work another structural
innovation appears: the cadenza is given a new function. Heretofore that free improvisatory device had come near the end of a movement and had provided the performer with opportunity to embel-
lish or comment upon the themes of the work, to elaborate upon the
composer's thematic manipulations—in short, to gild the lily. And it
had given him full opportunity to indulge in meaningless display, if
that were his desire. In the two piano concertos Mendelssohn had
avoided the problem by allowing no room for cadenzas, thus preserving the continuity of thought from beginning to end. Now, in
the violin concerto, the first-movement cadenza is written by the

composer himself, grows out of the development to lead into the recapitulation, and becomes a structural member of the form.

Mendelssohn's ten overtures represent two types: six which are connected with stage works, and four which may be called concert or descriptive overtures. Outstanding examples of the first type are the overtures to *A Midsummer Night's Dream*, Opus 21, 1826; and to Victor Hugo's play, *Ruy Blas*, Opus 95, 1839. The first of these remains one of his great monuments and is the work in which he reached the most mature style—in his seventeenth year. Perfect proportions, light and fairylike mood, great subtlety of phrase structure, full exploitation of string-instrument effects, and the utmost beauty of pure sound—these are its outstanding characteristics. The overture to *Ruy Blas* is decidedly heavier in tone. An introduction which is imposing and sinister in turn, a large sonata-form movement containing three contrasting and impulsive themes, an extended and dramatic development section, a periodic return of material drawn from the introduction—such elements combine to create a work which is among Mendelssohn's most dramatic compositions.

Among the overtures of the second type are *Calm Sea and Prosperous Voyage*, Opus 27, 1828; *Fingal's Cave* (or *The Hebrides*), Opus 26, 1830–1832; and *The Legend of the Beautiful Melusine*, Opus 32, 1833. These works are united by a descriptive quality Thus, the well-known motive which occurs throughout *Fingal's Cave* suggests the lapping of the waves; the "calm sea" of Opus 27 is reproduced in a quiet and melodious adagio; and a legendary, narrative quality permeates the *Melusine* overture.

Technically, these are Mendelssohn's finest overtures. Contrasting moods are wonderfully achieved through the simplest of figurations; and forceful, passionate moments are depicted either by rushing unison string passages, as in *Fingal's Cave*, or by vital, exciting development of short rhythmic motives, as in the "prosperous voyage" section of Opus 27. Among the most effective moments in these works are the quiet passages with which they end. This type of close must have been compatible with Mendelssohn's temperament, for the overtures to *A Midsummer Night's Dream* and *Son and Stranger* likewise end with passages in which quiet repose and lyric beauty are revealed.

Among Mendelssohn's last compositions for orchestra is one which is directly related to one of his earliest: the incidental music to *A Midsummer Night's Dream*, composed in 1843 as Opus 61. Seventeen years intervened between the overture to that play and the music now being discussed; and yet he was able to recapture the mood and style of the overture exactly. The music consists of a Scherzo, a work which with its miniature sonata-form and its perfect qualities has become one of the treasures of the literature; an Intermezzo with kaleidoscopic orchestral color and breathless pace; the *Notturno*, a piece which illustrates the nobility of Mendelssohn's melodic gifts and his unique ability to combine sweet sentiment with an undercurrent of deep feeling; the Wedding March, with two trios and an extended coda (a much longer composition than brides today are given an opportunity to discover); and a Dance of the Boors, a short, coarsely humorous piece whose theme is drawn from the overture composed in 1826.

The presence of many nicknames and descriptive titles in Mendelssohn's works may lead to the belief that he was a composer of program music. That belief is not founded on fact. For in Mendelssohn the external object, be it landscape or literary work or historical site, is not described; the object does no more than serve as a stimulus for his creative thought. The gloomy story of Mary Stuart, for example, may have given rise to a series of meditations in Mendelssohn's mind, meditations which eventually revealed themselves in the dark, reserved tone which permeates much of the "Scotch" symphony; but of direct description there is not a trace. The same is true of the "Italian" symphony and of other works inspired from without; we encounter the result of reflections rather than attempts at extramusical delineation.

The perfection of Mendelssohn's formal processes has long been appreciated; his sense of proportion, his good taste, and his unerring feeling for the right kind of expression are familiar aspects of his style. These are revealed as much in sonata-form movements as in miniatures; but in the former the composer's temperament left a characteristic mark. The essence of sonata-form, as has been pointed out elsewhere, is thematic conflict; and the arena in which that conflict is most clearly revealed is, of course, the development section. But in Mendelssohn conflict of any sort rarely occurs; his refinement, his equanimity of feeling, and his habitual elegance made the idea of conflict repugnant to him. As a consequence, the developments in his larger forms are seldom necessary to the full realization of the thematic material. Since the themes do not mirror conflicting emotional states, there is little Mendelssohn can do by way of development other than construct masterpieces of imaginative thematic manipulation which have no real emotional direction. Such developments remain fascinating in themselves, as do so many other passages in his music; but they do not achieve significance. And as a further consequence, the recapitulations, which in Mozart or Beethoven, for example, are on a higher level and throw new light upon thematic content and implication, are mere returns of the exposition with minor modifications. Symmetry is achieved, but a symmetry uninfluenced by the experiences which the themes (and the listeners) have undergone meanwhile.

It was Mendelssohn's fate to stand in two aesthetic camps at once. By education, temperament, and taste, he was a Classical composer; the keen awareness of relationship between form and content, the attention to detail, and the economy and perfection of his expression give evidence of his adherence to the ideals, say, of Mozart. But he was very much a man of his own time; Romantic currents are reflected in the sentimental and passionate quality of his melodies, and in his subjective interest in things outside music. Yet these conflicting elements are brought into harmony. Mendelssohn was not hampered by slavish adherence to sets of "Classical rules" of form; neither did undisciplined imagination and wild fantasy infect his music. Only in the quality of his emotion did he fall below the highest levels. Great depth of feeling is not reflected in his works, nor are the powerful tensions of human life. Charm, warmth, humor, and refinement, along with great technical skill devoted to making surface emotion seem attractive—such elements characterize Mendelssohn's orchestral compositions.

The career of Robert Schumann (1810–1856) well illustrates the splits and contradictions which were characteristic of the entire Romantic period. Schumann came to music after a desultory attempt at studying law; he had little of the basic training earlier musicians had taken for granted. For many years (1833–1844) he was active as an educator; his articles and reviews in the *Neue Zeitschrift für Musik* were important influences in raising the musical standards of Germany. In temperament he remained close to folk art, and he delighted in intimate, expressive miniatures; yet he tried his hand at all the larger forms of composition as well. His gift for originality was strikingly revealed over and over again; yet he could seldom organize or expand his inspirations effectively. He saw himself as having two personalities: the passionate, forthright Florestan and the dreamy, romantic Eusebius; and strains corresponding to these personalities appear in his music in rich profusion. Finally, the symptoms of schizophrenia are strongly suggested by his later behavior, and he died in a state of complete mental collapse at the age of forty-six.

Four symphonies, a set of three movements which all but constitute a sinfonietta, seven concertos of various kinds, and a half-dozen overtures—these are Schumann's orchestral works. It has long been popular, in discussing those works, to lay stress on his "bad orchestration"; endless pages have been filled with regrets that he was not more skilled in that branch of the art. The present author will contribute nothing to that subject, largely out of the conviction that Schumann's music need not be tampered with; in the hands of a skilled conductor and played by a competent orchestra, it can always be made to "sound" in spite of its thick scoring and its occasional lapses into acoustical miscalculation.

Schumann's first symphony, in B-flat major (Opus 38), is a product of his happiest years; it was written in 1841. In general tone and optimistic air, it well deserves the nickname which the composer himself gave to it, "Spring Symphony." An imposing introduction with distant and veiled harmonies gradually reveals a theme which brings to the fresh and energetic first movement a naïvely enthusiastic mood. Full of exuberance and free of dark conflict, the movement proceeds with great vitality to rousing climaxes; it carries the listener along in exciting fashion.

The second movement contains contrasts between long, soaring melodies and short, angular motives; a unique mood compounded of noble sentiment and restrained melancholy is achieved. A wealth of imaginative instrumental detail fills the movement; restlessly undulating figures in the strings and light syncopations in the woodwinds add a colorful charm. Second and third movements are connected, for the second ends quietly with an anticipation of the third movement's theme. The latter movement, a scherzo, is among Schumann's great inspirations. It is based upon a variety of melodies which are vigorous, intangible, short-breathed, and fleet in turn; it includes two contrasting trios, one of them in duple meter, and a coda which summarizes the whole in a truly masterful manner. The entire movement reflects the range, quality, and originality of Schumann's gifts as a composer. But it is not humorous, as are so many other works in scherzo form. The humor comes to expression in the finale, however; this is a light and deft movement full of conversational interchanges between woodwinds and strings, and it contains a miniature cadenza for the flute. Throughout the symphony, all is joyful and, at times, serene. Dark or passionate moments are missing, and the whole represents the most straightforward and healthy side of Schumann's nature.

Almost contemporary with the first symphony (1841) is a smaller work which is virtually a symphony without a slow movement: the *Overture, Scherzo, and Finale*, in E major, revised in 1845 and published as Opus 52. A first movement which is gay and impulsive somewhat in the manner of Schubert, a scherzo which is alive and rhythmical, and a finale which reveals Schumann's unfortunate lack of self-critical judgment—these constitute the work. In spite of many entertaining and charming passages, it does not reach the level of the first symphony.

The D-minor symphony was also composed in 1841. At its first performance it was properly called the second symphony. Schumann, however, was dissatisfied with its orchestral sound, withdrew it, and after a ten-year lapse reorchestrated large portions of it. The revised version was performed in 1853, was called the fourth symphony, and subsequently labeled Opus 120. Like Mendelssohn's "Scotch" symphony, its movements are designed to be played without pause between; indeed, at its first performance, when it bore the label "symphonic fantasy," its sections were listed as comprising one movement. But unlike Mendelssohn's work, Schumann's contains movements which are linked thematically; thus a continuous performance has its inner justification.

The work begins with a slow, brooding introduction which leads, in its closing measures, to a figure out of which the first movement's main theme is built. That movement is freely constructed with many fitful pauses; it is essentially a fantasia consisting of exposition and long developments of the theme's first measure. It illustrates Schumann's concentrated purpose as well as the scope of his imagination. The *Romanze* which follows contains a nostalgic theme and one which is derived from the material of the introduction; and in its middle part it presents a graceful, undulating figure which will later do duty in the scherzo's trio. The scherzo is vigorous, impulsive, and enchanting in turn, with quick changes of emotional direction and an originality of melodic line that shows Schumann at his best. It leads directly into a short section which precedes the finale; here again, the material of the introduction is employed. The finale's main theme is derived from the corresponding theme of the first movement and continues the rhythmic impulsiveness first heard in that movement as well as in the scherzo. Thus, the various sections are closely related thematically, and the cyclical form of the later symphonic poem is anticipated.

The outstanding impression received from the D-minor symphony centers around its variety of moods. First and last movements, for example, in spite of being based on similar themes, contain a fascinating array of subtle emotional shadings. One melodic fragment serves variously to introduce stormy, contented, agitated, powerful, and lightly graceful passages. Used in the main theme, in running figures, as a counterpoint, or merely as a punctuation device, that fragment is so employed that Schumann's masterful imaginative qualities come to full expression. The symphony departs widely from Classical forms; yet its proportions are well calculated and its flexible form is entirely suited to Schumann's purposes. In emotional content and in pure beauty of sound, it remains one of his finest compositions.

About 1846 Schumann completed a symphony in C major, Opus 61; this has become known as his second. In the years immediately preceding 1846 he had devoted himself wholeheartedly to contrapuntal studies and had composed a number of fugues for piano and organ respectively. Those studies also exerted influence upon other media, especially the symphony; for the latter depends upon imitative devices to a greater extent than do Schumann's earlier works. A single, imposing mottolike motive heard in the introduction reappears at striking points in the first, second, and fourth movements; but its successive reappearances do not contribute to a feeling of inner unity. On the contrary, the symphony is halting and fragmentary in its effect and uneven in quality. Magnificent themes and uninspired, routine developments; a moving, soul-searching adagio interrupted by a meaningless fugato; a forceful finale with foreshortened ineffective climaxes; imaginative melodic turns and general monotony of rhythm and tonality—such elements reveal the nature of that unevenness. Schumann's genius, already beginning to cloud over in forewarning of his later mental illness, was not able to overcome the weaknesses that this work reveals.

Schumann's E-flat symphony, Opus 97, known as his third, was written in 1850 at Düsseldorf. It reflects the composer's impressions of certain aspects of life on the Rhine, hence is called the "Rhenish" symphony. It approaches the B-flat and D-minor symphonies in general excellence of workmanship; but it does not achieve the same degree of animation. The first movement's imposing, syncopated main theme promises much; but its effect is weakened by constant repetition and by a degree of rhythmic monotony. The second movement, marked "scherzo," is a moderately paced, bucolic, and square piece which is interesting enough but scarcely striking; one is reminded of Schumann's smaller piano pieces. In the slow movement, however, the serenity which is often a factor of his sentiment comes to full expression in a texture that is rich and colorful.

Following these, and as an added movement, comes a pompous and majestic adagio, said to have been inspired by an ecclesiastical ceremony Schumann witnessed at Cologne. The finale, in decided contrast, is forthright and even jubilant; and despite close thematic connection with the fourth movement, proceeds on an ever-rising note of excitement to a rousing climax. The overall warm tone of this symphony cannot conceal the fact that Schumann's powers were waning. The inspired, exuberant, and truly original moments which are so copiously revealed in his earlier works are here largely absent. Routine craftsmanship of a high order remains; but the spirit is subdued and fatigued.

The works for soloist and orchestra, like the symphonies, show a gradual decline in quality. The piano concerto in A minor, Opus 54, Schumann's first work in this form, is by far his finest. There are external similarities between it and Mendelssohn's piano concertos: the last two movements are connected, the exposition in the first movement confines itself to a single presentation of the themes, and that movement's cadenza contributes to the flow of the music rather than interrupting it. But its general tone and emotional content are purely Schumann's. Its first allegro is roughly contemporary with the first symphony, 1841, at which time it was called a fantasy and was intended to stand alone. Four years later Schumann attached an andante and a rondo to the allegro; in that form it has become one of the best-loved of all nineteenth-century concertos.

Schumann's poetic, restrained manner is clearly revealed here. The piano is an equal partner with the orchestra, and all is on an intimate, charming level. No excess of emotion mars this piece, nor any ostentatious sentiment; and nowhere does it give way to shallow, virtuosic bluster. One of Schumann's avowed critical purposes was to drive empty, spectacular brilliance from the concert stage, and in this work he illustrated what could be substituted for the virtuoso's tricks. True, the solo part is full of rich figurations and often provides a running, embellished commentary to the thematic material; but technical "effects" are held to a minimum throughout. Schumann was at his best in inventing piquant or suave miniatures; the concerto contains its share of them, but they are held together by the underlying poetic mood. Particularly happy are such moments as the middle part of the andante and the waltzlike episode in the finale. Honest sentiment, grace, humor, and pure beauty distinguish the concerto from beginning to end.

The cello concerto in A minor, Opus 129 and composed in 1850, bears certain similarities to the piano concerto. It is primarily a lyric work and it contains a series of melodies which rank among Schumann's finest. But the rhythmic monotony which marks so many of his works is present also. We had noted, for example, in the D-minor symphony, his fixation upon a particular rhythmic fragment. The finale of the concerto reveals a similar fixation; and what was highly original and even charming on first hearing is dragged on unchangingly through large sections of the movement. Yet the concerto as a whole remains one of the half-dozen works in the repertoire which reveals the full resources of the cello; and again Schumann does not resort to empty display.

The violin concerto, written in 1853, was among the works which Schumann's musical executors did not make public. Not until 1937 was it published, at which time the wisdom of those executors stood fully revealed. The concerto contains a powerful first theme and a few lesser melodies; all else consists of routine developments of those themes or elaborate figurations built around them. Written at a time when his critical judgment had weakened, and preceding the complete collapse of his sanity by only a few months, it contains a few tender, inspired moments and a few flashes of genius. But they are not enough to keep the work alive; those responsible for the concerto's recent resurrection have done Schumann no great service.

Schumann's half-dozen overtures are products of his late years. The first of these, *Genoveva*, Opus 81, written about 1847–1848, is the overture to his only opera. That opera failed miserably, largely because of its dramatic weaknesses; but it contains individual moments of great beauty. Likewise the overture; somber and powerful passages occur, and a narrative mood pervades the whole. The overture to Byron's *Manfred*, Opus 115, written about 1848, is more successful, for it recaptures much of the drama inherent in the character of Manfred. The poem summarizes, in a sense, the struggle between good and evil; in true Romantic tradition, the good triumphs even as Manfred dies. This synopsis is adhered to in Schumann's overture, is set in a loose sonata-form, and results in an appealing work.

A survey of Schumann's orchestral compositions reveals the sad fact that he did his best, most original, and most significant work at the beginning of his career. The freshness and poetic exuberance of the first symphony were not recaptured in later works; and while vivid imagination and momentary inspiration remained with Schumann until his mental illness began, his logical sense and his power of self-criticism gradually declined. In Kretzschmar's phrase, pearls and sand are mixed in equal proportions in the later works; rhythmic monotony, cloudy developments, a less sure grasp of formal possibilities—those characteristics grew stronger. Yet these facts cannot affect the values contained in his finest works. Schumann rose to the heights for short intervals. He possessed enthusiasm, humor, charm, and eloquence. Such qualities have sufficed to keep his music alive and to provide its hearers with lasting pleasure, and much of that music represents the nobility and warmheartedness that characterized early Romanticism at its best.

VII

BERLIOZ AND LISZT

M USIC ORIGINATING in France has not figured prominently in the foregoing pages. The reason for this lies in the fact that seventeenth- and eighteenth-century French composers found their greatest interest in fields other than instrumental music. Ballet, opera, dance, and keyboard were media which had inspired composers from Lully to Gossec to their best efforts. But with the appearance of Hector Berlioz (1803–1869) instrumental music in France assumed world-wide importance. The originality, forcefulness, and new orchestral color of Berlioz's works combined to make him a controversial figure during his lifetime, and even today informed opinion is by no means unanimous in evaluating his orchestral compositions.

The novel element usually stressed in accounts of those works is Berlioz's attachment to programs, to his musical illustrations of literary or other extramusical stimuli. True, all his instrumental works carry descriptive titles, and many of them were written under the influence of impressions derived from outer events. But other composers had also been influenced by extramusical experiences; program music, or music which tells stories, is probably as old as the art itself. Vocal music, for example, insofar as it is narrative or is descriptive of emotional states, had never been far removed from program music; and instrumental music which describes the sounds of nature is at least as old as the fifteenth century. Bach, Haydn, and Beethoven, each in his own way, had contributed to the *genre*. Thus it is not the use of the program device which makes Berlioz unique; rather is it the strength, resourcefulness, and boundless imagination revealed by him as a musician.

One of the requirements of Romantic music in general, be it remembered, was that it should have an underlying purpose: a poetic idea, the revelation of an emotional state, or something similar. Further, the early Romantic period was far advanced toward becoming an age of spectators; the typical man of the period, no longer content to live within himself, looked for stimulation from the outside. Music, in the form of the public orchestra concerts which were coming into prominence during Berlioz's lifetime, provided much of that stimulation. Vicarious passion, excitement induced from without, noble or divine feelings based upon things heard or seen—these were to become essentials of standard Romantic diet. Parallel to the foregoing was the French flair, centuries old, for writing descriptive music. Berlioz was a Frenchman as well as a Romantic composer; he was sensitive to the needs of his generation, in fact reflected these needs in his own personality. Thus he could scarcely avoid writing music that was at once rich in descriptive suggestion and emotional power and based upon an underlying literary stimulus or a poetic idea.

The essential novelty in Berlioz's music, as has been seen, is not the program. In at least one notable case the program was written after the music—and that work is among the very few which is so burdened—probably in an attempt to justify or, in typical Romantic fashion, to explain what had been composed. The power and sweep of his musical effects, the revolutionary nature of his melodies and rhythms, the vivid colors of his orchestral works—those give a clue to his stature. The public of his time, or at least the more articulate spokesmen for that public, were often left far behind by the new qualities of that music. Berlioz's career was not marked by a series of successes in spite of the genius for orchestral writing which he revealed in three or four symphonies, seven overtures, and a variety of miscellaneous compositions.

The work by which Berlioz is best known is his *Symphonie fantastique*, subtitled "Episode in the Life of an Artist." Written in 1830, it was later revised and published as Opus 14 in 1846. Here, in his first full-scale symphonic work, he set out to write a dramatically unified composition; upon it he superimposed a program which was long considered to be partly autobiographical and to depict something of his relationship with Harriet Smithson, the actress who later became his wife. The supposed influence of that relationship upon the symphony has recently been demonstrated to be extremely weak, at best.[1] Let it suffice to say that the program which Berlioz forced upon the *Symphonie fantastique* is concerned with a young lovesick musician who has taken opium in a fit of despair. The poison plunges him into a vision-filled sleep; his emotions, memories, and fantasies are expressed musically. The object of his affections appears in his vision as a fixed melody (*idée fixe*, in Berlioz's own term) which recurs throughout the five movements of the work. Each of the movements bears a descriptive title which calls attention to episodes taking place within the opium-induced hallucinations.

The consistent employment of the *idée fixe* is one of Berlioz's great technical contributions to musical form. Beethoven had extended symphonic form to its limits—both in point of length and connected emotional content. It is likely that no early Romantic musician other than Schubert dared to compose works as large, say, as the "Eroica," seventh, or ninth symphonies without some unifying device, some mechanism which would "justify" or connect its parts. That device was at hand in the *idée fixe*. The most diverse of materials could now be combined; for running like a thread through a work, no matter how large, was the unifying melody serving as a point of continual new departure or as an external symbol of inner organization. And so powerful was Berlioz's demonstration of the fixed melody that the majority of later composers employed it in some fashion also. We have seen tentative appearances of a similar device in Schumann's fourth symphony (1841); and we shall examine Liszt's modification of the *idée fixe* later in this chapter.

The first movement of the symphony ("Reveries, Passions") begins with a slow introduction which suggests a variety of emotional states. A rich succession of melodic fragments set in colorful or-

[1] Barzun, *Berlioz and the Romantic Century*, I, 162–67.

chestral combinations leads directly to the principal allegro. This movement, in sonata-form, gives evidence that Berlioz was first of all a musician and only secondly a teller of tales: stripped of its attached program, it carries out all the requirements of a symphonic first movement. The main emphasis is laid upon the first theme, a long undulating melody of forty measures; it is this theme which becomes the *idée fixe* of the symphony. The group of melodies which serves as second theme is considerably less striking and finds relatively little employment in the long and forceful development section which follows. The recapitulation and coda are brief and are concerned largely with the *idée fixe*. The movement ends quietly (the program here introduces the idea of religious consolation).

The second movement ("A Ball") is an attractive, charming waltz. In a beautifully proportioned form the waltz melodies are twice interrupted by the return of the *idée fixe:* in the program the hero "finds the beloved one again amidst the confusion of a brilliant festival." An adagio ("Scene in the Country") is next in order. Here is a reflective, quiet movement, melodious and rich in rhythmic variety. Again the theme of the beloved appears. The program explains this, for "he is in the country, musing . . . then she appears once more. . . . Painful forebodings fill his soul. . . ."

For a greatly contrasting fourth movement Berlioz wrote a "March to Execution." Wild, sinister, and brooding in turn, this movement represents a new departure in depicting brutal, coarse, and extravagant emotions. Toward the end of the movement the *idée fixe* is presented again, but now in part only; for after four measures it is broken off by a sharp chord in a stroke of great dramatic power. The program subsequently explains the situation: "He dreams that he has murdered his beloved . . . been condemned to death, and is being led to execution. . . . For a moment a last thought of love is revived—and is cut short by the death blow."

The fifth movement ("Dream of a Witches' Sabbath") is free in form and extravagant in its dramatic variety. An eerie larghetto leads, after a noisy transition, into a section which has a caricature of the *idée fixe* as its theme. Then follows a forceful section in which fragments of the *Dies irae* [2] are introduced, after which a "dance of the witches" is begun. At the height of this fugal dance the *Dies irae* is heard as a counterpoint to the wild dance theme, and the symphony ends in an overwhelming climax. Berlioz's literary imagination was equal to the problem suggested by this fantastic array of episodes, for now the hero dreams ". . . he is present at a witches' revel, surrounded by grisly apparitions who have gathered to witness his burial. Strange tones, shrill laughter. . . . The melody of the beloved one returns, but it no longer retains its noble and shy character; it has become a vulgar, trivial, grotesque dance tune. . . . Bells toll for the dead. . . . A burlesque parody of the *Dies irae;* a dance of the witches. The dance and the *Dies irae* heard together."

The outstanding fact about the *Symphonie fantastique* is the revolutionary nature of its orchestral color, the sheer quantity of its instrumental effects. Berlioz's technique of writing for orchestra led to a completely new concept of the orchestra as a virtuosic musical instrument. First, the orchestra was greatly enlarged. A pair of cornets, two harps, English horn, clarinets in C and E flat, two tubas, an extra pair of both bassoons and tympani, and an augmented percussion section were added to the orchestra which had sufficed Beethoven in the ninth symphony. But this gives only an external picture of Berlioz's larger instrumental resources. For each of the harps was required to be doubled, the tolling bells which introduce the *Dies irae* section in the finale could be replaced by several pianos, and each string section was often divided into two or three parts. Thus Berlioz's orchestra is not only larger but also richer.

Berlioz understood, as no composer before him, the art of treating wind instruments as individuals. Devising new combinations at will and carefully or intuitively calculating the acoustic problems of tonal mass, he created new tone colors and exploited them fully.

---

[2] The thirteenth-century sequence, *Dies irae* (Day of Wrath), is a dramatic description of the Last Judgment. It is part of the Requiem Mass, in which it takes the place otherwise held by the *Credo*. The famous traditional plainsong melody has been employed in early polyphonic masses and has also been used in secular compositions by Liszt and Saint-Saëns, among others.

Among the more extreme of Berlioz's instrumental effects in this symphony are such combinations as solo clarinet accompanied by two tympani and bass drum, or by another clarinet and two oboes; full brass choir heard alone; and English-horn solo over a tremolo in the violas or over a rich and varied passage for four tympani. Elsewhere the quick interchange of string and wind colors, or isolated string-instrument chords in a context of winds, or even full-orchestra passages written in intricate rhythmic counterpoint, add tremendous vitality to the sound of his music. Truly, Berlioz was outstanding among the early masters of the new art of orchestration.

The quality of the music is another matter. Many of Berlioz's melodies, harmonies, or even extended passages will not bear close scrutiny. One finds, in the *Symphonie fantastique*, many a tawdry passage, many a coarse or ugly effect, which Berlioz later took pains to justify in his program. In his mind sheer ugliness deserved to be expressed musically also—as part of a larger dramatic truth. The squeamish listener or one who expects only beauty from music will be repelled by portions of this work. The program itself, addressed to the public of his own day, is certainly in doubtful taste, contains none of the nobility one has a right to expect of an art work, and is scarcely edifying in any particular. And yet, so great was the range of Berlioz's music, one finds expressive and refined passages in abundance also. The tremendous variety of his expression cannot be denied; one would, however, wish for a more convincing unifying device than the *idée fixe*, the occasional return of a melody with only "literary" justification.

The nineteenth century stressed the story-telling aspects of Berlioz's work and minimized the purely musical elements. Recent studies, on the other hand, have revealed that programs, in Berlioz's mind, were largely his concessions to an insensitive, unthinking audience and that the music must stand on its own merits. This is unfortunate, in a sense, for what remains, even within the well-organized forms, is a succession of dramatically moving, impulsive, touching or repellent, unpredictable, and sometimes illogical episodes. It is this impulsiveness coupled with the magnificent variety of sound and the unusual nature of Berlioz's melodic and rhythmic ideas which gives his music much of its fascination. But to think of that music as deriving from Beethoven's (which agrees with Berlioz's own estimation) is to misunderstand completely the unique qualities of both—in Beethoven, complete adherence to the musical requirements of his material and consummate formal and logical organization; in Berlioz, the musical description of emotional states, done with the full resources of a vivid imagination and an overwhelming technical facility. And although the end results—to the nondiscerning listener —may be somewhat similar in point of sheer power and emotional variety, the initial concepts are diametrically opposed.

Berlioz's next large orchestral work is of a different order. Often considered to be a viola concerto, it was referred to by the composer as his second symphony. He himself mentions an especially successful performance of the *Symphonie fantastique* in December, 1833, and after that performance, his first meeting with Paganini. A few weeks later the famous violinist asked him to write a solo for viola. After a first attempt which did not please Paganini (". . . I am silent a great deal too long. I must be playing the whole time") Berlioz "conceived the idea of writing a series of scenes for the orchestra in which the viola should find itself mixed up, like a person more or less in action, always preserving his own individuality. The background I formed from my recollections of my wanderings in Abruzzi, introducing the viola as a sort of melancholy dreamer, in the style of Byron's *Childe Harold*. Hence the title of the symphony, *Harold in Italy*. As in the *Symphonie fantastique*, one principal theme (the first strain of the viola) is reproduced throughout the work. . . . Harold's strain is superadded to the other orchestral strains, with which it contrasts both in movement and character, without hindering their development."[3] The work was completed in 1834.

Harold in Italy is cast conservatively in four movements. And although Berlioz supplied each movement with a descriptive title, he went no further toward supplying a program. The work must be understood merely as having been written under poetic stimulus.

[3] Berlioz, *Memoirs,* tr. by R. and E. Holmes, pp. 202-3.

For here again, as in the first symphony, he presents within the old musical forms a great variety of colorful episodes. The first movement, entitled "Harold in the Mountains. Scenes of Sadness, Happiness, and Joy," begins with a long, mournful adagio; a gently undulating and somewhat chromatic fugue sets the scene for the "Harold" theme—a slow melody suggestive of the hero's melancholy meditations. After a brilliant transition the main allegro ("happiness and joy") proceeds in free sonata-form through effective passages to a resounding climax.

The second movement, a "March of the Pilgrims," is a magical reflection of Berlioz's poetic imagination. An unpretentious tune, interrupted periodically by a rhythmic phrase suggestive of a fragment of litany, marches slowly through the movement. Beginning quietly, as if at a distance, it rises to noble expression and gradually subsides again; the dynamic pattern is that of an extended crescendo and diminuendo. As the climax subsides a *canto religioso* is heard over the reiterated bass of the march. And inserted within the texture is the solo viola part brooding on its first-movement theme, or embellishing the march with a free running figure, or providing a quietly agitated chordal accompaniment to the religious song. The dignified sound of bells is heard at beginning and end; the whole passes with an air of tranquility. It is Berlioz at his point of greatest refinement.

A "Serenade of an Abruzzi Mountaineer to his Mistress" serves as third movement. Here, between lively, brief introduction and epilogue, an English horn presents a nostalgic melody over a simple accompaniment; this is subsequently elaborated and extended. Harold, in the person of the solo viola, stands by with the melancholy theme and soon contributes an emotionally intense counterpoint to the serenader's melody. The movement ends in a moment of dramatic insight, for now the viola improvises on fragments of that melody, and the whole dies away quietly.

With the fourth movement we are abruptly returned to a world of wild brutality—"Orgy of the Brigands. Memories of Past Scenes." As in the finale of the first symphony, Berlioz here gave full sway to extravagant, unbridled expression. A forceful, rhythmically irregular passage is repeatedly interrupted by reminiscences of preceding themes—somewhat in the manner of Beethoven's ninth-symphony finale. Thereafter the wild abandon of the bacchanal sweeps everything before it in a riot of orchestral tumult. Yet Berlioz never loses control over his material. All is clear, wide-spaced, and—the concept of the orgy having been accepted—inevitable. Toward the end of the movement, at a great climax, a portentous pause is followed by a quiet return of the pilgrims' march; the procession passes by the brigands' grotto. "In a similar situation Tannhäuser flees; Harold dies. For the last time he fumbles for his theme. He finds the intervals no more." [4]

In no respect does Berlioz follow, in this work, the content of Byron's poem. The viola, as melancholy dreamer, is concerned with Berlioz's, not Byron's, mental images; in the words of the composer himself, it preserves its individuality intact. The music is colorful and expressive, evokes mood pictures, but is not bound to a program. Again the *idée fixe* is the external symbol for the unity which existed in Berlioz's own mind, for the dramatic relationship between the various scenes. The solo viola, provided with a variety of melodies and accompanying figures in addition to its own theme, steps in and out of the texture freely in the manner of an obbligato. Commenting, taking part, or merely observing, it is the spirit of Berlioz himself.

The *Symphonie fantastique* and *Harold in Italy* were autobiographical. In another work, written about 1839, Berlioz gave the symphony quite another function—that of illustrating a Shakespearian drama. *Romeo and Juliet* is a "dramatic symphony" for soloists, chorus, and orchestra. But the vocal forces are employed probably more extensively than in any other symphonic work written up to that time, and the form of the concert opera comes dangerously close. The orchestral introduction to the first movement is followed by a prelude for chorus and a variety of solo voices, and each of the four orchestral movements is preceded or followed or interrupted by choral interludes. Thus a total of twelve or more sections results. Only a few orchestral excerpts of this massive work have survived

[4] Kretzschmar, *Führer durch den Concertsaal*, I, 291.

in the repertoire, notably the "Love Scene" and the "Queen Mab" scherzo.

Another large work is of completely different character. In 1840 Berlioz was commissioned to write a composition suitable for a memorial to participants in the July Revolution of 1830. The *Funeral and Triumphal Symphony* resulted. A three-movement work originally scored for military band, it was supplied with string parts by Berlioz for an indoor performance and thus may be called his fourth symphony. The work has not yet attained a regular position in the repertoire (first American performance, 1947).

The *Damnation of Faust*, written about 1845, is a "dramatic legend," hence is not strictly a symphonic composition. Here again, as in *Romeo and Juliet*, soloists and chorus are combined with orchestra; but the form of this work is akin to that of a secular oratorio. A set of three orchestral excerpts drawn from the *Damnation of Faust* comes to frequent performance: "Hungarian March," "Ballet of the Sylphs," and "Dance of the Will-o'-the-Wisps."

Of Berlioz's seven overtures, a few have held honored places on the concert stage to the present day. In the overture to *Benvenuto Cellini*, his opera of 1838, and in *The Roman Carnival*, composed as an overture to the same opera's second act, the fluid imagination, vivid color sense, and striking melodic invention we have seen above as representing Berlioz at his best are again present. Other overtures, from the brilliant *Waverly* (Opus 1, 1827) to the dainty *Beatrice and Benedict* (1862), would, if they were properly known, do much to dispel the belief that Berlioz was a composer of only fantastic and bizarre music. He conceived and wrote on a grand scale, and the variety of expression in his music is great. It is to be hoped that his works will, in the future, be heard as widely as their qualities merit; he will then be recognized generally, as he is by a few, as one of the most gifted and significant composers of the nineteenth century.

Some years after the revolutionary ideas of Berlioz had begun to make themselves felt in western Europe, Franz Liszt (1811–1886) retired from the concert stage to take up his duties as court conductor to the grand duke of Saxe-Weimar. During the course of his stay at Weimar (1848–1861) Liszt turned, among other activities, to writing for orchestra. Two large symphonies, a dozen one-movement works to which he gave the name "symphonic poem," and several concertos were among the results of that activity. Those works reveal that Liszt had adopted the ideals of Berlioz and carried them to their logical conclusion.

Berlioz in his symphonies reflected the general Romantic idea that instrumental music must have a poetic content, that it must be reducible to direct meaning. But he was unable to free himself from the shackles of symphonic form. He attempted to superimpose the new aesthetic upon the old forms inherited from Beethoven. Taking structures which follow the laws of musical logic, he strove to saturate them with pictorial, sentimental, or fantastic elements. Further, he allowed his musical sense to be influenced by his literary programs; thus the illogical, episodic nature of his larger forms was an inevitable consequence. Berlioz's most successful movements are those in which musical considerations dominate: the "Queen Mab" scherzo and the "Ball" scene. One senses in Berlioz a struggle between an eighteenth-century feeling for form and a nineteenth-century desire for imaginative, form-free expression.

Liszt, facing the same problem, solved it quite differently. He came to realize early in his career that the new Romantic ideas required new forms. With characteristic energy and integrity he set about consciously to develop both. He proved that new forms were possible: the symphonic poem which he created is entirely suited to the expression of Liszt's aesthetic philosophy. It was not his wish to describe scenes, objects, and similar extramusical facts, but to translate into music his fundamental sentiments toward them. In that wish he had a worthy predecessor: Beethoven in the "Pastoral" symphony had expressed his feelings about country life, and in the ninth about universal brotherhood. And we have indicated above that certain of Beethoven's overtures lead to a realization of what the symphonic poem will be (see pp. 124–128). That composer's admiration for a character (Egmont) or sympathy with another's dilemma (Coriolanus) are strikingly revealed in these unified one-movement works. It is in this direction that Liszt progressed, but, unlike Beethoven and even more unlike Berlioz, he found himself most sympathetic to the contemplation of passive or poetic emotions. In *Mazeppa* and in the *Battle of the Huns* he did venture upon stirring actions, it is true, but even in those symphonic poems Liszt avoided effects comparable to the extravagances of Berlioz.

Liszt's principle of composition stems from Berlioz's *idée fixe*, but it is so greatly expanded that little connection with the latter remains. The essential element of Liszt's principle is a short motive or melodic fragment; out of it themes are constructed and developed. Accompanying figures, transitions, and similar technical devices often owe their origin to the basic motive also, thus a high degree of unity is assured. The whole transpires in a fluid, ever-changing texture which reflects the free-flowing sentiments basic to the composition. A continuous thematic transformation is at hand in the typical Liszt symphonic poem. A motive and the themes it occasions appear in contrasting tempos, in all ranges of the orchestra, in a variety of contexts and tonalities—subject only to their own inherent musical laws. Yet so great was Liszt's ability to characterize—be it a sentiment, a complex of feelings, or an idea—that the underlying emotional-poetic purpose of the music is clearly brought forward.

The twelve symphonic poems [5] in which Liszt demonstrated his aesthetic philosophy and his new principle of composing in free forms were completed between 1848 and 1857, although a few had been begun even before his move to Weimar. They differ widely in content and, as is to be expected, in structure. The mere listing of their titles is revealing: one sees the influence of Liszt's broad culture and literary sensitivity (as well as his Romantic yearnings) upon his choice of musical subjects. (It should be mentioned that the published order of the symphonic poems does not reflect their dates of

---

[5] A short orchestral piece written in 1883, called *From the Cradle to the Grave*, is sometimes included in this category. That work was an occasional piece, however (based on a sketch by Count Michael von Zichy), and Liszt himself did not include it among the symphonic poems.

composition. Liszt revised, experimented, and corrected his works ceaselessly; certain compositions were subject to two and even three drastic overhaulings.)

1. *Ce qu'on entend sur la montagne* (the so-called *Mountain Symphony*, inspired by a poem by Victor Hugo) [6]
2. *Tasso: lamento e trionfo* (inspired by Goethe's *Tasso;* it was followed, some twenty years later, by an epilogue concerned with the funeral of Tasso)
3. *Les Préludes* (inspired by Lamartine's *Méditations poétiques*)
4. *Orpheus* (based on the myth, but performed as an overture to Gluck's *Orfeo ed Euridice* at Weimar in 1854)
5. *Prometheus* (originally intended as an overture for a set of choruses based on Herder's *Prometheus Unbound*)
6. *Mazeppa* (based on Victor Hugo's poem, but in its original form it was one of the piano *Études* of about 1830)
7. *Festklänge* (an expression of the sentiments which surround any national—or, according to some commentators, a particular nuptial—festival)
8. *Héroïde funèbre* (an expression of homage to the brave)
9. *Hungaria* (a glorification of all that is Hungarian)
10. *Hamlet* (based on Shakespeare)
11. *Die Hunnenschlacht* (inspired by a painting by Wilhelm von Kaulbach)
12. *Die Ideale* (based on fragments of a philosophical poem by Schiller)

Les Préludes is perhaps the best-known of the series and the only one which has retained a place in the standard repertoire. It may well be examined here, for it reveals Liszt's principles of composition to perfection. The lines from Lamartine which inspired the composer begin, "What is our life but a series of preludes to that unknown song, the first and solemn note of which is sounded by Death?" Later the poet reflects upon love, nature, and the trumpet's call to arms. There is Liszt's "program"; without recourse to de-

[6] See p. 228 in this connection.

scriptive scenes he is yet able to recapture his own feelings toward
Lamartine's few sentences. One motive serves as the germ from
which many themes are derived (see Example 27), and a somewhat

EXAMPLE 27   LISZT, Les Préludes

derivative melodic idea ("love") provides contrast. The various subjects of the meditation (love, war, and the like) fall naturally into
sections of different tempo and mood. Thus four well-contrasting
divisions appear, with introductions or transitions inserted at appropriate places. The whole is roughly analogous to the four contrasting movements of a symphony, with movements connected and
unified by means of a common theme. The unifying theme is greatly
modified, of course, upon successive appearances to conform to the
mood requirements of the various scenes.

Thus Liszt made a final break with the symphonic forms developed by late eighteenth-century composers and succeeded, where

Berlioz did not, in creating a new form for the expression of the poetic "meaning" which both composers believed essential to instrumental music. But in so doing he also brought about a split in that important field. For the symphonic poem influenced a host of imitators from Saint-Saëns to Respighi even while another group, with Brahms at their head, strove valiantly to revitalize Classical forms and invest them with a new content. The details of that split belong properly in the following chapters.

In 1854 Liszt wrote *A Faust Symphony* consisting of "three character pictures (after Goethe)"; in the three movements of the work Faust, Gretchen, and Mephistopheles are depicted. Although it contains a few passages which are parallel to scenes in Goethe's drama, the symphony is not descriptive of external events. Rather does one obtain impressions similar to those received from reading the play—such was Liszt's intended purpose. The duality of Faust's nature and the struggle between idealism and materialism are suggested by the first movement—a dark and brooding lento-allegro and a fiery, impassioned agitato—for which Liszt found a sonata-form quite adequate. This is not Classical sonata-form, however, but a structure in which the conflicting ideas are transformed ceaselessly and find their most intense expression in the recapitulation. The "Gretchen" movement is a quiet, idyllic piece; in an eloquent love scene the second part of the "Faust" theme is wonderfully transformed in accord with the mood requirements. The "Mephistopheles" movement reveals a master stroke; here Liszt allows the first-movement themes to be parodied, mocked, distorted, and to stand as negations of their original meaning. Only the "Gretchen" theme survives unharmed and untouched; it becomes symbolical of the power which conquers evil. As an afterthought in 1857 Liszt added a closing section for tenor solo and men's chorus, to provide the listener with a "happy ending." This section has little organic connection with the rest of the work and adds nothing to its masterful qualities.

In the twelve symphonic poems, in the *Faust Symphony*, and in the *Symphony on Dante's Divine Comedy*, which followed a year or two after the *Faust*, Liszt revealed the full scope of his imagination, his musical intelligence, and his technical fluency. But with these laudable attributes a bombastic strain came to expression also. Liszt's method of theme elaboration included a large amount of declamation, of rhapsodic gesturing or posturing. It was perhaps an inevitable consequence that an empty rhetoric, a mere play with musical ideas, or a meaningless sentimental expression should emerge. Repetitiousness is characteristic of Liszt in these works and is based upon considerable use of melodic sequences. In a sense, Liszt achieves many climaxes not through musical development of material but by reiteration to the point of boredom.

Many of these negative aspects of Liszt's music may be attributed to the fact that the composer's character contained something of the charlatan and exhibitionist. Secure in his position as perhaps the greatest pianist of the nineteenth century and enjoying a reputation for musical wizardry, he relied upon the power of "effects" to make his music convincing. Isolated chords, dramatic interjections, sharp dynamic contrasts, abrupt changes of texture and mood—all employed in the interest of clarifying his poetic ideas—dominate large sections of his orchestral works. His skill in musical characterization led him to employ unusual intervals and far-reaching modulations. This led perhaps to his employment of a new type of chromatic harmony, a harmony based only slightly upon the old tonic-dominant or tonic-mediant relationships. But chromatic harmony in Liszt never became systematized; it remained for Wagner to organize a new harmonic language based upon chromatic relationships between chords, such as finally emerged in *Tristan und Isolde*. Many of the "modern" elements in Wagner's style owe their origin to Liszt's experiments; the use of chromatic harmony is but one of them.

The rhapsodic element present in large portions of the symphonic poems and the two symphonies found its most consistent expression in two piano concertos, in E flat and A major, both composed about 1848 and both subject to several revisions before publication in 1857 and 1863 respectively. In these works Liszt avoided even the semblance of programs, but the method of the symphonic poem was retained. The E-flat concerto, ostensibly in four movements with the second and third movements combined and the fourth connected with the third, is in effect a one-movement unified work. As in the symphonic poems, the various sections are joined by a theme or themes undergoing constant transformation. The A-major concerto is outspokenly a one-movement work divided into a half-dozen contrasting sections. In both works a bewildering array of cantabile passages, brilliant cadenzas, blatant tutti, and moments of rare sentiment and beauty are brought together. Scarcely a trace of form in the eighteenth-century sense infects these rhapsodic utterances. They are Romanticism at its most typical.

Finally, the *Danse macabre* for piano and orchestra, written about 1850, may be mentioned. This work marks a return to program music, for it consists of a set of free variations on the *Dies irae* theme and was inspired by a fresco in the Campo Santo cemetery in Pisa. Without foregoing in the least any of the virtuosic effects which make the concertos such dazzling compositions, Liszt raised the orchestra to a diabolical intensity and approached the frenzied expression Berlioz had introduced in his first two symphonies.

VIII

JOHANNES BRAHMS

We have seen how the innovations which came in the wake of Berlioz and Liszt radically altered the sound and structure of instrumental music. Among the elements which characterized that music in the middle third of the nineteenth century were a new concept of the orchestra, a new poetic purpose in composing, and a new principle of organizing musical forms. The novelty of those elements was immediately recognized—to such an extent that a "neo-German" party was formed; Liszt became its patron saint, Richard Wagner (1813–1883) its most outstanding adherent, and the *Neue Zeitschrift für Musik,* founded by Schumann about 1833, its mouthpiece. The successful furthering of "music of the future" became its avowed purpose.

The enthusiastic propagation of the new elements by an important group of composers after about 1860—Wagner chief among them—led to a kind of music which departed widely from Classical style. Proportion, relationship between form and content, economy of means, and fidelity to musical laws were all but forgotten by such composers. Many members of the neo-German party smugly assumed that their ideas were accepted by all composers, and the *Zeitschrift* reflected that assumption. One individual, however, held different views. At first out of training and temperament, later out of conviction, that composer opposed himself to the new theories and made it his life work consciously to revitalize Classical forms and expression and remain faithful to the methods and purposes of Beethoven. That composer was Johannes Brahms (1833–1897).

The scope, forms, and content of Brahms's instrumental music reveal fully the strength of that conviction. But its conservatism and its mixture of warmth and restraint are directly related to his character and to certain personal experiences. It may help to a fuller understanding of the music of Brahms if the man himself is kept in view.

Brahms came to public notice in his twentieth year through the publication of Schumann's famous eulogistic article, "New Paths," in the *Zeitschrift* of October, 1853. Such an enthusiastic introduction to the musical world might have turned the head of a lesser man; Brahms did nothing to exploit his sudden fame. He was warmly welcomed by Liszt—but his instinct for logical form, awakened by his earliest teachers and not lulled to sleep by the encounter with the famous man, allowed him to sense the structural lacks and dubious purpose of Liszt's music. He successfully resisted the blandishments of the leader of the neo-Germans and was not diverted from his own path. Thus even at the beginning of his career he exhibited the strength of character and purpose which marked him throughout his lifetime.

In his formative years he revealed normal warmhearted and sociable tendencies. It was perhaps inevitable that, thrown into close relationship with Schumann's family at the time of the composer's mental collapse (1854–1856), Brahms's friendship for Clara Schumann, fourteen years his senior, should develop into love. With Schumann's death, however, the young man's romantic infatuation ceased abruptly. The episode affected him deeply and apparently left permanent emotional scars. He was able to resume his warm friendship with Schumann's widow, but from about 1856 he took refuge behind a curtain of reserve which increased in the following years. A degree of gruffness and stoicism served as a mask to conceal his loneliness and, at various times, it estranged him from virtually all his friends. The concentration with which he pursued his goal, his seriousness and remoteness, and his unwillingness to display facile surface emotion—all of which qualities affected his larger instrumental compositions—may be attributed in part to these unfortunate circumstances. "He had found a champion for his music and had lost him; he had met a woman he could love, had wrought valiantly for her and lost her too. . . . He determined that never would he offer such hostages to fortune again." [1] Characteristically, he withdrew into himself and spent several years (1856–1860) in concentrated study—this in spite of the fact that his works up to Opus 10 had demonstrated a compositional technique which none of his contemporaries could match.

The principles of the neo-Germans continued to irritate Brahms. In 1860 he helped to draw up a protest against the basic assumptions of that party and circulated it for signatures. The premature publication of the protest, bearing only four signatures, called forth a vicious attack written by Wagner—but printed anonymously. Greatly embarrassed by the exposure of his ill-advised manifesto, Brahms resolved never to give way to impulse again. He cut himself off from the progressive group and became an avowed enemy of the merely colorful and picturesque in music. The restoration of Classical forms became the central purpose of his creative effort, and austerity its outstanding characteristic; in this he was aided by a tremendous self-critical discipline.

Brahms's first orchestral work was written during these years of emotional tumult. It was to be a symphony; beginning about 1854, Brahms first scored it as a sonata for two pianos, then proceeded with the orchestration. Even at this early age his self-critical sense was active, however, and he felt dissatisfaction with the work. Thereupon he cast it in the form of a concerto for piano and orchestra, and in that form it was completed. Known today as the first piano concerto, in D minor, Opus 15, it was completed late in 1858.

The concerto is a large, ponderous work and is somewhat ungainly; but it contains a full share of eloquent moments, and dignity and serious purpose mark its three movements. Display elements calculated to excite its listeners are completely missing—even though the solo part makes the utmost demands in skill and endurance upon the performer. Outstanding is its return to the form of the Classical

[1] Latham, *Brahms*, p. 23.

concerto; the movements are separated, the traditional double exposition is restored in part, and sonata-form is employed. But its
composer was a youth of his own time; various sections, especially
in the first movement, are miniatures complete in themselves—
structurally somewhat akin to the short, single-movement forms
which flourished throughout the Romantic period. And Brahms
could not avoid, in this work, heroic and grandiose gestures typical
of the best Romantic tradition.

A gloomy and dramatic first movement with contrasting lyric
themes is followed by a serene, quiet adagio; and this by a forceful,
energetic rondo full of rough vigor and a certain humor. Thematic
materials entrusted to the solo and orchestra respectively are often
clearly differentiated—and yet the two opposing elements are
treated as equal partners, almost as though this were a symphony
with piano obbligato. Its performance at Leipzig in January, 1859
(which followed the Hanover *première* by only a few days), was
a resounding failure—perhaps the greatest failure in Brahms's entire career. The Leipzig audience, accustomed to the flashy, virtuosic
concertos of the time, could make nothing of this profound composition. Characteristically enough, Brahms later wrote, in a letter
to his friend, Joseph Joachim, "It is the best thing that could happen
to one, I believe; it forces one to collect his thoughts, and it heightens
courage. Of course, I am still experimenting and feeling my way.
But don't you think hissing was too much?" [2]

Two serenades for small orchestra are roughly contemporary
with the D-minor piano concerto: one in D major, Opus 11, and
one in A major, Opus 16, both written about 1857–1860. The D-
major is a light and generally diverting six-movement work with
transparent texture and unpretentious themes. The A-major, in five
movements, is graver in intent and darker in color. Both serenades
conform outwardly to the eighteenth-century divertimento type,
but already in the late 1850s Brahms's markedly individual style was
so strongly developed as to affect even these experimental works.
His direction in earlier compositions had often been toward expan-

[2] *Johannes Brahms im Briefwechsel mit Joseph Joachim*, I, 227–29.

sion and Romantic extravagance (witness the D-minor concerto and the first version of the piano trio, Opus 8). Here, in the serenades, one senses a tendency to be economical both of thematic materials and orchestral resources. The A-major serenade, for example, requires no violins; Brahms had nothing for them to do, hence saw no reason for including them in the score. (Further, when that work was revised in 1875, he removed trumpets, tympani, and the second pair of horns.)

One may assume that it was Brahms's desire to experiment in the style of Mozart which led him to choose the obsolete divertimento form for these works, and one must admit that the experiment was not entirely successful. The perfect relationship between form and content has not yet been achieved here, and the development sections give the impression of being neither inevitable nor concentrated. These serenades should serve to allay the belief that Brahms had no interest in orchestral color, however. The wind instruments are employed as individuals, are given many delightful solo passages, and contribute to the graceful air and color variety which are typical. While they cannot be compared in intensity or purpose with the later symphonies, the serenades contain many charming moments which deserve to be heard more often than is the case today.

Over a dozen years elapsed before Brahms returned to orchestral composition. In the interval he had written a number of his finest chamber-music works, several sets of variations for piano, *A German Requiem*, and other choral works. His mastery of technique and expression was now assured. In the set of orchestral *Variations on a Theme by Haydn*, Opus 56a, written in 1873, that mastery was revealed in full measure. A suite for band (*Feldpartita*) in B flat, long held to be Haydn's composition, contains as second movement a chorale, "Saint Anthony"; it is this chorale which supplied Brahms with his theme. Here again the composer adhered to his custom of first writing out the work for two pianos and subsequently scoring it for orchestra. In this case he allowed the two-piano version to be published simultaneously with the orchestral; it bears the number Opus 56b.

The theme is one which must have attracted Brahms from the outset; a mixture of four- and five-measure phrases, a well-defined harmony, and a characteristic melodic contour made it well suited to his purposes. Set forth by the wind instruments and thus retaining something of its original open-air sound, it is followed by eight variations and an extended finale. These variations are not merely ornamental repetitions of a tune, however, but are in the nature of character variations. One salient feature or musical characteristic of the theme is seized upon in each variation and becomes the subject of a short, meaningful development. Thus, the first variation is concerned with the rhythmic pulsation of the theme's cadence; the second, a development of the theme's first three notes; the fourth builds out of the theme's second and third measures a quiet counterpoint to a new melody. Similar subtle variants are afforded in later sections of the piece; these are not always easily perceptible, it is true, yet the relationship of each variation to the theme is unmistakable.

The finale, constituting about one quarter of the composition's length, is a contrapuntal masterpiece. Here a new five-measure bass line is derived from the original melody and bass together, and is treated in the style of a *basso ostinato* in seventeen different settings (quasi variations). The eighteenth setting returns slyly to the original theme of the piece, and the movement ends brilliantly with rushing scale passages. The entire work is one of Brahms's great achievements. Transitions between successive variations do not exist; yet the mood and expressive content of the several sections are so adjusted that a continuous unfolding of beauty occurs and the emotional effect is perfectly satisfying. Polyphonic imitations, canons, sections in double counterpoint, and similar strict devices do not detract from the melodic charm of this work; on the contrary, they give it lasting musical significance. As an example of Brahms's intention—namely, to reveal the *musical* possibilities of material without reference to any extramusical suggestions—it is superb. His skill in writing for orchestra and making full use of his instrumental resources, and his mastery of expressive variety were fully demonstrated. He now felt himself ready to present a full-scale symphonic work to an eager public.

It is quite in keeping with Brahms's conservatism, his self-discipline, and his self-knowledge (which included a definite strain of insecurity and lack of confidence) that he had been for years unwilling to accede to public demand for a symphony. Brahms had set himself no small task in assuming to follow Beethoven's path; he was aware of the seriousness of his self-imposed responsibility. Thus, he had begun work on a symphony in C minor at least as early as 1856, and Clara Schumann had seen portions of its first movement in 1862; he delayed its completion, however, until 1876, when it appeared as Opus 68. And having embarked successfully on a symphonic career, he exerted himself strenuously in the new medium. The period of Brahms's devotion to the orchestra began about 1876. A few each of piano solos and chamber-music works and about a dozen sets of songs were composed during the following decade, but his main preoccupation was with large orchestral works. The three remaining symphonies, three concertos, and two overtures were all completed between 1877 and 1887.

The C-minor symphony begins with a massive, slow introduction which presents much of the first movement's thematic material. The intensity, seriousness, and power of the introduction are carried forward in the allegro which follows. Apart from its weighty emotional content, the elements which make the strongest impression here are those of thematic integrity and formal construction. Melodic fragments heard consecutively in the introduction are combined, inverted, and expanded unceasingly in the allegro. The inexorable, systematic exploitation of the motives' musical characteristics, the polyphonic combinations and recombinations they are permitted to undergo, the logical and compelling nature of the climaxes themselves, and a host of similar technical details are responsible for the tremendous effect of this dark movement. Yet all such matters are forgotten in hearing this work; the rugged grandeur of the music speaks its own message.

The second and third movements offer complete contrasts to the first. The broad, lyric adagio is deceptively simple in structure; for although it moves smoothly in a mood of unbroken serenity, it gives evidence of Brahms's fondness for phrases of irregular length, his genius for melodic construction (not melodic invention, it may be noted), and his feeling for rhythmic freedom. A glance at the score will reveal that various single-measure inserts or extensions are contained within the first section of the theme—to such a degree that twelve measures are expanded to seventeen; yet so logically and imaginatively is the expansion made that only one's sense of beauty is affected.[3] Similar cases abound in Brahms's works.

The third movement is not the expected scherzo but an allegretto in duple meter full of surprising irregularities of form. The relationship of the middle part to the first, the incomplete return of the third, the key relationships between the first and second parts (A flat and B major)—these are chief among them. Brahms was no mere imitator of Classical forms; like his illustrious predecessors, he found the proper relationship between his musical material and its treatment and modified his forms accordingly—as this movement strikingly reveals. The attention to small, unifying detail which is demonstrated throughout Brahms's works may be seen here also. To give only one example, the movement's first phrase (five measures) is simply inverted to produce the second phrase (measures 6 to 10)—without in the least destroying the limpid charm of the whole.

With the finale Brahms returns to the power and forcefulness of the first movement. Here again a slow introduction presents successively the thematic materials which will later be developed. No fewer than seven motives or melodic fragments are set forth,[4] the first six of which are employed in various capacities in the main allegro. Only the seventh, a chorale phrase, is reserved for the climax in the coda of the movement, where it is shouted out by the full

---

[3] This concept is elaborated in Evans, *Handbook to the Chamber Music and Orchestral Works of Brahms*, II, 10–13.

[4] In measures 1, 5, 19, 21, 26, 29, and 46, respectively.

orchestra. Strength and overwhelming optimism characterize this movement. The depression, morbidity, or gloom of the first movement are washed away by the courage and triumph inherent in the last. And again Brahms's most tremendous emotional outbursts are achieved by means of vigorous thematic manipulation, logical development, and adherence to the formal practices of Beethoven. Yet this is no sonata-form movement in the style of that composer but one in which development and recapitulation are in part intertwined, in which one is incorporated in the other.

As a listening experience, Brahms's first symphony is unforgettable. The composer's ability to bring intellect and emotion together to serve his musical purposes demonstrates his fitness to follow in Beethoven's path. Brahms's inclusion of introductions which are thematically related to first and fourth movements, respectively, may be taken as a backward glance at the symphonies of earlier decades. We have seen that Schubert and Schumann connected introduction and first movement thematically; and Brahms was strongly influenced by both these men. The C-minor symphony, however, is the only instrumental work in which he made this concession to his Romantic predecessors.

Having spent about twenty years in intermittent work upon the somber first symphony, Brahms now changed his direction and purpose radically. The second symphony, in D major, Opus 73, was composed in 1877 and presents moods which contrast in all essential details with those of the first. It has been called a "pastoral" symphony and is generally conceded to be the most approachable of his major works. True, it is melodious throughout, it is clear in form and intent, and it represents perhaps the highest point Brahms attained in sheer brilliance and variety of orchestral color. But these qualities are achieved without the least departure from rigorous structural logic and the principles of absolute, nonprogrammatic music.

The first symphony was, as we have seen, rhythmically and melodically complex and was constructed out of a rich supply of thematic material; in this sense it is related to Brahms's early years.

The second symphony, in contrast to the first, is clear in its rhythmic structure, lyric in tone, and exceedingly economical of thematic materials. A three-note motive dominates the first movement's themes. Example 28 shows the close relationship between the motive

EXAMPLE 28

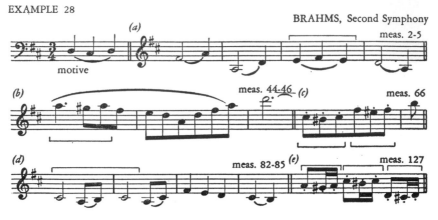

and the melodies dependent upon it. These melodies are expanded, manipulated, and combined in many fashions, the movement becoming an outstanding example of lyric charm enhanced by intellectual vigor.

One might further point out the passage in which overlapping of the motive occurs (measures 224–226), and the passage in which the fragments given in Example 28 (a) and (b) are developed simultaneously (measures 455ff.). It is with such carefully worked-out details that Brahms makes his emotional meanings clear. No account of his music dare fail to stress its calculated nature. The power and convincing emotional effect of his larger works are achieved through the perfect balance of heart and brain; Brahms does not set down momentary musical impulses or rely upon dubious inspiration. Everything is the result of considered judgment, keen knowledge of the effect of details upon the listener, a masterful technique in counterpoint, and, above all, a thorough appreciation of the fact that art results from the meaningful manipulation of materials.

The second movement, an adagio with serenity and sheer beauty as keynotes, illustrates Brahms's essential independence of bar lines. Throughout his compositions he disclosed a tendency to write phrases which, whether through syncopation, extension, or irregular length, do not coincide with the metrical grouping of the context in which they appear. His chamber music is especially rich in such rhythmic subtleties; [5] here, in the symphony, we see phrases consistently shifted across half a measure (measures 6–10, 45–51, 73–77) and thus negating the effect of the strong beat at the beginning of each metrical group. One of the great beauties of Brahms's style lies in his manipulation of rhythms just in this manner. A free, flowing lyric expression results from these deviations; yet its rhythmic complexities also challenge the attentive listener.

The third movement, like the first, is economically written. It is a folklike, somewhat angular, and short triple-meter allegretto twice interrupted by contrasting "trios," one in fast duple meter and the other in fast triple. Here again virtually all thematic material is directly related to the movement's first phrase, so that the abrupt transitions from triple-meter allegretto to duple-meter presto, for example, are melodically justified. As a whole, the movement offers great contrast both to the serene adagio and the energetic finale.

The fourth movement provides the concentration and brilliance which the symphony had lacked up to this point. A disproportionately long exposition section, in which the themes are sufficiently exploited, makes a complete development unnecessary; the recapitulation is also shortened somewhat, the whole attention being thus directed toward the coda. The latter, although brief, is forceful beyond any previous section; here Brahms rises to new heights of instrumental effectiveness. For sheer power, it has few peers in his works. The lyric, serene, and bucolic moods of the earlier movements are here transformed, and the symphony ends in a mood of triumph.

A seven-year gap in Brahms's composition of symphonies exists

[5] See, for example, the piano trio, Op. 8, 1st mvt.; the string quartet, Op. 51, No. 1, 3d mvt. A rare opposite case is provided in the piano trio, Op. 101, 3d mvt.; here a composite meter clarifies the irregular phrase length.

at this point; not until 1883 was the third symphony completed. Four other orchestral works fall into this interval, however. First among them is the violin concerto in D major, Opus 77, written in 1878. One may be sure that Brahms had not forgotten the complete failure of his first piano concerto, Opus 15, some twenty years earlier. That heroic and serious work had required more than a decade to win even grudging recognition and respect. Characteristically, now in the violin concerto, Brahms wrote as uncompromisingly as he had in the earlier work. A certain similarity of form and intention (but not of content) connects Opus 15 and Opus 77. The traditional problem of the concerto's double thematic exposition is again solved, as it had been in the 1850s, by an abridged thematic statement by the orchestra and a full statement by the violin. Further, a virtuosic display is completely absent: although the solo part makes great demands upon the technical ability of the performer, it does not present violinistic effects for their own sake. Rather, a noble and dignified mood prevails, one which is created entirely out of the logical, musical manipulation of the themes.

The first movement, in sonata-form, dips deeply into the past; for it leaves room to insert a traditional improvised cadenza. The adagio is a movement of simple construction but with great lyric charm; the finale is a freely constructed rondo. Throughout the work one senses Brahms's reserve and integrity, along with his firm resolve to remain faithful to musical requirements even at the cost of external brilliance. Fully aware of contemporary developments in instrumental technique, and in fact committed to employing an advanced technical style by the nature of the concerto, he yet brought violinistic idioms and a firm structure into harmonious relationship. The concerto is serious without being heavy, melodious without being sentimental; and it ranks among the half-dozen great masterpieces for violin and orchestra.

The awarding of an honorary doctor's degree to Brahms by the University of Breslau in 1879 occasioned the writing of the *Academic Festival Overture*, Opus 80, in the following year. This well-known work is often believed to be merely a potpourri of student songs. Quite the contrary, however; for an analysis [6] reveals that only about one quarter of the composition is concerned with the quotation of such songs, the rest being Brahms's own material. Beginning somberly with a number of original thematic fragments, the overture then presents the first of the traditional melodies. Thereafter, original and derived materials are introduced alternately, are expanded and in part developed. In this work, one of Brahms's rare deviations from a logically developing form, the proportions remain satisfying and the climaxes are well distributed. The overture requires a larger orchestra than any other work of Brahms; third trumpet, third tympani, bass drum and cymbals, and both contrabassoon and tuba are added to the regular orchestra, and a richer variety of scoring than usual is the result. A lusty, good-natured air pervades the work; in spite of its somewhat sectional form and its overabundance of material, it is uniformly successful in performance.

The latter is not the case with the next composition, the *Tragic Overture*, Opus 81, completed shortly after Opus 80. Here is a work of serious import (the title was given by Brahms himself with no clue to its significance) in sonata-form and with eloquent themes. Yet its effect is strangely dry and disappointing. Developments and transitions are somewhat perfunctory—most unusual in Brahms—and the unity of the work is threatened by the large number of melodic bits it contains. These defects are usually attributed to the fact that the *Tragic Overture* was written in close proximity to the *Academic Festival* and was designed to have the same loose structure. But Geiringer points out [7] that sketches for the work probably date back at least to the late 1860s. One must look upon this composition as one in which Brahms's treatment does not measure up to his purposes.

The fourth work of the symphony-free period is the second piano concerto, in B flat, written in 1878–1881, and published as Opus 83. The austere, serious qualities of the D-minor concerto are

[6] For example, that of Evans, in *Handbook to the Chamber Music and Orchestral Works of Brahms*, II, 70–76.
[7] *Johannes Brahms*, pp. 260–61.

noticeably absent here; this is a serene and joyful work. So close is the relationship between the two component elements that it has been called a symphony for piano and orchestra. The first movement illustrates that relationship: the piano shares in announcing the theme, then plunges into an interlude which prepares for the exposition proper. Throughout the movement the piano carries solo, obbligato, and accompanying passages with equal facility. The second movement presents additional evidence that the work is closely allied to symphonic form, for it is a fully developed scherzo in sonata-form, with contrasting trio and written-out recapitulation. This is the only scherzo to be found in Brahms's orchestral works—the miniature scherzos of the two serenades (1857–1860) excepted.

The adagio which follows is lyrically inspired; a suave melody announced by the solo cello dominates the movement. Simple in construction and sparing of themes, this movement is one of the most expressive and satisfying pieces in Brahms's instrumental music. In the finale, Brahms returns to the large rondo form; animated, rhythmically alive, and full of subtle melodic turns, the movement reveals to a great degree an equal partnership between piano and orchestra.

Brahms's conception of the concerto, as we have seen, is far removed from that of his contemporaries. He strove to restore the form to its Classical position as a symphonic work for two opposing instrumental bodies; yet he took advantage of Beethoven's example in tightening the relationship between the two. Whereas the typical Romantic concerto had become a display piece that reveled in sentimentality and virtuosic effect, the Brahms concertos rigidly avoid just those elements. And praiseworthy as Brahms's intentions in this direction were, one must admit that the very element which gives the concerto its *raison d'être* is missing. The technical idiom of the solo instrument is altered—through sheer will power and compositional facility—not to reveal the individual characteristics of the instrument but to serve the musical form. And although many pages of superb music emerge in the process—some of them the most eloquent Brahms ever wrote—the musical effects he intended might

better have been realized if he had not employed the concerto form
at all.

The subordination of characteristic solo elements may be seen to
an even greater degree in Brahms's last orchestral composition: the
A-minor double concerto for violin and cello, Opus 102, written
in 1887 (after the third and fourth symphonies, which will be discussed below). The first movement of this work marks a return to
pre-Classical concerto form, for it consists essentially of an alternation between passages for full orchestra and for the solo instruments
—analogous to the old concerto grosso—with, of course, wide-
ranging developments in both types of passage. The great technical
difficulty of the solo parts is not compensated for by a corresponding gratefulness or even melodiousness; themes are rigorously
pursued, a number of subsidiary melodic ideas are presented briefly,
and the movement rises to a great climax. The second movement, a
quiet andante, proceeds in rather routine fashion in spite of many
rhythmic subtleties brought about by masterful extensions of odd-
length phrases. Brahms's gift for pure lyric writing, on the wane
since about 1865, had long since been superseded by a gift for
manipulating melodic fragments in a shifting rhythmic context. It
is this characteristic which gives the andante its charm—a charm
which is revealed not necessarily at first hearing but only after long
study of the work. The finale is a movement in free rondo form
with certain sonata-form elements added. Lighter in mood than the
other movements, it still does little to rescue the solo instruments
from their bondage to the orchestra.

We return now to an account of the symphonies. The first and
second, we have seen, were completed close together (1876 and
1877) and differ markedly in content. Similarly, the third (Opus
90), completed in 1883, was followed closely by the fourth (Opus
98), written in 1884–1885. Again a contrast of mood and texture is
apparent.

The third symphony, in F major, represents a perfect fusion of
Brahms's Classical tendencies and his Romantic temperament. With-

out allowing any deviations from strict musical logic to infect his writing, he was yet able to invest the work with a warm, lyric mysticism in the best Romantic tradition. Further—and this is extremely rare in his larger works—a melodic motive drawn from the first movement casts its shadow over the inner movements as well, and is outspokenly quoted at the end of the finale. This must not be looked upon as a late concession to his contemporaries, however, but as an element made necessary by his musical purpose.

Unlike Brahms's other symphonic first movements, this one proceeds in confident, clear fashion from beginning to end. Emotional conflicts are little more than hinted at; the movement is a prime example of the composer's skill in abstracting more expressive contrasts from his themes than they would at first seem to possess. A three-measure "motto" precedes the main theme (see Example 29)

EXAMPLE 29

BRAHMS, Third Symphony

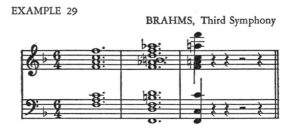

and appears at significant places throughout the movement. But this single structural detail is in no sense an arbitrary addition to the texture, such as Berlioz might have composed; rather does it become an integral part of the entire symphony. The bass of the first theme is derived from it, and it enters into developments and transitions within the first movement.[8]

Likewise, the "motto" is again suggested in the tranquil, serene slow movement, namely in the third measure (and in the fourth, which serves as an "interlude-by-extension") of the theme, and in other passages as well. It may be pointed out here parenthetically that suggestions of this movement's second theme reappear in the finale (compare measures 41ff. of the second movement and meas-

[8] See passages beginning in measures 49, 101, 216, and parallel passages.

ures 20ff. of the fourth movement). Various accompanying, ornamental figurations in the third movement outline the contour of the
"motto." Even though the perception of this effect is not always immediate, evidence of close thematic relationship between this charming, melodious movement and the preceding movements is given.

It was Brahms's usual practice to proceed from dark to light, to
work out conflicts in the first movement of a large composition and
to employ the last movement as an epilogue, a summation, or merely
as a lighthearted contrast—quite in the late-eighteenth-century manner. In the third symphony that process is reversed, for now the
greatest emotional tension is reserved for the finale. Here, in a large
and dark sonata-form movement, the emotion and drama noticeably
absent in the three preceding movements come to full expression.[9]
A number of "interpretations" have been attached to this symphony. It has been called Brahms's "Eroica"; the top line of the
"motto," namely F–A–F, has been taken to be his personal motto,
frei, aber froh (free but happy), in distinction to Joachim's *frei,
aber einsam* (free but lonely). Regardless of these, the impression
here is of a mood of growing intensity extending across the symphony's four movements. The culmination of this mood is followed
by quiet reflection (measures 267ff.) on the mood with which the
first movement ended.

Brahms's fourth symphony, in E minor, is more economically
written than any of his others. As he matured and gained greater
insight, he strove to simplify his forms and condense his themes. The
extravagance and superabundance of themes which had characterized his earlier works find little expression in the later. Three themes
each in the sonata-form movements of the third symphony had
sufficed. Now, in the fourth, two themes each and a few derived
motives allow Brahms to write three economical and concentrated
movements; and the fourth movement is even more sparsely laid

[9] According to Evans, *Handbook to the Chamber Music and Orchestral Works
of Brahms*, II, 140ff., the opening phrases of this movement constitute an introduction, the first theme proper being announced in the thirtieth measure. The recapitulation, from measure 172, is then quite regular. This analysis runs counter to many,
but Evans's observations are well founded.

out in respect to thematic material. The spare, two-note motive which animates the first theme of the opening allegro casts its shadow over large parts of the movement. The emotional tensions and great climaxes achieved here are the direct results of Brahms's masterful processes of thematic manipulation; he found no need to call upon rhapsodic utterance or striking orchestral color to achieve a dark narrative mood here. The second movement, a lyric andante, carries forward the elegiac nature of the first and contains many references to archaic patterns: hints of Phrygian mode, major and minor in quick succession, and sectional form. The third, an *allegro giocoso* in full sonata-form, substitutes for the scherzo. Although it is boisterous, at times lighthearted, and sometimes impulsive, it contains little humor.

In a sense, the symphony is complete at the end of the third movement. The elegiac mood of the first, revealed in all its darkness by the contrasting sublimities of the second, is canceled, as it were, by the sparkle and brilliance of the third. But a three-movement symphony would have been abhorrent to Brahms. There remained but the possibility of writing a fourth movement which concentrated upon a single mood and contained no conflict, and hence no anticlimax. A sonata-form would scarcely have served his purposes here; characteristically, he reached back into the Baroque period and revived the monothematic chaconne form.[10]

The movement consists of thirty-one settings of an eight-measure chord sequence, plus a coda. To allow the gradual and consistent elaboration of a short theme to continue through an entire movement might have resulted either in dullness or a disproportionately large climax. Brahms avoided both dangers by providing a quasi-symmetrical three-part form. The first part, containing twelve settings (in a sense, variations upon a musical idea) rises in rhythmic and contrapuntal complexity and falls again. In the middle part, with four settings of the theme, the measures are expanded to double their original value and give the impression of a slower tempo. The

[10] See Apel, in *Harvard Dictionary of Music*, pp. 126-27, for an account of the chaconne-passacaglia controversy.

third part, restoring the normal measure length and leading to a great climax, embraces fifteen settings—which are to some extent variations of the first twelve. Then follows a brilliant coda which includes essentially four further settings of the theme, but now expanded and developed to the highest point of emotional tension.

Brahms remains a "difficult" composer largely because he makes great demands upon his listeners. Daydreaming, superficial attention to the music being heard, a desire merely for sensuous listening pleasure or for musical excitement are attitudes that make it impossible to approach the real content of his music. Brahms's greatness is to be found in the sincerity of that music, in its freedom from tawdriness, and in its strong, masculine content. His meticulous concern both for the tiniest detail and the overall conception, along with his rare combination of reticence and warm-heartedness, stamp him as unique among Romantic composers. A summarizer rather than an experimenter, a composer who brought an unwilling public to revere the past even as he did, Brahms epitomizes all that is noble in the late nineteenth century. He will be remembered as an individual who overcame the limitations of his temperament and his times, determined upon a firm course, and composed profoundly and beautifully out of the depth of inner conviction.

IX

THE LATE ROMANTICISTS

THE SECOND HALF of the nineteenth century was, musically speaking, a time of dissension, violent partisanship, and vicious diatribes. Brahms's firm rejection of the tenets of the neo-German party was but one manifestation of the quarreling which extended well into the twentieth century. It was, in fact, a by-product of the major musical controversy of the time, namely that between Richard Wagner (1813–1883) and Eduard Hanslick (1825–1904), an influential Viennese music critic. Hanslick's position was that music had its own laws, was not concerned with extramusical delineation of feeling, and should not be burdened with psychological "meanings." His strong opinions and his eloquent pen earned him the undying hatred of Wagner, for that composer held views almost diametrically opposite to Hanslick's.

The innovations which Wagner brought to music originated entirely in the operatic field. Yet so strongly did certain elements of his "music of the future" influence instrumental composers in the period after about 1870 that the new style may be discussed here briefly—particularly since instrumental portions of his operas have won places in the symphonic repertoire. In Wagner's aesthetic philosophy, music is the expression of feeling even though it cannot designate the object or idea which gives rise to the feeling. Particularly is this true in the music drama, which results from the fusion of music, speech, and the related arts. The inner psychological action of the drama exists in the music (which is to say, in the orchestra), while the outer, perceptible action is defined by word and gesture (as set forth by the singers). Since the psychological action is continuous, the music must be continuous; transitions between scenes become orchestral interludes.

This philosophy first came to total expression in *Der Ring des Nibelungen* (1849–1874), a massive cycle consisting of a prelude, *Das Rheingold*, and of three music dramas, *Die Walküre, Siegfried*, and *Die Götterdämmerung*. In that cycle Wagner created a complex polyphonic texture. Its constituent parts are "leading motives"— short musical fragments each of which is related to a particular object or idea—and the inner action of the drama is revealed through the contrapuntal combination, development, and expansion of the motives. The whole, which creates a web of "endless melody," is dressed in a rich orchestral garb, constantly varied in sound and requiring a huge orchestra. The number of wind instruments is greatly increased, the string group is on occasion divided into twelve or sixteen parts, harps are added, and all instruments—particularly the brasses—are employed with consummate virtuosity.

In Wagner's early works—at least in those portions which appear on the concert stage—these far-reaching ideas were not yet evident. In *Eine Faust Overtüre* (1839) he composed a one-movement work in sonata-form with contrasting themes and extended development. Prefaced by a slow, somber introduction, the main movement draws a picture of "Faust in solitude," as Wagner later described the piece to Liszt. In the overtures to the early operas— *Rienzi* (1842), *Der fliegende Holländer* (1843), and *Tannhäuser* (1845)—he adopted Weber's overture plan to some extent. A selection of the opera's themes is presented in a form which provides for dramatic development and thus allows the principal conflict of the opera to emerge. By the time he composed *Lohengrin* (1850), Wagner's plan had been modified: the preludes to Acts I and III of that opera do no more than prepare the mood of the following scene.

In the prelude to Act I of *Die Meistersinger von Nürnberg* (1867) various motives drawn from the opera are introduced in a free form and are sonorously and contrapuntally developed in a manner that epitomizes the entire opera in all its rich humor, sentiment, and vitality. The *Siegfried Idyl* (1870) may be mentioned here; designing it as a birthday present for his wife Cosima (Liszt's daughter) and as an expression of happiness at his own role as a father, Wagner skillfully combined a cradle song with motives from *Siegfried*. The one-movement work, for small orchestra, is a charming and eloquent tribute.

The many orchestral excerpts from works of the late years bring to full expression the new method described above. As varied as the dramas from which they are taken, but uniformly of masterful construction and enormous dramatic power, they have achieved their place on the concert stage simply as orchestral compositions. Miniature symphonic poems for the most part, they are effective and satisfying even when separated from the operatic stage. The prelude and "Love Death" from *Tristan und Isolde*, the "Entrance of the Gods into Valhalla" from *Das Rheingold*, the "Ride of the Valkyries" and the "Magic Fire Music" from *Die Walküre*, the preludes and the "Forest Murmurs" from *Siegfried*, the "Funeral Music" and the "Immolation Scene" from *Die Götterdämmerung*, the prelude to Act I, the "Transformation Scene," and the "Good Friday Spell" from *Parsifal*—each in its own way shows a new facet of Wagner's musical genius. Whatever its expressive intention—be it in the direction of sheer excitement, tenderness and passionate warmth, dark mood, or imposing utterance—such an excerpt reveals the full-blown, programmatic, and eloquent Romanticism of which Wagner was the greatest master. And it was in opposition to such rich, form-free, pictorial music that Hanslick inveighed most vehemently.

To bring his opposition to a sharp focus, Hanslick was equally severe with anyone who claimed artistic friendship with Wagner or with the latter's methods. And among those who revered Wagner was Anton Bruckner (1824–1896). Now it will be noted that Hanslick's views about music agreed strongly with those of Brahms. The critic's championing of Brahms did much to raise the latter to a dominant position, especially in Vienna. Thus a Brahms-Bruckner controversy came into being. Furthered by the overenthusiastic partisans of the respective composers rather than by the principals themselves, this controversy has done much to obscure the true historical position of Bruckner. For that composer has been linked arbitrarily with Wagner's methods and aesthetic purposes and has been held to be the direct opposite of Brahms—incorrectly so, as will appear below. The bitter enmity of Hanslick was probably influential in keeping Bruckner's music from enjoying a fair hearing at the time of its writing, and much of the suspicion and prejudice that greet the performance of a Bruckner symphony even today may be traced to that enmity. To combat the resultant hostility, numerous Bruckner societies have been formed; adherents to the cause customarily proclaim their idol to be among the truly great. Bruckner's real position probably lies somewhere between the positions taken respectively by his detractors and his disciples.

The figure of Bruckner is an anachronism unique in recent music history. Living in a century in which versatility, rich culture, and sophistication were the earmarks of a composer, Bruckner remained a childlike, narrow-minded peasant. Revering Wagner almost to the point of idolatry, he apparently remained unaware of the revolutionary nature of Wagner's music and heard only glorious sound, imposing and festive moods, and modulatory freedom. Enthusiastically on the side of the neo-Germans—as represented by Wagner— he yet avoided any programmatic content or symbolism in his music. When he did attempt to "explain" his symphonies, as seemed to be required by the times, his accounts of programmatic intention bordered on the simple-minded. Of his ten symphonies (including the "No. O," written a year or two before the work numbered as the "first"), three are in C minor and three in D minor—in an age which prided itself on variety of mood. And finally, he adhered to strict forms and four-movement symphonies and composed scherzos externally similar to Beethoven's—in the face of one-movement symphonic poems, interest in realistic expression, and many other Romantic characteristics.

Yet in spite of these anachronistic elements—many of which he shared with Brahms, be it noted—he felt himself drawn to certain contemporary ideals as well. Chief among them is the principle of expansion of form along Schubert's lines and in direct contrast to Brahms's. Where the latter tended to economy in thematic statements, Bruckner was lavish with themes and derived subordinate themes from principal ones in the manner of Liszt. Further, he showed an interest in pure sound, enlarged his orchestra almost to Wagnerian dimensions, and made possible a richer variety of tone color—to a far greater extent than Brahms. His method of thematic development hinged largely upon the use of simple repetition with changed orchestration, or the contrapuntal combination of two themes, or harmonic sequences, or unmotivated modulation—again a unique combination of Schubert's and Liszt's practices, as well as of Wagner's. Finally, in their dimensions, breadth, and variety of material, Bruckner's symphonies brought a new type of expression to Romantic instrumental music.

Bruckner's first numbered symphony was written about 1865–1866, a few years before his eventful move (1868) from an obscure position as organist at Linz to a teaching position at the Vienna Conservatory. The last of his additional eight symphonies remained without a finale at his death in 1896. These nine works were subject to many revisions and were in part reorchestrated by well-meaning friends; some were published not at all in accord with the composer's manuscripts. Although Bruckner enjoyed a fair number of performances of his works during his lifetime—with varying responses from public and press—his first great success came with the performance of his seventh symphony in 1884, when he was sixty years old. So great a degree of similarity characterizes all nine symphonies that a description of the seventh may pass as a description of all—within limits, of course.

That work, in E major, begins with a broad allegro in sonata-form. Three themes, fully developed and recapitulated, and a coda based upon fragments of the first theme constitute the first movement, which is extended to about fifteen minutes of length. It was Bruckner's habit to begin with a soft tremolo or a quiet rhythmic figure, to announce the theme or theme-generating motive in a reflective mood, to rise to a great climax, and then to subside again. The resulting three-part division (soft-loud-soft) was then employed in succeeding sections of each movement as well, to such an extent that it is almost axiomatic to say that every major formal division of any Bruckner symphonic movement begins softly.

A typical Bruckner first theme is wide-ranging and clearly defined in harmony; it stresses intervals of fifths and octaves. The majestic air of proclamation that characterizes the Bruckner style is a direct result of this thematic type. A selection of first-theme beginnings is given in Example 30 to illustrate this point.

EXAMPLE 30

The slow movement of the seventh symphony is an expressive and heartfelt composition. An unusual color results from the addition of a quartet of Wagner tubas (two tenor, two bass) to the regularly employed contrabass tuba. Again as in the first movement, a slow increase of sonority is followed by a decrease, after which a new theme is announced quietly. Extreme breadth and imposing climaxes make this one of the most effective and moving pieces in all of Bruckner's works.

Next is a large scherzo with several thematic fragments and an extended form. Animation without humor, repetition and modulation as development techniques, and colorful orchestration prevail throughout the first part. The trio is quietly lyrical with a naïve, peasantlike tone; it is followed in the usual manner with a full recapitulation *da capo*. The scherzos in Bruckner's symphonies are among the most successful movements; yet concentration in a structural sense was not among his gifts. Thus there is a degree of reiteration, of pounding away at the obvious, which works against the best interests of the respective movements. The trios, often being nothing more than bucolic dances, seldom have any connection —musical or emotional—with the energetic, forceful scherzos proper.

The finale of the seventh symphony is a long, sonata-form movement with an extended coda which, at its end, quotes a portion of the first movement's main theme. A forceful rhythmic figure dominates throughout large sections; a quieter, chorale-like theme affords contrast. In several of Bruckner's symphonies the finale gives an impression of a new beginning, gives a feeling that much had been left unsaid in earlier movements and deserved to be set down before the work's conclusion. In a sense, the principal weight is laid upon these finales—the finale of Brahms's third symphony is similar to many of Bruckner's. The finale of the seventh, however, is an exception to this general observation; for here one encounters a movement which neither continues nor summarizes what had gone before. It is a finale which presents no new problems but is given over solely to capping the climaxes heard earlier; as such it develops great rhythmic energy and a truly fearful sonority.

Bruckner represents to perfection a type of composer extremely rare in music history: a "natural" musician, one who is unconcerned with intellectual, philosophical, or even structural matters. The forms he inherited sufficed for his purposes. One may well imagine that he never questioned them. A sense for eloquent melody scarcely surpassed by any composer—and an inability to make it progress significantly; a keenly developed feeling for true polyphony—often employed merely to pad the already sonorous texture; an ear for subtle nuances of tone color and harmony—and a complete lack of self-critical judgment in employing them; great skill in building effective climaxes—and largely unmotivated ones: with such characteristics, Bruckner was a paradox and bundle of contradictions. In listening to a Bruckner symphony, a work dedicated to the conviction that only the highest thoughts are worthy of symphonic treatment, one must give up the usual critical attitudes; one must not look for musical logic, for motivation, for sophisticated expression. A sincerity and nobility of intention, along with devout Catholicism, come to light; a truly divine patience—Bruckner's first major success found him a man of sixty—and a childlike joy in beautiful sounds are basic.

When Bruckner's symphonies are analyzed and their harmonic mannerisms and symmetrical phrases, their redundancies and mawkish contrasts, laid bare, an incredible naïveté is revealed. In his unworldliness he resembles Schubert; in his pretentiousness and love of color he is akin to Wagner—without, however, any of Wagner's ability in large-scale organization. It may be that Bruckner's masterful counterpoint, his instrumental effects, the majesty and religious air which are seldom missing from his works—unless they have been pushed aside by a crude, peasantlike passage—were derived from his organ playing. His improvisations and contrapuntal learning were his great claims to fame during much of his life. Whatever their source, the above elements contributed to a set of symphonies which have no counterparts in music history. Bruckner marks, to a certain extent, a synthesis between the neo-German party of Liszt and Wagner and the neo-Classicists with Brahms at their head. And as long as intellect and emotion are opposite poles which must be brought into harmony to create significant music, Bruckner will have both admirers and detractors.

There are certain striking parallels between the lives of Bruckner and César Franck (1822–1890). Franck was born at Liége, moved to Paris in 1835 and, with the exception of two years (1842–1844) spent as a touring virtuoso, lived the remainder of his life in the French capital. Like Bruckner, he was a devout Catholic, a church organist, and a teacher. Like Bruckner, his first major success as a composer found him in his sixties. Again like his Viennese counterpart, he was ignored, misunderstood, and even mocked when his mature compositions were first performed. In a musical sense, however, there is little connection between these two elderly, sincere, and lonely composers.

Franck's orchestral compositions are few in number. The first, written about 1845–1846, but not published, seems to have been a symphonic poem based upon a literary work which had also inspired Liszt—Victor Hugo's poem, "Ce qu'on entend sur la montagne." [1] Thirty years elapsed before Franck returned to the field; then he composed three additional symphonic poems at long intervals: *Les Eolides* in 1876, *Le Chasseur maudit* in 1882, and *Les Djinns* in 1884; the last work includes a part for piano solo. This was followed a year later by the *Variations symphoniques*. In 1887–1888 came the last symphonic poem, *Psyché*, for chorus and orchestra; and about the same time Franck's only symphony was completed.

These works vary greatly in content and style. *Les Eolides* is a delicate, refined, and subtle work with none of the bombast made familiar by Liszt's works in this form. Its program is concerned with gentle zephyrs, the daughters of Aeolus; and its chromaticism and extended modulation are in Franck's mature style. Indeed, certain

[1] Norman Demuth, in *César Franck*, pp. 25–26, believes Franck to have precedence in the creation of the symphonic poem. He gives evidence that Franck employed devices of thematic transformation and noisy climaxes in Liszt's best manner. The exact date of Liszt's composition (about 1848) is nowhere clearly given, however, and the point remains dubious. In any case, Franck did not exploit the form.

of its harmonic effects and instrumental colors serve as a preview of the Impressionistic works of the following generation.

Le Chasseur maudit ("The Accursed Hunter") is in quite a different category. Here is an extravagant, macabre piece with a typical Romantic program. A hunter profanes the Sabbath, rides roughshod through a crowd of worshippers, and is thereafter condemned to be hunted perpetually by the emissaries of Hell: ". . . the Count, mad with terror, flies away . . . pursued by demons; by day through abysses, by night through the air"—thus the literary background of the piece. Making use of thematic transformation in the best Lisztian manner, remaining faithful to the program and thereby achieving a high degree of pictorial accuracy, Franck emerged with a piece that holds its own with any of the pre-Straussian symphonic poems. The two remaining works in this category, namely *Les Djinns* and *Psyché*, have not attained great success.

The *Variations symphoniques* belong to a small but important category of works in variation form for piano and orchestra; Liszt's *Danse macabre* (1850) is a forerunner. But unlike that work, which is programmatic, Franck's is an abstract composition without literary background. A one-movement work with three thematically connected sections (see Example 31), it is beautifully constructed and

EXAMPLE 31

FRANCK, Variations Symphoniques

reveals all that is best in Franck's style. The form is a unique combination, for its sections are respectively a fantasia, a set of variations, and a sonata-form with coda—all brought into close connection by subtle thematic transformations and made emotionally satisfying by the high quality of the expression and rich variety of texture. Brilliant without being shallow, moving without being sentimental, noble without being pretentious or cloying, it brings piano and orchestra to a new level of partnership.

There had been no significant French symphonies between Berlioz's massive works of the 1830s and Saint-Saëns's C-minor symphony of 1886—unless one wishes to include Georges Bizet's charming, Mozart-influenced symphony of 1850 in this category—largely because of French negative attitudes toward instrumental music. Thus, when Franck turned to that form about 1886–1888 and composed a serious, tightly constructed symphony in D minor, he was writing an unwanted work. At its first performance in 1889 the symphony was ridiculed for its chromatic harmony, its free modulations, and its part for English horn. One wonders whether the critics had forgotten that Berlioz had used that instrument and whether they knew that Haydn had employed two English horns in his "Philosopher" symphony of about 1765. But Franck's composition has outlived its critics and remains one of the dozen most popular symphonies of all time.

Franck is linked so closely to the use of the cyclical-form principle that he is often thought to have invented it; that belief is completely false, of course. For under that principle, successive movements of a composite work are given themes in common, and that device had been employed by many composers before him. One need mention only Bach's *The Art of the Fugue*, Beethoven's last string quartets, Opus 130 to Opus 133, and Schumann's D-minor symphony to realize that cyclical form is of long standing. In one-movement sectional works, an adaptation of cyclical form becomes the underlying structural principle; Liszt's symphonic poems and Franck's own *Variations symphoniques* are examples. But Franck was perhaps more consistent in the use of the form than composers before him; the symphony is but one case in point.

The first movement, an allegro which is thematically connected with the adagio that serves as an introduction, makes much use of its first motive, a motive which Beethoven (in Opus 135) and Liszt (in *Les Préludes*), among others, had employed also (see Example 32).

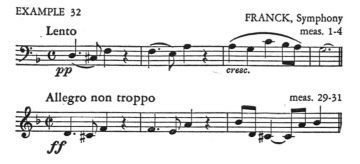

EXAMPLE 32

FRANCK, Symphony

Its content ranges from quiet and mysterious through sweetly sentimental to broad and pompous. The second movement, an allegretto with the well-known solo for English horn, contains a lightly agitated middle section with humorous overtones; one might speak of slow movement and scherzo being intertwined here. The finale begins and ends brilliantly; it contains, in addition to its own themes, quotations from the second movement and further development of the first movement's principal theme. Thematic transformation, cyclical form, and slight hints of a widespread symmetry thus serve closely to connect one movement with the others.

In Franck's later orchestral compositions one feels the presence of a master organist and improviser. His characteristic, restless modulation, his thick, chromatic harmony, and a style which is basically polyphonic are elements that fall naturally into the compositions of organists. There is little of the long line and the soaring melody which are the marks of an orchestral composer. Rather are there short phrases, usually two or four measures in length, a constant starting and stopping which grows out of improvisatory technique, and a type of climax which depends upon increased sonority instead of emotional growth. Harmonically dark and tense passages are followed by cloying and melodious ones; and although a rich variety of textures and expressive content is always present in Franck, one finds little of the sustained, cumulative organization typical of the best symphonic music of the time. Such organization is found to a greater degree in the orchestral works of two of his pupils.

Vincent d'Indy (1851–1931), foremost spokesman of what may be termed the "Franck cult," contributed to an extension of cyclical-form principles and introduced an intellectual, dry quality which French instrumental music had seldom possessed earlier. His *Symphony on a French Mountain Air*, Opus 25 (1886), is for piano and orchestra; the piano part, while soloistic and bristling with technical difficulties, is an obbligato and adds merely another series of tone colors and idioms to the already rich and varied orchestral palette. Two other orchestral compositions are heard occasionally. *Istar*, Opus 42 (1896), is a set of variations in which the theme is gradually unclothed, as it were, and is heard in pure form only at the end of the piece. The second symphony, in B flat, Opus 57 (1902–1903), also testifies, like the *Istar* variations, to D'Indy's solid gifts as a severe composer of the contrapuntal, modulatory, Franckian school.

Whereas D'Indy was clear and definite in all his compositions, Ernest Chausson (1855–1899) remained somewhat of a dreamer and a cautious predecessor of free and lyric Impressionism. Chausson's only symphony, in B flat, Opus 20 (1890), reveals a rare combination of forthrightness and diffidence. Themes are noble and melodious and are developed "correctly"; yet the work is not moving or productive of great enthusiasm. The *Poème*, a one-movement quasi concerto for violin and orchestra is, with its rhapsodic themes and impassioned developments, perhaps his finest work. Chausson, D'Indy, and other pupils of Franck did much to establish a love of symphonic music in the French public. They were also instrumental in passing ideals of solid workmanship, contrapuntal skill, and standards of formal construction to a generation of composers in the 1920s who reacted against the style founded by Debussy. In that intermediary role is to be found their greatest value.

Charles Camille Saint-Saëns (1835–1921), although a contemporary both of Franck and Brahms, remained largely untouched by the Romantic expression of those men. Throughout an enormous number of works extending across a sixty-five-year period which began in 1855, he revealed a fluency, versatility, and formal clarity virtually unmatched by any other recent composer. From his first symphony (1855) to a set of sonatas for various woodwind instruments and piano (1921) one finds a lightness of expression, a degree of refinement, and a sameness of style that are strongly reminiscent of Mendelssohn. Of his more than three dozen orchestral works, only a few have survived in the repertoire.

Chief among them is his third symphony, in C minor, Opus 78, written about 1886. It was not in Saint-Saëns's nature to experiment blindly. He went no further than modifying existing forms to meet his own somewhat narrow expressive requirements. Thus, although the symphony is based on cyclical-form principles and is apparently in two movements, it actually contains four: an agitated allegro (with a slow introduction) connected to a sonorous and sentimental adagio, and a brilliant scherzo tied to a triumphant finale by means of an interspersed chorale. An organ and two pianos are required in addition to an orchestra almost of Berlioz's dimensions; thus Saint-Saëns provided himself with resources sufficient for the powerful and striking effects with which the symphony abounds. His facility of invention, his gift for writing spontaneously ("as an apple tree produces fruit," he once declared), leads to a typical stylistic feature: one rhythmic figure or melodic idea is repeated ceaselessly throughout a movement. This practice, while it serves to unify, also makes for monotony. Vigorous, imposing, and melodious as this symphony is, it cannot be said to have eternal significance.

The same reservation applies to Saint-Saëns's symphonic poems, *The Spinning Wheel of Omphale*, Opus 31 (1871); *Phaëton*, Opus 39 (1873); and *Danse macabre*, Opus 40 (1874). Here are attractive, fluent, and melodious accounts of the various programs, carried out with good taste, a minimum of the chromatic and harmonic restlessness that animates Franck's music, and a flair for "describing" extramusical elements. The spinning wheel in *Omphale*, the wild ride through the skies in *Phaëton*, and the grisly dance in the *Danse macabre* are all suggestively depicted.

The many concertos of Saint-Saëns (six for piano, three for violin, two for cello) are somewhat alike in their graceful brilliance, avoidance of extreme virtuosic effects, and unfailingly refined and problem-free expression. Virtually all these works reveal the outstanding mark of Saint-Saëns's style—adherence to one basic figuration. Several (the well-known A-minor cello concerto among them) make use of cyclical form and appear with connected movements.

The orchestral works in general reveal the composer's mastery of unassuming counterpoint, his sense for clear form, his desire to avoid emotional extremes—and a high degree of superficiality. Great competence in all technical matters is offset by little real inspiration in melodic writing and no great depth of feeling. Enjoyable, outwardly effective, and graceful and charming though they are at times, the works of Saint-Saëns are scarcely destined for a permanent place in the literature.

One may respect the convictions of Liszt and Brahms toward the programmatic symphonic poem and the abstract symphony, respectively. As realized by those men, the two forms were mutually antithetical and represented two utterly opposed aesthetic points of view. With Peter Ilyich Tchaikovsky (1840–1893) one senses a lack of conviction in this regard; his constitution embraced little of the thoughtful, reasoning approach to music that distinguished both of his older contemporaries. For Tchaikovsky wrote in both fields with equal facility. In half a dozen free, descriptive pieces and an equal number of symphonies, he gave himself up to the requirements of both positions with the greatest ease. And yet, no essential difference between the two opposing types is apparent in his music. Thus, outwardly representing a bridge between the two nineteenth-century musical philosophies, he remained true only to his own confused musical sense, and succeeded only in revealing his neurotic, hyperemotional personality.

One aspect of programmatic music which became prominent in the years after about 1870 was that of nationalism (this will be discussed fully in the following chapter). An important group of Tchaikovsky's Russian contemporaries, calling themselves "The

Five," set themselves the task of exploiting purely Russian elements in their music. Now, Tchaikovsky at times made use of Slavic folk songs, and a color and sound which pass as Russian impart a national flavor to his music. But he remained aloof from the aggressive, conscious nationalism of this group and turned his face toward the west.

With this mixture of programmatic and abstract musical intention, with his universalism and unwilled nationalism, Tchaikovsky stands revealed as an uncertain, vacillating composer whose work is strangely uneven. Aware of his lack of control in structural matters and particularly inept in the matter of thematic development, he yet attempted to remain faithful to preexisting musical forms—the few evidences of cyclical-form principles in his works notwithstanding. An unashamed and impulsive emotional intensity, perhaps the most striking characteristic of his larger works, often interfered with his desire to write in traditional forms. It is this conflict which caused him to set the tawdriest, most bombastic passages against refined and beautifully melodious ones.

Three early symphonies (No. 1, G minor, 1866; No. 2, C minor, 1872; No. 3, D major, 1875) reveal a Tchaikovsky who was as yet unwilling to progress beyond the externals of symphonic form. Harmonic sequences, a great deal of empty rhetoric, and brassy climaxes substitute, however, for the careful, calculated manipulation of thematic fragments which is the major aspect of the style, say, of Brahms. It is generally agreed that those symphonies are immature; as such they are seldom performed today—except that the second, the "Little Russian," with attractive Ukrainian folk tunes, still has its devotees.

Now, immaturity is not related to Tchaikovsky's youth or inexperience. Maturity, in a musical sense, may be taken to mean evidence of the ability to write both effectively and significantly; and that quality came and went throughout the composer's career. Immature passages occur in his last works; and in at least one of his early works Tchaikovsky found a type of expression which is truly mature. That work is the overture-fantasy *Romeo and Juliet*, written about 1869–1870 (roughly contemporary with the piano works before Opus 10) and revised in 1880. Here the composer is seen at his best, in a combination of rhapsodic fantasy and sonata-form. The structural plan of this work became almost a standard in the single-movement compositions as well as in the symphonic first and last movements of later years. Its elements are as follows: a slow and lugubrious introduction; an allegro with two themes, each of which is worked over at some length after its first appearance; a development section proper; a recapitulation; and a coda, either slow or fast, which often refers back to earlier thematic material.

In adhering to this rather fixed form, Tchaikovsky necessarily departed from Shakespeare's drama, in that the poet's proportions between major and minor episodes of the plot were altered. To some extent this is true also of the other programmatic works: *The Tempest* (1873), *Francesca da Rimini* (1876), and *Hamlet* (1888) among them. Since the same form is found in supposedly abstract, non-programmatic movements also, and since works of both types were susceptible to the same structural principles, one realizes that programs as such were of little influence upon Tchaikovsky. The essential element is the rather narrow range of emotional states he was at great pains to express.

Tchaikovsky brought to the most intense expression a tendency which affected most of nineteenth-century concert music. We have seen that in the early 1800s the public had found in the concert hall a source of vicarious experience. Beethoven had inspired them with noble, powerful, and significant emotions; Berlioz had given them spectacular scenes; Liszt often introduced poetic platitudes; and Brahms recapitulated Beethoven on a personal, subjective level. It remained for Tchaikovsky to bring frenzied or hysterical writing to its highest pitch—mingled with the emotions evoked by melancholy or sentimental melodies, and occasionally by striking, original instrumental effects. It is such moods which unite *Romeo and Juliet* with the other single-movement pieces—*Marche slave* (1876), *The Year 1812*, and the *Italian Caprice* (both from 1880)—in addition to the works mentioned above.

The "favorite" symphonies (No. 4, F minor, 1877; No. 5, E minor,

1888; No. 6, B minor and nicknamed the "Pathétique," 1893) bring to expression emotional states similar to those in the programmatic works—with, of course, additional moods contained especially within the inner movements. It is in the latter that Tchaikovsky's occasional lightness of mood and deftness of expression are best revealed. Thus in the slow movement of the F-minor symphony, a somewhat melancholy mood is relieved by a lilting, staccato embroidery of the principal melody (see Example 33). The scherzo of

EXAMPLE 33

TCHAIKOVSKY, Fourth Symphony, 2nd movement
meas. 85-89

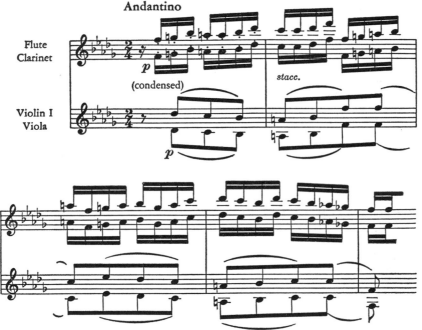

that symphony, with its consistent pizzicato figures in first and last sections and its balletlike wind passages in the trio, contains nothing of his customary frenzy, nor does the graceful waltz which serves as third movement in the E-minor symphony. Here he is refined, eloquent, and melodious; that movement does much to relieve the morbid, saccharine, and brutal moods which prevail elsewhere.

It is unfortunate that the work which is probably Tchaikovsky's best is also among his least-known: the four-movement symphony or symphonic poem, *Manfred* (1885), based on Byron's poem. In place of the typical repetitions and redundancies, there is in this work a breadth achieved without padding, a structure which satisfies the musical needs of his program and his thematic material at the same time, and an imaginative array of romantic, fairylike, and narrative episodes. Diffuseness is avoided, and a degree of unity is achieved both by the use of cyclical-form principles in the first and last movements and by the air of refinement which pervades the whole. Tchaikovsky's handling of the orchestra—larger than in any other of his works—reaches new heights of brilliance and variety. There is scarcely a tawdry or vulgar passage in *Manfred*. The subtle charm of the scherzo and the open, pastoral tone of the slow movement are among his finest inspirations. Since public demand for Tchaikovsky's music must be satisfied in the decades which lie ahead, one might wish that *Manfred*, the noblest and most extensive of his works, could become more familiar.

The B-flat-minor piano concerto (1875), perhaps the best-known of all concertos, achieves its popularity largely through its theatrical effectiveness and unrestrained exhibitionism. Structurally among the weakest of his works, it presents a collection of contrasting tunes which it repeats and elaborates without ever ascending to subtle or even thoughtful expression. The familiar theme of the introduction, for example, is shouted out at great length and gives promise of being basic to the whole. But thereafter it disappears from view; its pretentious posturing remains merely an oratorical flourish which has no connection with what follows, and it contributes to the unbalance which is the weakest feature of the work. A high degree of extremely effective and brilliantly virtuosic writing in the solo part cannot conceal the shallowness of the themes or the poverty of workmanship.

The D-major violin concerto (1878) is essentially a lyric work in spite of its external effectiveness. It moves pleasantly and brilliantly, and is at no time as bombastic or trivial as the piano concerto. Tchaikovsky made full use of the technical possibilities of the violin, but he also succeeded in establishing a tuneful, narrative air relieved by moments of attractive sentiment and driving rhythm. The *Variations on a Rococo Theme* (1876), for cello and orchestra, reveals the composer in a graceful and deft mood.

Tchaikovsky's virtues as a composer derive from his melodic sense and his imaginative employment of orchestral resources. A real gift for writing tunefully, for casting his melodies into broad, lyric patterns, and for scoring and harmonizing them so that their particular mood qualities are enhanced—it is this which makes his music attractive at times. The fact that such melodies are not suitable as symphonic themes did not escape the composer; he repeatedly complained of his inability to manipulate them and thus to create larger forms. But no matter how weak the structural element in Tchaikovsky's music, a worse feature is the vulgarity and coarseness of what he substituted for thematic manipulation. In place of thematic development one often finds long, arid passages full of padding, of sequence repetition, of tautologies growing ever more hysterical—and, to the ear attuned to sensational effect, ever more exciting. The works in which such devices are kept to a minimum, in which he revealed a degree of sensitivity and restraint—namely the serenade for string orchestra (1880) and certain movements in the first three orchestral suites (1879, 1883, and 1884)—are not "typical," hence are rarely performed. The suite from the ballet, *The Nutcracker* (1892), belongs in this category, except that the closing waltz shows Tchaikovsky at his very worst insofar as clichés and platitudes are concerned; yet it has remained in the repertoire by reason of its exotic appeal.

X

THE NATIONAL SCHOOLS

THE ART OF MUSIC is in a certain sense analogous to a language; indeed, it has often been called a "universal language." Two closely related possibilities of furthering the analogy may be noted: a language may be spoken with personal or regional accents, or even with different dialects; and out of its dialects new languages may be formed—somewhat in the way that the several Romance languages developed out of Latin. A glance at music history reveals how the first of these possibilities was realized. Composers from Haydn to Schumann "spoke" with a German accent, so to say, but remained within the language through the universal appeal of their utterances. At the same time such diverse composers as Rameau, Rossini, and Chopin "spoke" respectively with French, Italian, and even Polish idioms and inflections, yet remained universal. The music of these composers recaptured in an intangible way something of the national characteristics, spiritual sense, and personal aspirations of their respective people.

In the second half of the nineteenth century other groups of composers went some distance on the path of the second possibility, namely that of creating regional languages out of the universal tongue. Their method was to make overt use of their own folk songs, idioms, dances, and legends and to transform the universal aspects of the language to fit the new expressive material. These composers, unlike those of the first group, were active in geographical areas where political oppression or personal subjection were the order of the day—notably Russia and Bohemia. This tendency to employ indigenous materials is called "nationalistic" in music. Nationalism represents in a sense the pugnacious, self-assertive denial of a cultural inferiority; it is a form of artistic self-consciousness.

Certain necessary preliminaries to the formation of musical nationalism took place in earlier decades. The urge, in the late eighteenth and early nineteenth centuries, to preserve folk songs on a national basis had resulted in many collections of source material. The composers of that time had shown how the material might be used. Haydn and Schubert had turned in a few works, for example, to Hungarian Gypsy idioms; Beethoven had on occasion quoted Russian tunes; and both Haydn and Beethoven had interested themselves in folk songs of the British Isles. And now the nationally minded composers in the period after about 1860 found it necessary to consider the musical worth of their own material in order to utilize and exploit their respective folk heritages. This was doubly desirable; for many composers of the time, faced with the tremendous accomplishments of Haydn, Mozart, and especially Beethoven, and unable to meet those giants on their own terms, were thus forced to express themselves on a smaller, more intimate scale.

A national music does not come into being as soon as folk materials are employed, however; for an essential part of national self-expression consists of unveiling the nation's soul in the music. This requires a composer of genius who, if he is to write music that will hold its own upon the universal scene, must present a universally significant content even though it is couched in national idioms and, perhaps, in national forms and color. The earliest of such composers were Michael Ivanovich Glinka (1804–1857) among the Russians and Bedřich Smetana (1824–1884) among the Czechs. Glinka in his operas, *A Life for the Tsar* (1836) and *Russlan and Ludmilla* (1842), introduced Russian, Polish, and oriental colors, painted a succession of brilliant nationalistic pictures, and made liberal use of Russian melodic and rhythmic idioms. The overture to *Russlan and Ludmilla* has survived on the concert stage. It is, however, not typical of the opera itself; its Italian brightness and energy as well as its universal humor and melodiousness are scarcely representative of Glinka's essential nationalism. Truly Russian orchestral music did not emerge until later in the century; it will be discussed in due course.

Smetana, on the other hand, was active in the orchestral field and was the creator of a Czech national music. His earliest works in the field, however, gave only faint promise of that accomplishment: the three symphonic poems written between 1858 and 1861 were inspired by western European literature and reflected the composer's admiration for the music and methods of Liszt. Theme transformation and a quantity of sequence repetition characterize these forgotten works. From 1863, after several years spent in Gothenburg, Smetana lived in Prague and was active in supplying the Czech National Theater with repertoire material. In eight operas, among them the well-known *Bartered Bride* (1866), he disclosed his fondness for Czech legend and literature and placed a great variety of folk songs and dances upon the operatic stage. More importantly, however, he revealed the Czech temperament in all its rhythm, color, and emotional vitality. These operas are nationalistic even when they do not embody folk songs. Yet at the same time the universal appeal of *The Bartered Bride*, for instance, is felt keenly; its characters are human beings, and a close relationship exists between Smetana's style and the lyric style of the Viennese masters, particularly Schubert.

His great contribution to symphonic literature is the cycle of six symphonic poems with the collective title *Má vlast* ("My Country"), written between 1874 and 1879 in spite of his complete loss of hearing. Here Smetana strove to recapture the spirit of Bohemia itself. The cycle is compounded of legend (*Vyšehrad* and *Šárka*), history (*Tábor* and *Blaník*), and description of landscape (*The Moldau* and *From Bohemia's Fields and Groves*). The Vyšehrad motive, quoted at the beginning of the cycle, is employed throughout the first poem and is mentioned in the second as well as the sixth; it plays little part in the thematic materials of the others, for one may do no more than trace a faint resemblance (based upon a sequence of falling intervals) between the motive and subsequent themes.

All six poems of the cycle are devoted to revealing the glories of the Czech heritage; it is this poetic idea rather than the Vyšehrad motive which unifies the cycle. Within each of the six symphonic poems, faint echoes of Liszt's practices are heard; a considerable amount of theme transformation is undeniable, and each work is divided into several sections which are often marked by contrasting tempos. Yet the sections of each work constitute in effect a four-movement connected symphony; and the harmony, the melodic and rhythmic elements, and the general color of the cycle are Smetana's own and hence stand for the Czech national style. Polkas and other dances appear on occasion—but also, notably in the love scene of *Šárka*, a breadth of melody that is closely akin to Wagner and has little in common with Czech idioms.

Smetana, like many others who adhered to the ideals of the neo-German party, depended upon poetic stimulus for his musical inspiration. Without relying upon realistic description or departing from clear, well-organized forms, he yet remained faithful to his programmatic ideas. Never obscure, always melodious or rhythmically alive, Smetana was content to remain on a somewhat local, intimate level. He showed little interest in posing problems of universal emotional significance and solving them musically. Thus he cannot be reckoned among the Promethean composers whose music benefits a larger group. It is perhaps inevitable that outside his own country *The Moldau* is the only work of the *Má vlast* cycle to have survived in the standard repertoire.

Antonín Dvořák (1841–1904) was far more prolific in the orchestral field and composed in a greater variety of forms and styles than Smetana. Influenced in turn by virtually all the great composers of the nineteenth century, he consistently returned to a fresh, problem-free expression and a love for his Czech homeland after each digression. In nine symphonies, five symphonic poems, several concertos, and almost two dozen miscellaneous works for orchestra, Dvořák disclosed a gift for pure melody and a grasp of the relationships between form and content unequaled by his nationalistically minded contemporaries.

Dvořák's nationalism is not outwardly as perceptible as that of

Smetana—at least not in the orchestral works; nor was his interest in literary stimulus and programmatic content as consistent. The majority of his symphonies are in the sphere of abstract music. They are dedicated to presenting attractive, forceful, and contrasting melodies in forms which are basically those of the early nineteenth century. Occasionally a symphonic movement 'suggests dance rhythms or is an outspoken dance form—notably the *furiant* which serves in place of a scherzo in the so-called "first" symphony. But actual quotation of folk songs is held to a minimum. It is rather the Czech spirit, with all its impulsive alternation between gaiety and gloom, with its rhythmic vitality and physical energy, that comes to expression.

The first four of Dvořák's symphonies were not published during his lifetime; the remaining five, along with many works in other categories, were arbitrarily treated as to chronological order and opus number by his publishers.[1] Thus one ordinarily gains a distorted view of Dvořák's development as a composer. The great maturity and considerable technical mastery revealed by the first symphony, for example, are truly astonishing—unless one realizes that it is actually his sixth work in the form.

Early works—insofar as they are available, and including categories other than the symphonic—reveal a Dvořák who was greatly attracted to the style of Wagner. Free, expansive forms and long, flowing melodies set in a rhapsodic manner are typical. A period in the late 1870s saw him greatly concerned with Czech folk materials; this phase is seen in the four *Slavonic Rhapsodies* and in the first set of *Slavonic Dances* (originally for piano four-hands, but later orchestrated), all of which were written between 1874 and 1878. The F-major symphony of 1875 makes lesser use of national elements, it is true; yet its slow movement is closely allied to the Slavonic and melancholy *dumka*.

[1] The proper order of the symphonies, with approximate dates of composition, is as follows: C minor and B flat, both from 1865 and both unpublished; E flat, 1873, and D minor, 1874, both published posthumously; No. 3, F major, 1875; No. 1, D major, 1880; No. 2, D minor, 1884–1885; No. 4, G major, 1889; No. 5, E minor ("From the New World"), 1893.

About 1877 Dvořák was befriended by Brahms and became, in a sense, the latter's *protégé*. Thereupon he tended to shake off the earlier influences, develop his own style, and follow a musical ideal which in many ways resembles that of his great contemporary. The D-major symphony gives evidence of the program-free, eloquent, and logical manner of Dvořák in the 1880s; it is a joyous, sparkling work. And yet the A-minor violin concerto of about the same years reveals a free, rhapsodic expression combined with unmistakably nationalistic elements in a form which owes much to Liszt. Conversely, the *Scherzo capriccioso* of 1883 represents Dvořák at his imaginative and formal best. Cast in the form of a scherzo with trio, but containing long developments and brilliant transitions, it is a breathless, effective—and difficult—movement for large orchestra. The work deserves to be restored to the high place in the repertoire it once enjoyed.

With the D-minor symphony of 1884–1885 Dvořák reached new heights. Here is a "universal" work, as opposed to a national or purely personal one; the emotional scale of this symphony is far above any other of his orchestral compositions. From a technical point of view, he revealed himself here to be a master of thematic manipulation devoted to intense emotional expression; only Brahms among his contemporaries could write more concisely and logically. It is unfortunate that the D-minor symphony is not as well known as the ever-popular "New World."

The G-major symphony of 1889 marks a complete contrast to the foregoing. For here is an easygoing collection of unrelated material, developed without any great emotional compulsion. Enjoyable in the manner of virtually all of Dvořák's music and containing a few enchanting passages, it cannot compare with the symphonies which precede and follow it. A cycle of three related pieces from 1891–1892 may be mentioned here. At first united under the title, "Nature, Life, and Love," the pieces were later issued as overtures with separate titles: *In Nature's Realm, Carnival,* and *Othello.* Bound together by a pastoral motive which appears at appropriate moments in the works, they mark a return of the programmatic element to Dvořák's music. The *Carnival*, especially, has retained its place in the repertoire; it brings to expression the composer's exuberant spirit and mastery of orchestration.

The E-minor symphony, the ninth of his works in this form, was written in 1893 during the first year of Dvořák's stay in the United States; its subtitle, "From the New World," is thus justified. As he had done elsewhere, he expressed the spirit of a people—this time the American people instead of the Czech, of course, but American as reflected in the life of the Czech community of Spillville, Iowa—without quoting folk melodies. A deliberately naïve air pervades the themes of this work; its melodies are not so much developed as repeated, and sequence repetitions and routine climaxes play a larger part here than in any other of his major works. This type of treatment is perhaps made necessary by the shape and content of the themes; the latter are in the main scarcely adapted to true symphonic treatment, and one may be sure that Dvořák was aware of this. For, almost as if to compensate for this type of theme elaboration, he makes a bow to sophisticated cyclical form: themes from the first movement appear in the second and in the third, and the coda of the fourth quotes liberally from all three preceding movements. The symphony as a whole is a brilliant, effective, and satisfying work; but it is not the most significant of Dvořák's compositions.

The B-minor cello concerto of 1894–1895 also belongs to the American stay; but his third year in the United States found Dvořák homesick. One may surmise a loss of interest in the American scene, and this is reflected in the romantic, somewhat melancholy tone which predominates in the concerto. A colorful, rhapsodic work resulted, one which exploits the solo instrument's technical possibilities without exceeding the bounds of good taste. It remains one of the most attractive works in the cello repertoire.

Dvořák's interest in program music was revived after his return to Prague. In 1896 and 1897 he wrote no fewer than five symphonic poems. The immediate stimulus was a collection of folk ballads. Terror, death, and fantasy are characteristic of the ballads he selected, yet he exercised great restraint and thematic economy in setting them to music. These works have not held their place in the repertoire; they are mentioned here only to give evidence of Dvořák's uncertainty as to his true mission as a composer.

An eloquent melodic quality shines through all of his works; in a sense, his lyric gifts were akin to Schubert's. His instinct for form and proportion was as highly developed as his melodic sense, and he possessed a technical ability and an imagination which allowed him at all times to balance these opposites. Extreme contrasts, embracing abrupt changes from dark melancholy to wild joy, are typical of his music; yet such contrasts are usually justified by the contexts in which they appear. Seldom did he allow mediocre passages to remain in his works; his self-critical sense was almost as keen as Brahms's. It is only by comparison with the very greatest—with a Beethoven or a Mozart, say—that the personal, subjective nature of his emotional palette is revealed. In all respects save those of profundity and eternal significance, Dvořák must be ranked among the finest of nineteenth-century composers.

To express Russian life and feeling, following the work of Glinka and Alexander Dargomijsky (1813–1869), became the underlying purpose of a group of enthusiastic musical amateurs who came under the influence of Mili Balakirev (1837–1910). The latter, together with Alexander Borodin (1833–1887), César Cui (1835–1918), Modest Moussorgsky (1839–1881), and Nicholas Rimsky-Korsakov (1844–1908), formed the nucleus (called "The Five") of a nationalistic school which exercised a great influence upon later generations of Russian composers. The technical training and musical abilities of this loosely knit group were so varied, however, and their central purpose was so vaguely stated, that little solid, systematic work came from their respective pens.

Balakirev, largely self-taught, became interested in teaching and conducting; his compositions are few, and his function was principally that of acting as a gadfly to the others. Only Rimsky-Korsakov felt it necessary to pursue organized musical study later in life. The main preoccupation of the others seems to have been the

composition of operas; and it is in the operatic field that their true
worth as nationalists and musicians is to be measured. In every case,
the quantity and quality of their purely orchestral works falls below their operas. Since none of Cui's works have survived in the
repertoire, the following discussion will concern itself only with
Borodin, Moussorgsky, and Rimsky-Korsakov.

In Borodin one encounters an element which runs through much
Russian music: economy of thematic material, and with it, deliberate,
monotonous repetition of melodic fragments. We have seen this in
Tchaikovsky. This trait is not to be looked upon as a weakness in
Borodin, but as the expression of an aesthetic creed different from
that of German composers since Haydn. Borodin had demonstrated
his ability to write along Classical lines and to develop themes in the
German manner in his first symphony, in E-flat major, composed in
1862–1867. In the second, however, the repetitive method is fully
revealed. The symphony is in B minor, was written between 1872
and 1876, and is his most important orchestral work.

A striking motive heard at the very outset impresses itself upon
virtually the entire first movement (see Example 34). The few bits

EXAMPLE 34   BORODIN, Second Symphony
    Allegro   meas. 1-7

of contrasting melody which are introduced play little part in the
structure of the whole; rather is there a constant dwelling upon or
reflecting upon the first motive. Outwardly in sonata-form, in that
the principal divisions of that form are well marked, the movement
develops little thematic conflict. The scherzo is an orchestral tour de
force in which themes are of minor importance; a few melodic fragments do appear, but they become lost in the rich, kaleidoscopic
orchestral color. The slow movement is more orthodox and expresses something of a melancholy, quasi-oriental character that has,
since Borodin, been taken to reflect the Russian temperament. The

finale is a series of vivid, exciting episodes, based in part on contrasting themes but unified by the unfailing brilliance of the orchestral sound. Harmonies are free throughout the symphony, and a typical alternation of barbaric and intimate moods gives the work much of its national character. A third symphony was left incomplete at Borodin's death.

It is remarkable that the second symphony should be so closely knit both in structure and intention; for it was written across a four-year interval, was interrupted by work on other compositions and by Borodin's scientific studies and medical-administrative duties. There is a certain similarity in all of his works, it is true, in that his melodies are generally of folk-song type and tinged with oriental color, and that constant repetition with changed orchestration is the chief organizing principle. This basic similarity may be seen when two other orchestral works are compared to the symphony: the ever-popular set of "Polovtzian Dances" from the unfinished opera, *Prince Igor,* and a small symphonic poem, *On the Steppes of Central Asia,* the latter written in 1880.

Moussorgsky is even more sparsely represented in the orchestral literature than Borodin. A single composition, *A Night on the Bare Mountain,* is his principal representative. It was designed originally (1860) as incidental music for a lurid drama called *The Witches;* it suffered many modifications at the composer's hands (including one version for piano and orchestra, and a place in two operas) and, about 1882, at Rimsky-Korsakov's. Its present form as a symphonic poem is largely the work of the latter. The thematic material of the work is unified by a harsh, macabre quality which goes far toward carrying out the implied program—an orgy of witches and grisly apparitions, finally dispersed by the chimes of the village bells. The material and framework are Moussorgsky's, the sequence and arrangement Rimsky-Korsakov's. But the fantastic nature of the composition, its dramatic transitions, and its sheer excitement are undeniable, regardless of the author. *A Night on the Bare Mountain* is not, strictly speaking, within the body of nationalistic music. It does, however, testify to Moussorgsky's interest in Russian legendary subjects, an interest which animates the greater part of his operas.

Pictures from an Exhibition was originally a set of piano pieces composed in 1874; it was orchestrated about 1922 by Maurice Ravel, and in its new dress has added considerable luster to Moussorgsky's name. The ten pieces are descriptive sketches, and several of them are connected by a "promenade," a short interlude which represents the composer moving from one picture to the next. Quite apart from Ravel's masterly orchestration, the set reveals the depth of Moussorgsky's insight, his vivid imagination, and his forward-looking harmonic sense.

Rimsky-Korsakov, the youngest of "The Five," served a double function. As musical executor of Moussorgsky's fragments and unfinished works he prepared a number of compositions for practical performance; and as the most industrious and best-trained musician in the group he wrote more systematically and in greater quantity than his colleagues. About a dozen Russian historical and legendary subjects were made into operas and performed during his lifetime. But more than a dozen orchestral works were written also; several hold respected places in today's symphonic repertoire. One of them, *Antar*, began its career as Rimsky-Korsakov's second symphony in 1868, was revised and reorchestrated several times, and emerged finally in 1903 as a symphonic suite of four movements. It is constructed somewhat on the Berlioz model: it is a programmatic work, it contains a basic motive or *idée fixe* which appears in each movement, and it brings to expression four episodes in the adventures of the legendary Antar, an Arabian poet and desert hero. The movements describe Antar's encounter with the queen of the fairies, and his moods of revenge, power, and love, respectively.

Three compositions of 1887–1888, however, are the works upon which Rimsky-Korsakov's orchestral fame is most largely founded. A *Capriccio espagnol* was at first planned as a fantasy on Spanish themes for violin and orchestra—perhaps to serve as a companion piece to the *Fantasy on Russian Themes* for the same instrumental combination, completed in 1886. That plan was discarded, and the

Capriccio was composed as a virtuosic set of five movements for orchestra. The composer was careful to point out that the brilliance of the work lay in the structure of the themes and in the piece itself: "It is the very essence of the composition, not its garb or orchestration." His considerable knowledge of instrumental idioms and technical possibilities, gained in part as an inspector of naval bands, stood him in good stead; he knew the difficulties and inmost nature of the instruments as perhaps no composer before him. As a result, the many gay, wild, or sentimental tunes in the *Capriccio* are well adapted to form an orchestral work of the greatest effectiveness.

The symphonic suite, *Scheherazade*, followed directly upon the *Capriccio*. For its literary subject-matter Rimsky-Korsakov turned again, as he had done for *Antar*, to the *Arabian Nights*. The suite is based upon the story of the sultan Schahriar, who is diverted from his habit of murdering one of his wives each night by the charm and narrative ability of Scheherazade. The movements are entitled "The Sea and Sinbad's Ship," "The Tale of the Kalendar Prince," "The Young Prince and Princess," and "Festival at Bagdad." Two themes run through the suite: a hard, brutal one, carried by full orchestra and symbolizing the sultan; and a suave, florid cadenza for violin and harp, representing Scheherazade. The themes appear in the manner of Berlioz's *idée fixe*, either to introduce the various movements or at significant moments within. It may be pointed out that the transformation of the sultan's theme in the course of the work represents the gradual weakening of his murderous resolve; the composer has written character sketches of the two protagonists rather than drawn simply a series of brilliant, fanciful oriental pictures.

The richness of color and orchestral mastery which characterize all of Rimsky-Korsakov's larger works are nowhere so clearly revealed as in *Scheherazade*. An orchestra of standard, pre-Wagnerian dimensions sufficed him; yet he achieved a great variety of sonorous, delicate, massive, and even overwhelming effects. Like his contemporaries, he was much given to thematic reiteration and showed little interest in developing themes to provide closely knit forms;

but the monotony dangerously inherent in this practice is avoided by the flexibility of his orchestration. Indeed, the virtuosity he revealed in this respect became something of a weakness. One becomes surfeited with the constant change of color and sound, one realizes that in Rimsky-Korsakov such elements are ends in themselves. Of all the Russian nationalists, he was perhaps the most effective in a superficial sense, yet his dramatic ability did not compare with Moussorgsky's, for example, or his perception of form and proportion with Borodin's. He possessed a full measure of sentimental and lyric qualities; yet these are often overlooked because of the exciting, forceful expression which is seldom absent from his music.

The remaining composition of 1888, called *Easter Overture* and *Russian Easter* among other variants, is essentially a fantasy on Russian liturgical themes and is designed to contrast the gloom of the days preceding Easter with the joy and merriment of Easter Sunday itself. A slow and somber introduction, in which a chantlike theme is presented in company with florid cadenzas for a solo violin, leads directly into an allegro that is brilliant, dark, and majestic in turn. Several themes, all suggestive of liturgical moments, are treated in Rimsky-Korsakov's usual manner: fragmentary repetition with changed orchestration. A large percussion section in which bells are featured adds to the festive mood of the final portion, and the composer's purpose of depicting the rejoicing on Easter is well achieved. The *Russian Easter* is a satisfying composition.

The type of symphonic suite introduced by Rimsky-Korsakov is found in the works of many Russian composers of a later generation. One of these is by Michael Ippolitov-Ivanov (1859–1935), a pupil of the former and for some years a conductor in Tiflis, the chief city of Transcaucasia. His familiarity with the music and topography of the region came to expression in the *Caucasian Sketches*, a suite of four descriptive movements. An array of Georgian (hence, partly oriental) melodies gives pictures of the mountains, villages, and mosques of the area, and a pleasant but scarcely significant work results.

The movement toward musical nationalism in the Scandinavian countries was neither as vigorous nor as productive of lasting results as in Russia and Bohemia. Further, leading Scandinavian composers were usually sent to Germany for their education; there they came under the influence of the German Romantic tradition and remained largely in its thrall. Niels Gade (1817–1890), the foremost Danish composer of his time, was typical in this respect. He became essentially a transplanted Mendelssohn "speaking" with a mild Danish accent. Sweet sentiment, a graceful style, and a narrow emotional range characterize many of his works—eight symphonies and several overtures among them. But an essential lack of virility and an avoidance of dramatic conflicts in those works have doomed them to virtual oblivion.

Edvard Grieg (1843–1907) was alone successful among Norwegian composers in impressing his individual yet nationalistic style upon the international concert stage. Two orchestral suites, arranged from music composed for Ibsen's play, *Peer Gynt*, about 1874–1875, have become universally popular. They reveal Grieg's full mastery of smaller forms and disclose the lyricism which was his outstanding characteristic; the eight pieces which constitute the suites are filled with charming melodies set to colorful and piquant harmonies. Grieg was primarily a composer of mood pieces in which a faint air of melancholy predominates; such moods come to full expression in the *Peer Gynt* music as well as in the suite, *Aus Holbergs Zeit* (a set of miniatures composed for string orchestra), and in the incidental music to *Sigurd Jorsalfar*.

Grieg, like many other composers of his time, received his training at Leipzig; Schumann's poetic, short-breathed style remained of great influence upon him. The fresh, open-air, and rhapsodic aspects of that style left their mark principally upon the A-minor piano concerto, composed in 1868—the work which best represents Grieg in the repertoire of today and which is one of his very few compositions in large form.

The concerto is representative of nationalism in that it breathes the spirit of Norwegian folk music. Folk songs as such are not quoted; but the subtle, often modal harmonies, the melodic lines which have a contour all their own, plus the dark and melancholy moods which prevail—these are national in their color and effect. The restraint and economy typical of Grieg elsewhere are less evident in the concerto. Forceful, brilliant, and even exuberant passages abound, and the virtuosic solo part is in the best Romantic tradition. In common with nationalists of other lands, Grieg showed little interest in thematic development and structural logic. Sequence repetitions of the kind found in Czech and Russian music are found to an even greater degree here—the material so repeated being Norwegian rather than Slavic, of course.

The first and last movements of the concerto are vigorous and are compounded of many short melodic fragments; the middle movement is songful, and is based largely upon a single melody. But regardless of tempo and type of treatment, warm lyric qualities are seldom absent. It was Grieg's great accomplishment to develop a unique, truly personal style; its basis is a type of melody that hovers about the fifth of the scale rather than the keynote, and a piquant harmonic system. These, together with his penchant for sequences and his fragmentary, episodic forms, give Grieg's music an individuality possessed by few other composers. It is that individuality of style plus the eloquent and attractive melodic material which raise the concerto to its high place as one of the best-liked concertos in the repertoire.

The Spanish folk-music heritage, perhaps the most colorful in western Europe, was even later in coming to the notice of significant orchestral composers than any of the foregoing. And it is ironic that three French composers were among the first to include Spanish idioms in their larger works. Bizet, in his opera, *Carmen* (1875), had recaptured the characteristic melodic patterns, the inexorable rhythms, and the intense expression of Spain. At about the same time, Edouard Lalo (1823–1892) introduced a synthetic Spanish quality in his *Symphonie espagnole,* a five-movement concerto for violin and orchestra. The vivid orchestral colors as well as the exotic themes and rhythms of this work provide it with a picturesque quality that justifies the title in part. In the finale of his D-minor cello concerto of 1876, Lalo quoted a Spanish folk song; and many passages in the two other movements are filled with a type of rhapsodic expression that suggests the same national temperament. And finally, Emmanuel Chabrier (1841–1894) composed *España*, a rhapsody for orchestra, in 1883; this work is overtly Spanish in all its rhythmic and melodic aspects.

To such composers, who appropriated a national idiom purely for its qualities as entertainment, one may scarcely attribute a desire to solidify or preserve Spanish folk culture. And the Spanish-flavored works of such composers are, with the exception of *Carmen*, purely occasional pieces. To this group we may add Rimsky-Korsakov's *Capriccio espagnol*, discussed above. Not until about 1885–1890, in the time of Isaac Albéniz (1860–1909), was the basis for a Spanish national school established. Albéniz was active primarily in the field of piano music, however; significant orchestral compositions are not to be looked for before the end of the nineteenth century.

Nationally minded composers continued to appear in the years after 1900, both in the countries already spoken of in this chapter and in other regions even more remote from the larger cultural centers. Indeed, one of the striking facts about the early twentieth century is that national musical interests continued to be served no less strongly than they had been in the period after about 1860. The works of many such composers were purely of local interest; as such they cannot be discussed here. Other nationalistic compositions have won and held places in the standard repertoire. They give evidence that national and universal appeal are still as compatible as they were in the music of Dvořák, for example, and that national idioms and dialects had not, in the nineteenth century, reached the limits of their respective expressive possibilities. Such works will be discussed in a later chapter.

XI

POST-ROMANTIC COMPOSERS

The chapters concerned with the progress of symphonic music since Liszt have given a faint picture of the confusion, lack of uniformity, and contradictions which beset the last half of the nineteenth century. Liszt had created a new form and a new texture, and Wagner had synthesized a new expressive concept—all of which Brahms had ignored; Bruckner had attempted to enlarge the old forms in the light of a naïve religiosity; and the nationalist composers had sought a new idiom and impressed it upon the forms they had inherited. Toward the 1890s a reaction against these various aspects of Romanticism took place and the confusion was heightened. The end result in the field of instrumental music was a further modification of the content and style of the symphony. The methods and principles of composers from Haydn to Mendelssohn were abandoned; a massive, composite form which still bore the name of "symphony" but which had little in common with its predecessors, slowly took shape.

The essential principle of the old symphony had been the manipulation of contrasting themes; of thematic material which differentiated between dramatic and lyric elements, between the incisive and the melodious. Now, in symphonic works of about the 1890s, that principle was forgotten. An amorphous texture emerged, compounded of motives or melodic fragments which generated new fragments in an endless stream without reference to contrasts of contour or quality; the texture was not unlike that produced by Wagner's "endless melody." Principal and subordinate theme, theme group, transition—such concepts were virtually lost sight of in the new texture; and clearly defined "form," as the Classical composers had understood it, became meaningless. The only possibility of revealing a structural plan lay in unifying the mood of one section and contrasting it with another. Further, the formal divisions that had been marked by basic changes of harmony (in the sense that a first-theme group lay in the tonic, a second in the dominant) became swallowed up in a free harmonic style. This style, based upon enharmonic and chromatic modulation and tending toward weakening the tonal integrity of a movement, had begun with Liszt and was to end with Debussy.

Thus it became impossible or pointless to continue with Classically derived concepts of the symphony; only Brahms had been successful in that effort. In the face of this impasse and in the absence of sustained musical inspiration, a number of composers sought salvation in technical virtuosity and in expanded orchestral means. Such composers illustrated the erroneous belief that the larger the means, the more important the ideas expressed. A great flexibility in orchestration marks the work of these men, along with detailed verbal and dynamic guides for the player, and, in some cases, a sincere idealism in utilizing the enhanced resources. Gustav Mahler (1860–1911) is the foremost composer of this group.

After a wretched boyhood and great hardship Mahler became the director of the Viennese Imperial Opera and spent parts of four seasons (1907–1911) as conductor at the Metropolitan Opera and of the New York Philharmonic Society. In those positions he demonstrated his skill and insight as one of the great conductors of his generation. But his heritage as a Bohemian Jew, plus his dictatorial, egocentric behavior, gained him a host of enemies. Misunderstood and maligned, he became one of the loneliest and most unhappy of men. His nine (or ten) symphonies and his orchestral song-cycles reflect the spiritual isolation in which he found himself, as well as the personal idealism and grandiose conceptions to which his career was dedicated. Intellectual vigor and emotional vitality loom equally large in his works. To his orchestra, which exceeded the dimensions even of Wagner's instrumental group, he often added vocal solos and choruses. Yet in spite of his monumental resources and grandiose effects, he was essentially a lyricist struggling with forms that were alien to his nature. To this day he remains a controversial figure; his music is idolized or ridiculed in turn, and one can scarcely take a neutral position toward it.

Insofar as Mahler's utterances about his symphonies are to be believed, he attempted nothing less than to express the universe, to write music of such dimensions "that the whole world is actually reflected therein." The experience of nature, of the essential being of man, of the power of resurrection—such concepts animate his works. His tremendous enthusiasm, energy, and imagination were directed to this idealistic task without thought of self or of public acclaim. In his attempts to embrace all facets of cosmic experience, Mahler juxtaposed the most diverse kinds of music. Coarse military-band effects, bird calls, solemn chorales, restrained or sentimental melodies, bitter and ironic passages, overwhelmingly majestic climaxes, and folk songs—such are some of the elements out of which he constructed his works. His adherents believe that he was justified in depicting the vulgar side by side with the sublime, the sentimental with the ironic, the folk song with the most sophisticated strains— for, they claim, universal experience includes such disparities. And his detractors point to banal or crude passages scornfully and ignore the nobility of other sections.

Mahler's first four symphonies are respectively in D major, 1888; C minor, 1894; D minor, 1896; and G major, 1900. They are in a sense bound together, for a lyric, folk-song quality is basic to them. Indeed, the first symphony contains themes from his song cycle (of 1884), *Lieder eines fahrenden Gesellen* ("Songs of a Wayfarer"); the others contain texts (soprano and alto solos and chorus in the second, alto and two choruses in the third, soprano solo in the fourth) drawn from *Des Knaben Wunderhorn* ("The Youth's Magic Horn"), a collection of folk poems made about 1805. The lyric themes go far toward determining the structure of the free, sectional forms that are typical of Mahler in these works, even in the movements which contain no direct folk-song references.

In other respects, however, each of the four symphonies is unique. For where the first freely employs the sentiments of the love-sick "Wayfarer," the second suggests questions about the meaning of life and suffering, and ends with an account of the glories of resurrection. The third, an enormous work with a forty-five-minute first movement, is a song of nature. Its six movements represent, according to Mahler's original indications, the symbolic emergence of summer over the opposition of an inert nature, and the meaning of flowers, animals, angelic purity, and love to mankind in general. The much smaller and more intimate fourth symphony, finally, gives an account of joy arrived at through struggle and proceeds, in its last movement, to a naïve song about the pleasures of life in heaven.

This is not to say that the symphonies are programmatic in intent. Mahler found it distasteful to provide a composition with a program, just as he deemed it ridiculous to set a literary experience to music. But he could—and did in his letters—give an indication of the "origin of a musical conception . . . which is certainly concrete enough for verbal description." [1] Bruckner had found it expedient to write programs for some of his works in order to "explain" them to a puzzled audience. Mahler, however, did no more than provide his eventual listeners with a verbal framework upon which they could construct the moods that the works express. In a sense, his explanations run parallel to his symphonies and are not superimposed upon them.

The fifth (C-sharp minor, 1902), sixth (A minor, 1904), and seventh (E minor, 1905) symphonies constitute another phase in Mahler's career. They are purely instrumental works with themes no longer of folk-song quality, and while they are not in the least programmatic, they may be said to symbolize certain personal conflicts in the composer's life. The fifth symphony, with its chorale-

---

[1] Alma Mahler, *Gustav Mahler; Erinnerungen und Briefe,* pp. 187–88. See also Newlin, *Bruckner, Mahler, Schönberg,* pp. 140–43.

like finale, depicts a gradual transition from morbid despair to vigorous *joie de vivre* and religious faith (but it is the Catholic faith, which
Mahler assumed as one of the requirements of his post at the Vienna
Opera and to which he became sincerely devoted). The sixth is
tragic in every respect; it suggests the victory of harsh destiny over
the human will. The seventh, on the other hand, is hopeful and romantic, and culminates in an energetic finale somewhat in the manner of the fifth symphony. It is significant that in these works, which
are unaccompanied by verbal elucidations or sung texts, Mahler
returned to some extent to Classical principles. Among the least
extravagant of his works (in the sense that restrained mood and
thematic economy are typical), they are also among the most approachable.

The eighth symphony (E flat, 1907), the so-called "Symphony
of a Thousand," stands alone. Here Mahler called upon a tremendous
array of forces, including a greatly enlarged orchestra with an
auxiliary brass choir, two double choruses, a boys' choir, and seven
vocal soloists. The Latin hymn, "Veni creator spiritus," and the
closing scene from Part II of Goethe's *Faust* provide the texts for
this massive work. Similar in mood to the second symphony, in that
it is dedicated to an allied spiritual problem (the resurrection of man
in the second, Faust's ascension to heaven in the eighth), the E-flat
symphony yet brings a new concept of enormity to music. Closely
related to a cantata in style in spite of its adherence to symphonic
structural principles, the eighth represents a synthesis between
choral and instrumental music. As such, and as perhaps the most
ambitious and monumental work of the post-Romantic decades, it
marks the end of a development which began at least as early as Beethoven's Choral Fantasy, Opus 80.

Das Lied von der Erde ("The Song of the Earth"), composed in
1908, is at once a song cycle and a symphony. But Mahler, although
he called it a symphony, did not number it as the ninth out of super-
stitious fear of death (neither Beethoven nor Bruckner had written
more than nine symphonies). The text is taken from a German version of a set of melancholy Chinese poems by Li Tai Po and requires,

in the six movements of the composition, tenor and alto soloists alternately. Here the synthesis between lyric and instrumental elements is brought to a culmination, for the vocal phrases are intertwined with orchestral themes and the whole is unified both by the cyclical form of the work and the hopeless, despairing mood of the several movements.

The ninth symphony, D major, of 1909, which depends only upon instruments to carry its message of resignation, comes as Mahler's farewell to a world which misunderstood the nobility of his aims and the sincerity he brought to bear upon them. To a greater extent than elsewhere, moods of bitterness and restraint are overcome; and the quiet movements are even reflective and reminiscent in quality. A tenth symphony remained incomplete at Mahler's death—thus, incidentally, justifying his superstition.

It is scarcely possible in this brief account to do more than mention the richness and variety of the orchestral sound with which Mahler clothed his musical ideas. Virtually every instrument is treated soloistically and is made to add its individuality to a transparent, glowing texture. The most ethereal as well as the most forceful effects abound, along with every intermediate shade of expression. The sum total of his work reveals a composer whose tremendous technical gifts and high ideals cannot be disputed, but whose purposes seem empty and whose structural methods puzzling to all save his most ardent disciples. Mahler's place in music history has not yet been determined to everyone's satisfaction. To determine that place will require repeated performances of his music and a stifling of the prejudices which rise against virtually every composer who contains within himself both the culmination and decline of a musical style.

Richard Strauss (1864–1949) had, like Mahler, great technical skill in composition and a predilection for massive orchestral effects; and his career as a conductor was equally successful. But unlike his contemporary, he found the symphonic poem most compatible with the expression of his musical gifts, and those gifts did not lie in the field of lyricism—this in spite of many successful operas and over a hundred songs. It is in the manipulation of themes rather than in the invention of melodies that Strauss reigned supreme during his lifetime.

Of the many compositions of Strauss' youth, those written in the period about 1880–1886—including an F-minor symphony and three concertos for violin, horn, and piano, respectively—betray a warm Romanticism in the best traditions of Schumann and early Brahms. With a "symphonic fantasia" called *Aus Italien*, written in 1887 after a visit to that country, Strauss began to cast off conservative influences and take the technical paths indicated by Liszt and Wagner. The four movements of *Aus Italien* reveal his feelings about various aspects of Italian life; more importantly, they served as a bridge whereby he passed from the field of absolute music to that of program music. In subsequent works, however, he avoided the Berlioz-inspired multiple-movement form and wrote one-movement symphonic poems on the Liszt model. The first of these, *Macbeth* (about 1887), was delayed in publication until after *Don Juan* (1888) had appeared; the latter to this day remains one of the most popular—and also the most inspired—of his compositions.

In many cases Strauss' symphonic poems were first performed—and even published—under only descriptive titles. But the public's desire to have the puzzling works made comprehensible resulted in his being deluged with requests for verbal props. He complied reluctantly, but only after asserting repeatedly that his works were to be listened to as music, not as descriptions of external events. Later editions, then, bore bits of poetry, explanatory headings, and the like—to such an extent that the source of his inspiration is fairly well determined in each case. Except in a few passages where physical happenings are depicted with a high degree of realism, the several symphonic poems must be judged by musical standards alone. Since *Don Juan* illustrates Strauss' subsequent method, it may be treated here in some detail.

Strauss, like Wagner, possessed great skill in inventing melodic or rhythmic bits which have the power to suggest emotions or character traits. Broken-scale passages, pungent rhythmic figures, melodic fragments of striking contour—such thematic material is developed at length and allows the composer to draw a succession of musical scenes or character sketches. One may read into them the psychological changes his characters undergo, as well as the impact of the environment upon his musical personages. Thus it was not difficult for various commentators to seize upon elements found in the background literary work and attach labels to the various motives and scenes. In the case of *Don Juan*, Nikolaus Lenau's poem was Strauss' inspiration. Lenau's hero, unlike the Don Giovanni of Mozart's opera, is an idealist who seeks the perfect woman. Wilhelm Mauke, the author of the "official" commentary on *Don Juan*, borrowed two female characters from Mozart's libretto, discovered motives of satiation, drunken stupor, remorse, new resolve, and the like; and he emerged with a hero who has little in common with Lenau's character.

When one ignores such labels and listens to the music as Strauss would prefer, one finds that the composer is concerned essentially with sonata-form, theme transformation, and development. Transitional material is derived from the themes, motives are often combined contrapuntally, and a closely knit texture emerges. But Strauss' fluency in the invention of small details results in a complex, heavily laden score; only his great skill as an orchestrator keeps the details from overwhelming the essentials. The pure sound of Strauss' orchestra is unique: brilliant, colorful, or glowing when the music demands such qualities, and dull or appropriately muffled in other passages. Strauss was at first content with the standard orchestra of his time: three of each woodwind, the usual string, brass, and percussion sections, and a harp or two. Only later did he find four of each woodwind and heavily reinforced horn and trumpet sections necessary.

Death and Transfiguration, composed in 1889, is technically similar to *Don Juan*. Here again the program came after the event, for Alexander Ritter's poem of a sick man struggling with death was written after the earliest performances of the music. Here, too, the addition of a program was quite unnecessary, for *Death and Trans-figuration* scarcely requires such a program, in that it is essentially in sonata-form with slow introduction and epilogue and contains fewer of the extraneous elements which become so disturbing in Strauss' later works.

The next orchestral composition, from 1895, is in the realm of medieval legend; its full title is *Till Eulenspiegel's Merry Pranks, in the old roguish manner—in rondo form—set for large orchestra by Richard Strauss*. Till, in German folklore, was a practical joker and wag who lived by his wits and engaged in adventures of all kinds. It was Strauss' wish to go no further in elucidating a program than may be surmised from the title; again he was persuaded other-wise, and a full set of labeled motives exists to define Till's various pranks. These may be ignored in the interest of the pure humor and fantasy which the work reveals. *Till Eulenspiegel* is a virtuosic piece which makes great demands upon orchestral players. But it is no longer "unplayable"; virtually all of Strauss' "impossible demands" upon players have been met, and today's performer takes Strauss' music in stride without the head-shaking and defeatism which soured the lives of his predecessors in the 1890s.

With the next three symphonic poems Strauss' structural frame-work was almost doubled in size, his melodic invention took a step backward, and his musical textures became more complex. The first of these, *Thus Spake Zarathustra* (1896), inspired by Nietzsche's book, outlines Strauss' avowed purpose to "convey musically an idea of the development of the human race . . . up to Nietzsche's idea of the Superman." [2] Even the titles of the eight sections of the com-position are drawn from the book—for example, "Of the Great Yearning," "Of Joys and Passions," and "Song of the Grave." In an endeavor to follow this program, Strauss departed from his previous manner. The music, first of all, goes where it is led and not where its inner nature demands; subsidiary and unessential detail tend to crowd out the principal musical ideas; the ideas themselves become angular, stark, and tuneless; and the variety of scenes is so great that

[2] Quoted by Finck, *Richard Strauss*, p. 181.

unity and coherence become impossible. As a technical achievement it is superb; as a work of inspiration or insight it leaves much to be desired. Except for an eloquent passage ("Of the Dwellers in the Back World") near its beginning, *Thus Spake Zarathustra* is strangely unappealing and pompous.

Don Quixote, subtitled "Fantastic Variations on a Theme of Knightly Character" and written in 1897, is based on episodes in the life of Cervantes's comic and pathetic hero. The work is Strauss' contribution to the new concerto literature, for Don Quixote is personified by a cello solo, and virtuosic demands are made upon the performer. Here the blatancy and vulgarity which often mar Strauss' scores are kept to a minimum. Passages of mock pathos, effective in their delicacy of texture and sentimental charm, reveal Strauss' sympathetic attitude toward the misguided Don Quixote. Highly descriptive moments—notably those which illustrate the hero's encounter with the herd of sheep and his attack on the windmill—testify to the composer's skill in setting ordinary sounds and noises to music in a realistic manner.

The quasi-autobiographical *Ein Heldenleben* ("A Hero's Life") of 1898 is perhaps the most pretentious of Strauss' orchestral works and the most questionable as to subject matter. Of the idealism that marked Mahler there is no trace. It is a long work in six sections, each of which shows one aspect of the hero's life—his adversaries, his helpmate, his battles, and his death among them. All of Strauss' great skill in pungent thematic invention is revealed here, and, in addition, an even greater mastery of musical characterization and appropriate orchestration. Yet the complexity, strident climaxes, and rich sound of this work cannot conceal a rather decadent, materialistic quality. Technique and resourcefulness have here triumphed over artistry and inspiration.

The *Sinfonia domestica* of 1903 and the *Alpine Symphony* of 1915—both descriptive symphonic poems in spite of their titles—carry the process still further. The orchestra grew ever larger (twenty horns, six trumpets, and six trombones are required in the second of these works), the texture ever more complex, and the colors ever more brilliant. And Strauss' expressive aims sank as the resources were expanded. It is significant that he reached the greatest development of his technical skill at the time when his musical values reached their lowest ebb. Strauss exemplifies the spiritual poverty of the period after about 1890. As a composer of great orchestral music he was virtually finished after *Till Eulenspiegel.* Becoming progressively less melodic in his choice of themes, relying to an increasing extent upon intellectual activity, he reached the point where he possessed only technical skill. Effective as his works are from the standpoint of orchestral excitement and riotous color, they cannot be of lasting interest to the sensitive listener who seeks spiritual refreshment from a musical composition.

Max Reger (1873–1916) may be grouped with Mahler and Strauss largely because he, too, possessed a fabulous compositional technique and a keen sense for orchestral color. In other respects he was quite unlike his contemporaries, however. He felt himself drawn to the past even more strongly than did Brahms; he virtually ignored program music, strove for objective expression, and developed an orchestral style which is almost organ-like in color and texture. Reger was active principally as a pianist, conductor, and teacher; in spite of his early death he composed a great number of works in all fields but opera. More than a dozen orchestral compositions fall relatively late in his career, all having been written after 1900.

Early works, notably those for organ and for piano, reveal a strong Romantic influence combined with that of Bach. Among his first important orchestral compositions, the *Variations and Fugue on a Merry Theme by J. A. Hiller,* Opus 100, discloses an amalgamation of those influences and the full emergence of Reger's unique harmonic style. Somewhat in the manner of Brahms, elements of the theme are abstracted and developed separately in successive variations, and the whole is crowned by a massive fugue. It is in the two forms represented here, namely, the variation set and the fugue, that Reger's attachment to the past is most clearly indicated; one may surmise that the combination was a sympathetic one for him, for he wrote a similar and better-known work on a theme by Mozart (and on themes by Bach, Telemann, and Beethoven for piano).

In one group of his early organ works Reger attempted to restore the spirit of Baroque polyphony, in which melodies created their own harmony—as opposed to the Romantic polyphony which had become essentially a horizontal diffusion of vertical (harmonic) elements and which thus resulted in an apparent rather than a real polyphony. This desire accounts for the usual description of Reger as a "nineteenth-century Bach." But a thick, polyphonic style is by no means characteristic of the later Reger, as many commentators [3] would have one believe. On the contrary, Reger was typical of his period in his fondness for pure sound and his willingness to place expressive content above clarity of form. In this sense he was as truly a Romantic composer as were Schumann and Chopin. And for Reger, expressive content was determined largely by the harmony.

Harmonically, he owed little to a past any more remote than Liszt's. His systematically developed, eternally shifting harmonies (to clarify which he published a *Beiträge zur Modulationslehre* in 1903) are required to explain and justify the tight, chromatic melodies he often employed. Conversely, those melodies are outgrowths of the sliding, chromatically connected, and freely modulating chords which constitute the chief expressive elements of Reger's style. In few composers are melody and harmony as mutually dependent as in Reger. In order to reveal the progressions of his harmonically conceived melodic line he employed a somewhat contrapuntal texture which is quite unlike the "Bach style" of one group of his organ works. The tonality of the orchestral compositions is often relatively obscure, particularly in fast movements where harmonic changes occur with great rapidity.

The many instruments specified in his orchestral scores are usually employed in carefully calculated and meticulously shaded blocks or closed groups of sonority; one may trace here the influence of the Classical composer upon the Romantic. Occasionally, however, as in the *Romantic Suite*, Opus 125, Reger creates a rich, somewhat

[3] Including the present one. See Ulrich, *Chamber Music*, p. 361.

ethereal sound that represents modern orchestral writing at its finest. And in the *Serenade for Orchestra*, Opus 95, as well as in the first of *Four Tone Poems*, Opus 128, inspired by paintings of Arnold Böcklin, one encounters a unique division of the string section into two "orchestras," one muted and the other not. Such instrumental effects, produced in a context that is extravagant in its chromaticism and free modulation, and singularly devoid of true contrasts in material and mood, stamp Reger as a gifted, imaginative composer. Yet his emotional range was neither great nor compelling.

Reger has attained little representation upon the concert stage outside his native Germany. One may attribute this in part to his somewhat precious, overladen style and to the uneventfulness—even tediousness—of his harmonic mannerisms. But his chronological position was also unfortunate. At about the time his later works came to wider notice, namely about 1911 to 1914, the first World War brought international diffusion of his music to a virtual standstill. And from about 1920 new styles superseded the old and an appreciation of Reger became even more difficult. Opinion about his worth is by no means unanimous to this day, and the final word about the place of Reger's music and the value of his technical contributions has probably not yet been said.

The gradual musical awakening of countries on the periphery of the great European nations was, as we have seen, one result of Romantic developments. The Scandinavian countries had awakened less vigorously than, for instance, the Slavic, and were represented in the late nineteenth century largely by Grieg. Now, Grieg was primarily a lyricist, at his best in small forms. Northern Europe produced no large-scale compositions until Jean (or Jan) Sibelius (b. 1865) arrived upon the international stage. Sibelius is the first Finnish composer to achieve wide renown; and, in spite of long lists of compositions in many fields, he is primarily a symphonist. It is to be expected that national feeling should have entered into his early orchestral compositions.

Among such works is a series of short pieces based upon episodes in the *Kalevala*, the Finnish national epic poem. Sibelius had begun to write an opera on that subject about 1893, but he abandoned the project after he had composed a rhapsodic prelude, now known as *The Swan of Tuonela*. This was followed two years later by *Lemminkäinen's Homecoming*. The well-known tone poem *Finlandia* (1899) may be mentioned here as belonging to the group of works which reveal Sibelius' intermittent interest in national concerns. But Finnish idioms play a minor part in his career; such works as the suite, *Karelia*, the symphonic fantasia called *Pohjola's Daughter*, and a few others are not among his most important. It would be stretching a point to consider Sibelius merely as a late arrival among the nationalist group of composers.

The seven symphonies that were composed between 1899 and 1924 constitute, on the other hand, a unique set of works. Each one is essentially different from the others; size, number of movements, and mood content vary greatly from one to another. Yet the seven are bound together not only by common style characteristics—which is to be expected in so individualistic a composer as Sibelius—but also by a single organizing principle or structural method. That method emerged gradually and came to fullest expression only at the end of the twenty-five year period; and having achieved it, Sibelius apparently found himself creatively exhausted. Virtually no significant composition has appeared since *Tapiola* (1925), a symphonic poem that is constructed on the same principle as the later symphonies.

The first symphony (E minor, 1899) may be taken as Sibelius' starting point. It contains the usual four movements, is related to Tchaikovsky in contrasts of somber mood and brilliant expression, and is rather loosely constructed in large sections. Lyric melodies, exuberance, and emotional outbursts are found in greater abundance here and in the second symphony (D major, 1901) than in later works. But the second already reveals the direction of his interest in the new method of construction. It is as though Sibelius gathered the theme's component motives and fragments together in the first part of the first movement, assembled them in the development, and allowed them to disperse again in the recapitulation.[4] And the scherzo leads smoothly into the finale to form a connected whole.

The third symphony (C major, completed in 1907) shows a continuation of the process introduced in the second; now it is achieved more subtly, in that the scherzo and finale are actually combined into one movement. But the entire content of this symphony is more restrained; Sibelius has become somewhat economical in the employment of musical material and has derived transitional passages and subsidiary ideas from the principal themes throughout. The fourth symphony (A minor, 1911) marks a return to four-movement form; however, the first movement is an adagio in abridged sonata-form and the work contains not themes so much as theme fragments which undergo continual transformation. In content it is somewhat cool and remote; and its harmonies are often obscure and thick—to such an extent that one may speak of polytonality.

The happiest results of Sibelius' method of compressing and unifying the elements of symphonic style are arrived at in the fifth symphony (E-flat major, 1915–1919). A slow first movement begins normally in sonata-form; but out of its development section—and closely related to it—a scherzo emerges, complete with trio and recapitulation. The second movement is a set of variations on a rhythmic figure; the finale is a straightforward movement in sonata-form with a coda apparently in slow tempo (but this is caused only by a change in notation: three measures of the main movement are now compressed into one). Like the fourth, the fifth symphony is a meditative work characterized by freely shifting harmonies. Themes as such find little employment; rather do homogeneous blocks of sound, compounded of the whole complex of harmonic, rhythmic, and instrumental elements, serve in place of themes.

In the sixth symphony (which, completed in 1923, swings between D minor and the Dorian mode) Sibelius returned to a four-movement form; but style characteristics which had marked earlier works are here present to an enhanced degree. Blocks of sound again serve as themes; and such isolated melodies as do occur are integral

[4] See Abraham, ed., *The Music of Sibelius,* for detailed accounts.

elements of the context out of which they emerge. In mood and content, the sixth symphony avoids the gloom and sheer power that are so often present in Sibelius and substitutes a mild melancholy carried by a nervous, bustling texture; but it is no less tightly constructed.

With the seventh symphony (C major, 1924), finally, Sibelius achieved the—perhaps unconscious—goal of his symphonic writing: ultimate compression in form and unity of expressive content. The seventh consists of one movement only; the tempo is slow at times and fast at others, but each shift in speed is made gradually and smoothly. Thus one cannot speak of sections as one can in other single-movement works—Schumann's D-minor symphony and the majority of symphonic poems among them. But it is open to demonstration that the symphony begins in the mood of an adagio which, after a development, imperceptibly becomes a scherzo; the latter, in turn, is transformed into a clear-cut allegro out of which a second scherzo develops; and the whole ends with a recapitulation of the adagio mood and material. Thus it contains considerable contrast within its organic unity, even though all its thematic material has a common origin; and in the process, considerable emotional tension and great climaxes are achieved.

The symphonic style which Sibelius employed so consistently has its roots in the nineteenth century. Cyclical-form principles and thematic transformation are basic to it, for the composer's thematic material often wanders from movement to movement and is appropriately modified on successive appearances. The device of connecting one symphonic movement with another is also old: we have given examples in the works of composers from Beethoven to Saint-Saëns. And finally, the use of short motives as source material for longer musical ideas is often found in composers as early as Liszt. Thus the structural elements in these symphonies are not new; it is Sibelius' consistent use of them, and the subtlety with which they are employed, that set his style apart from other composers. Transitions between parts that are already closely related are carried out in a smooth, masterful fashion, and thematic material undergoes almost constant transformation. These characteristics enable him to achieve the effect of continual, restless growth in his larger works.

Yet with all this relationship to the immediate past, and with a harmony that is essentially conservative, Sibelius possesses an individual means of expression. The stern and severe mood of his larger works, and the almost complete lack of humor they reveal, are supposedly reflections of the harsh and forbidding northland; the influence of nature—of pine forests, granite rocks, and glacial lakes—upon Sibelius is well documented. Certain habits of orchestration are illustrated in almost every work; among them we may mention his use of families of instruments in closed blocks, of the low register of the woodwinds, of extended pizzicato passages, of abrupt alternation between strings and winds, and of fast, driving passages for the string group.

Sibelius' harmonies are often static; long sections based upon one chord are typical, and he reveals a great fondness for *ostinato* devices and pedal points. Melodic mannerisms abound also: the downward skips of a fifth in the melodic line, the use of many repeated notes, a phrase which begins slowly and "explodes" into rhythmic animation at its end (see Example 35). Outstanding also is the

EXAMPLE 35

SIBELIUS, Fifth Symphony, 1st movement

Tempo molto moderato   meas. 58-60

presence of passages which are neither thematic nor transitional, but contain merely a slowly shifting harmony which is rhythmically vitalized by a fluttering or tremolo of the string section; the finale of the fifth symphony and the allegretto of the sixth illustrate this device.

Perhaps the most important and individual of Sibelius' style traits, however, is his method of causing series of apparently unrelated themes to grow and develop out of melodic or rhythmic motives. Often a group of a few tones or even a single interval provides the germ out of which a large work is constructed; and unlike Beethoven, from whom the device is obtained, Sibelius does not always place the germinal motive in a prominent position. Considerable similarity in texture results from the habitual use of this principle, of course; yet the latter provides his works with a consistency and expressive unity that even his impulsiveness, his seemingly arbitrary juxtaposition of contrasting material, and his fragmentary melodic lines cannot destroy.

Orchestral composers in England during the late nineteenth century had been strongly influenced by German Romanticism. The spirits of Mendelssohn and Schumann remained very much alive even as late as the time of Charles H. Parry (1848–1918) and Charles V. Stanford (1852–1924). In the compositions of Edward Elgar (1857–1934), however, a new and individual tone made itself felt— one that is said to be peculiarly English in its mixture of restraint and sentiment, in its conservatism in texture and harmony. Elgar's symphonies (A flat, 1908, and E flat, 1911) as well as his overtures (*Cockaigne*, 1902, and *In the South*, 1904) are rarely performed in the United States. But his *Variations on an Original Theme* (the so-called "Enigma Variations," written in 1899) come to frequent performance and are worthily representative of his style.

The "Enigma Variations," fourteen in number, contain a variety of beautifully melodious passages, refined orchestral colors, and a great amount of rhythmic energy. Separate variations are inscribed with initials or nicknames of Elgar's friends and are based upon a theme which is only partially revealed by the composer—hence the enigma. Their content ranges from the delicate and fairylike "Dorabella" (No. X) to the forceful and strident finale, and includes many intermediate shades of noble expression. The whole is a work which testifies to Elgar's skill as an orchestrator and to the conservative, even aristocratic nature of his musical idiom.

Among many post-Romantic Russian composers, Alexander Glazunov (1865–1936), Reinhold Glière (b. 1875), and Sergei Rachmaninoff (1873–1943) may be singled out. Glazunov, whose fame is diminishing with each passing decade, composed eight symphonies, several concertos, and a great variety of orchestral music in the smaller forms. He remained close to the ideals and methods of the Russian nationalist composers in his descriptive works, and equally close to the German concepts of symphonic style in others. His violin concerto of 1904 is still heard with pleasure, as are the *Overture solenelle* of 1901 and one or two of the early symphonies.

The work by which Glière is probably best known to present-day audiences is his monumental, richly scored, and sensationally effective third symphony (B minor, 1909–1911). Entitled *Ilya Murometz*, it recounts episodes in the life of the legendary Russian hero of that name. A variety of dramatic and descriptive passages are unashamedly Romantic; others are frankly Impressionistic; and the work contains some of the most grandiose climaxes in recent music.

Rachmaninoff, one of the greatest pianists of his age, is remembered chiefly for his second symphony (E minor, 1907) and his second piano concerto (C minor, 1901). Both works reveal a composer richly endowed with melancholy sentiment, given to extreme emotional expression, and possessing great technical skill. The entire symphony is built around a motive consisting of three notes; virtually all its themes, across four long and concentrated movements, are subtly related to that figure. The expressive unity achieved thereby is considerable, but a certain degree of monotony results from the overuse of a single germinal motive.

XII

NEW APPROACHES

ONE MAY GATHER FROM the accounts in the preceding four chapters that the field of symphonic music had lost a single, unified direction in the period after about 1860. Mutually opposed aesthetic principles flourished side by side; innovators and reactionaries had their respective partisans. Although the universal stream of music continued its course, it had been severely undermined by the nationalistic. Miniatures and monstrosities alike came to public hearing, and extreme sophistication went hand in hand with extreme naïveté. Throughout musical Europe, individualists had broken away from common cultural patterns, and excesses of all sorts became commonplace. The personal, intimate sentiment of Chopin, say, had through successive steps become the turgid, often vulgar, and sometimes hysterical subjectivity of Tchaikovsky. The eloquence of Schubert had been replaced by the garrulousness of Strauss and Mahler, and the trenchant epigrams of Schumann by the blunt and uncompromising pronouncements of Sibelius.

In spite of the period's great lack of a unifying thread, however, one may fairly make the following generalization. The intense, subjective expression that animated virtually all composers of the period had its roots in the Romantic heritage they shared in common, no matter what form that expression took; and yet the technical means whereby it was achieved departed ever further from the system of tonality that lies at the base of the Romantic period. One has but to recall the chromaticism of Liszt and the chromatic harmony employed by Wagner to realize that the tonal relationships which had served earlier composers had been loosened considerably. The expansion of harmonic resources after about 1860 led to the increased use of altered chords, to rapid and continual modulation, and to vagueness of tonal feeling. The end result, by the 1890s, was a demonstrable decline in the importance of tonal centers, in tonal integrity itself. With its content inflated out of all proportion and its technical basis all but destroyed, the Romantic movement in music ceased to be. Even though certain of its exponents composed well into the twentieth century, Romanticism as a positive cultural force was finished well before the end of the nineteenth.

A number of composers moved into the resultant cultural void; the period beginning about 1890 was marked by many attempts to create a new kind of music. But the breakdown of a common musical culture which had begun to disintegrate even in the time of the nationalists made it difficult to find a common goal or procedure. Composers reacted as individuals, and many different approaches having little relationship to each other were made in the following decades. Not one "modern" style, but several styles appeared, and a chaotic, experimental state persisted through the years of the first World War. About 1920 a degree of agreement was achieved, and even then it was founded upon community of purpose rather than of technique. Thus there is no single line of connection between the period about 1890 and the present. In this chapter an attempt will be made to describe the styles of the principal innovators of the time. The concluding chapter, then, will be concerned with composers whose work has been influenced by those styles, and with those who have in the years since about 1920 emerged with stylistic elements of their own.

The first important reaction against the excesses of the period was set in motion by Claude Debussy (1862–1918). Even as a student Debussy took strong exception to the rules and formulas of musical composition. His questioning, iconoclastic nature was at first not hampered by his admiration for Wagner; but later he became a leader of anti-Wagner forces in France and strove to remove the heavy hand of German tradition and to substitute new musical principles. His acquaintance with many poets and artists—Verlaine and Monet among them—led him to embrace the tenets of a group of painters called Impressionists and to develop the musical counterparts of their purposes and techniques.

The Impressionism of Debussy was not anti-Romantic in its basic premise, for it was still subjective in that it sought to express the emotion—or impression—evoked by thoughts, ideas, or external objects. And since Debussy relied heavily upon objects as sources of inspiration, his works remained closely allied to the descriptive, programmatic compositions of the Romanticists. The emotions expressed, however, were far removed from the bombast and pretentiousness of his German contemporaries, and the forms in which they came to expression had little in common with earlier forms. Indeed, Debussy seemed more concerned with a color, an isolated harmony, or an acoustic effect than with patterns and structures. Cool restraint, suggestion rather than statement, and preoccupation with individual sounds—such factors animate the greater part of his music.

In a technical sense, however, the music was new. Debussy introduced several stylistic innovations that were of great influence upon his successors and that affected the course of twentieth-century music for several decades. The sources of those innovations were varied. His independence of musical thought was strengthened by his encounters with Russian music (he was engaged as pianist by Nadejda von Meck, Tchaikovsky's patroness, from 1880 to about 1882), and later acquaintance with the music of Moussorgsky stimulated him afresh. Pentatonic and whole-tone scales and other exotic effects probably derive from his infatuation with a Javanese orchestra which he heard repeatedly at the Paris Exposition of 1889. The harmonic ambiguity, the shimmering tremolos, and the colorful glissandos that are important elements of his style are in a sense counterparts of the vagueness of the French Symbolist poets. To this array of elements Debussy added series of dissonant, unresolved seventh- and ninth-chords moving in parallel, chords with added tones, chords foreign to the tonality, and similar devices. The end result was a musical style that hinted at emotional experiences, that hovered mysteriously, that contained new color combinations, and that seldom came to grips with problems of form as earlier composers had understood the term. In place of traditional structures, Debussy employed a free, rhapsodic manner which is not easily subject to formal diagramming.

The first important orchestral work, written in 1892 and performed two years later, was the well-known *Prélude à l'après-midi d'un faune*, based on Mallarmé's symbolic poem. At about the same time Debussy began the composition of three *Nocturnes* for orchestra—*Nuages, Fêtes*, and *Sirènes*—the last of which required a chorus of women's voices vocalizing and humming without text. The set was completed in 1899. It is in these *Nocturnes* that the full range, sensitivity, and variety of Debussy's style can best be seen.

In *Nuages* ("Clouds"), the composer imagines cloud formations drifting slowly across a dark sky, changing form and texture as they progress; the quiet mood is nowhere disturbed. *Fêtes*, by contrast, is vigorous and joyful. Its "program" is given by Debussy himself: [1] "The restless, dancing rhythms of the atmosphere, interspersed with abrupt scintillations." There is also a procession, "a dazzling and wholly visionary pageant, passing through and blended with the revelry; but the background of the uninterrupted festival persists; luminous dust participating in the universal rhythm." And in *Sirènes*, "the sea and its innumerable rhythm; then amid the billows silvered by the moon, the mysterious song of the Sirens is heard; it laughs and passes." It is this type of imagery which Debussy caught and translated into music. The contrast between this and the programs of Strauss, for instance, is obvious.

La Mer, composed in 1903–1905, consists of three symphonic sketches entitled "From Dawn till Noon on the Sea," "Play of the Waves," and "Dialogue between the Wind and the Sea," and is Debussy's largest orchestral work. Here, various aspects of the sea are presented: eerie, bright, joyful, powerful, and tumultuous in turn. *La Mer* is more closely knit, more complex in texture, and at

[1] Quoted by Oscar Thompson, *Debussy, Man and Artist*, pp. 320, 321.

times more polyphonic than either of the earlier works. It contains theme fragments, of course, and a few extended melodies; it even makes some use of cyclical-form methods and devices. But themes undergo continual modification—in keeping with the ever-changing moods of the sea—and ordinary standards of formal construction do not apply. A fanciful, imaginative, and wonderfully suggestive picture of the sea is given; yet the appeal of this work as a piece of absolute music is also great. One cannot fail to be impressed by the refinement and beauty of the textures and by the many varieties of sound Debussy was able to draw from the orchestra.

Between 1906 and 1912 he composed a series of three unrelated *Images* for orchestra. *Ibéria*, the first of these (although published as the second), has retained its place in the repertoire; the two others, *Rondes de printemps* and *Gigues*, have all but disappeared from view. Possessing only a vicarious familiarity with Spain, Debussy succeeded, in *Ibéria*, in writing music that has an authentic Spanish flavor and that recaptures the moods and colors of the country. The three sections of *Ibéria* are connected, and they contain thematic material in common; the sections are entitled, respectively, "In the Streets and By-Ways," "The Fragrance of the Night," and "The Morning of a Festival Day." To perhaps a greater extent than elsewhere, Debussy here relies upon scraps of melody and rhythm to describe his colorful imaginings. A constant ebb and flow of movement, a piecing together of fragments, and a transparent, kaleidoscopic texture—these constitute the work. But the most important element—in *Ibéria* as in his other compositions—is the harmony.

One may find, occasionally, examples of tonic-dominant relationships and of traditional chordal progressions. But such old-fashioned elements are only incidental to Debussy's purposes. Chords—consonant and dissonant chords alike—are employed as units, as individualities; the resolution of a dissonant chord plays little part in his theories, nor does a harmonic progression in the old sense. Rules are thrown overboard, and harmonies are created with one criterion in mind: their effect upon and appeal to the human ear. With whole-tone and pentatonic scales, with a negation of the principles of chord progression and resolution, with little concern for part-writing, with an untrammeled harmonic imagination, with no attention to older principles of thematic development or symmetry —small wonder that Debussy's music represented an entirely new direction in the period after about 1890. And small wonder that it influenced scores of composers in France as well as in other countries. But in such composers, it was the technical aspect of Debussy's work that was most often imitated, not the refined subjectivity and Impressionism out of which the technique emerged. And in many such composers the unifying power of a basic tonality, the integrity of tonal centers, or the reliance upon connections of chords within a key was often lost sight of. The end result was an abandonment of the tonal system and the substitution of a new principle of atonality.

Alexander Scriabin (1872–1915), Russian-born pianist and prolific composer, was a unique transitional figure, one who was only slightly influenced by Debussy, yet one who reflects a similar departure from the harmonic devices of German Romanticism. Because of the mixture of old and new in his music, Scriabin is difficult to label or classify. In early works he adhered to the style and technique of Chopin; but an interest in expanding harmonic relationships led him to experiment with new methods of chordal construction. In innumerable piano works as well as in his orchestral compositions (his third symphony, "The Divine Poem," of 1903; and the *Poem of Ecstasy*, 1907–1908), he introduced various arbitrarily made scales and employed chords ever more freely. The experiments culminated in *Prometheus*, a symphonic poem with the subtitle, "Poem of Fire." This work, written in 1909–1910, is based upon one "mystic chord" built in fourths: C, F sharp, B flat, E, A, and D. In the employment of that chord Scriabin went far beyond the bounds of tonality; his later works bore no key signatures, and diatonic passages are rare in them.

Yet in spite of his harmonic boldness and experimental bent, Scriabin remained an adherent of Romantic formal principles. Regu-

lar phrase structures, well-defined sections, and thematic development somewhat along traditional lines are important elements of
his style. And his harmonic innovations, employed at first with restraint and subtlety, soon degenerated into mannerisms—to such an
extent that his freedom in harmonic expression was virtually lost.

The element of Theosophical mysticism played a great part in
Scriabin's later career; his orchestral works had esoteric, occult
significance in his mind. Thus "The Divine Poem" represented the
struggle of the human spirit to free itself from bondage to the
physical body; the *Poem of Ecstasy* revealed the joy of the spirit
in being creatively active. *Prometheus*, in which a color organ is
added to the orchestra, attempted to depict the spiritual connection
between color and sound. Performances of Scriabin's orchestral
compositions take place with lessening frequency at the present time.
To a generation accustomed to the clear-cut if dissonant content
of truly modern music, Scriabin's works seem strangely Romantic
in outlook, massiveness, and quality of subjective expression. His
harmonic style has found few imitators, and it has not made a lasting
impression upon composers who succeeded him.

Arnold Schoenberg (1874–1951) was an innovator of quite a
different calibre. Schoenberg, too, took his departure from Romanticism, but it is the Romanticism of Brahms and Strauss out of which
his early works emerged. In a string sextet, *Verklärte Nacht*
("Transfigured Night"), composed in 1899, he applied the form of
the symphonic poem to chamber music. This composition, as well
as the first string quartet (D minor, 1907) could only have been
the work of a fluent, impassioned Romanticist. Eloquent, intense,
and subjective expression is characteristic, along with a thick contrapuntal texture, rich chromaticism in melody and harmony, and
Wagnerian climaxes. The symphonic poem, *Pelléas and Mélisande*,
written about 1905, recalls the work of Strauss in form and content;
but it goes even beyond that composer in fervid melodic utterance,
in chromaticism, and in contrapuntal complexity. With this group

of works the last step in subjective emotional expression was taken. Yet in some respects even these early works point to the path Schoenberg was to take in the following years.

The first *Kammersymphonie*, written in 1906, marks a large step forward on that path. One revealing element is the compression in form and instrumental resources; for this is a one-movement work divided into five connected sections, scored for only fifteen instruments, and economical in its employment of thematic fragments. More important, however, is Schoenberg's departure from traditional methods of chord construction. A series of fourths becomes both the melodic and harmonic basis for the composition; and although it has a tonal basis (E major), it makes little use of a tonal scheme or a clearly defined tonal center. The *Kammersymphonie* marks an abandonment of the grandiose style of Mahler and Strauss, even though in the massive *Gurrelieder* of 1900–1913 Schoenberg had still required an enormous orchestra and had combined the elements of song cycle and cantata on a large scale.

Compression, thinness of texture, and economy of means became increasingly important to Schoenberg, and his style was modified from one work to the next. In the *Five Pieces for Orchestra*, composed in 1909, the chromaticism gained complete ascendancy over diatonic elements, and one can now speak of atonal music (although Schoenberg always preferred the term "pantonality" [2]). Simultaneously, extremely angular melodic lines became a feature of his style. Intervals of sevenths and ninths in the melody, shifts from one octave to another, and a virtually continual succession of wide skips are typical.

In the years after the first World War, Schoenberg strove to systematize his atonal, experimental accomplishments. A group of chamber-music works appeared at intervals from 1924 in which his discovery and development of the "method of composing in twelve tones" was clarified. This method, with its fixing of the "tone row," thereupon became the chief compositional principle of Schoenberg and his disciples. The twelve tones refer to the complete chromatic

[2] See Newlin, *Bruckner, Mahler, Schönberg*, pp. 259–61.

scale; and it is a cardinal element of the principle that all the tones are of equal importance: there can be no tonic or dominant in Schoenberg's system. The tones are arranged arbitrarily in a manner determined by the expressive requirements of a particular work; the resultant rearrangement of the chromatic scale is then the "tone row" for that composition. The row may be inverted, may be played backward, and the retrograde version may be inverted. Repetition of a single tone, for rhythmic or expressive reasons, is generally permitted. The row, or portions of it, may be employed both vertically and horizontally: the first group of tones may form one chord, the second group another, and so on.

The twelve-tone system describes only the technical aspects of this music, of course. Every variety of music has its own principles and formulas; and Schoenberg merely substituted his formulas for those which had served earlier composers. In his view, consonance and dissonance represent merely different degrees of harmonic tension and are not related to the terms "pleasant" and "unpleasant." In works to about 1930 the system was used uncompromisingly, almost mechanically, and the content of those works is singularly devoid of lyric, rhymthic, or emotional appeal. In later works one finds evidence of a tentative return to tonality, to subjective expression, and even to a degree of lyric attractiveness. The *Suite* for string orchestra, of 1934, is in G major; a tonal center may thus be looked for. Tonal harmonies emerge occasionally in the violin concerto of 1936 and often in the *Theme and Variations* for orchestra of 1943. These works, however, are still predominantly restrained in emotional utterance, tight and compact in structure, and clear and dissonant in their contrapuntal textures.

Igor Stravinsky (b. 1882) has for about four decades been among the most important of contemporary composers. His association with Sergei Diaghileff (1872–1929), the founder and director of the Ballet Russe in Paris about 1909, led to a series of ballets the music of which exerted a tremendous influence upon a later generation of composers. Stravinsky had been a private pupil of Rimsky-Korsakov; his early works, including a symphony in E flat (1905–

1907), were traditional in form and content. The first two ballets written for Diaghileff—*L'Oiseau de feu* (1910) and *Petrouchka* (1911)—substituted another set of influences. The first is full of Russian color and orchestral brilliance, and the second contains a few polytonal passages and striking examples of humor and irony.

A ballet written in 1913, however, entitled *Le Sacre du printemps*, abolished with one stroke many of the preexisting formulas of musical construction. Here, in a series of "pictures of pagan Russia," Stravinsky introduced a great variety of revolutionary materials. Reiterated rhythmic figures and also unmetrical, freely changing rhythms; sequences of ninth- and eleventh-chords; melodic passages set in parallel sevenths and ninths; ugly polytonal clusters; quiet and weird chordal sequences; and tumultuous climaxes—all these are interspersed in a loose, sectional form. This work, introduced to a public in Paris which was saturated with the superrefined and delicate traceries of Impressionistic music, came as a tremendous shock. The disturbances, even the riotous behavior, that accompanied the early performances of *Le Sacre du printemps* are matters of history.

The outstanding accomplishment of Stravinsky lay in bringing a new concept of rhythmic vitality to music. Either hypnotic in their primitive reiteration or chaotic in their freedom, the diabolical rhythms contributed to the frenzy caused by sheer, unrelieved dissonance. With these elements came a hard, mechanical, objective quality: Stravinsky generally avoided any expression of sentiment or lyric beauty. This was primitive, elemental music, in keeping with its ballet plot, and its composer was labeled a "neoprimitive." The critics of the time failed to see that his technical procedures were largely logical extensions of nineteenth-century methods, and that only his attitude of nonsentimentality was new. The orchestra of *Le Sacre* and the two earlier ballets was huge, and Stravinsky proved himself able to handle his instrumental resources. Instruments are used as individuals or are set in groups which exhibit the greatest possible contrast in color and sonority, and instrumental technical possibilities are exploited to the utmost.

In a series of smaller compositions written during the years of the first World War, Stravinsky turned away from the massive orchestra and an extremely dissonant content and composed with restraint both in means and style. *Pulcinella*, a ballet based on the music of Pergolesi and written in 1919, is one example of the new trend. Shortly thereafter he became enamored of the past, adopted older ideals of form and proportion, and began to employ dissonant counterpoint wholeheartedly. In the piano concerto of 1923–1924, these elements may be seen. But the work which best reveals the direction of Stravinsky's postwar interests is the *Symphonie de psaumes,* for chorus and orchestra, completed in 1929.

The symphony consists of three movements which are to be played without interruption. Portions of Psalms 38 and 39 and all of Psalm 150 provide the texts for the respective movements, and the words are sung in Latin. It is a serious work. Its intense moods are carried by stark and mildly dissonant harmonies in a texture that is thickly contrapuntal and rhythmically diverse in turn. The chorus is employed in austere fashion; its parts are intertwined with the instrumental voices, and a dark color results. The somber qualities of the work are enhanced in that neither violins nor violas are required in the orchestra; and the whole stands in great contrast to the wild and colorful ballets of the prewar period.

The *Concerto in E Flat* for orchestra (subtitled "Dumbarton Oaks" at its first performance, Washington, D.C., 1938) is still farther along Stravinsky's path into the past. Notable is the return of a definite tonality in the title of the work; but here as in his other "tonal" compositions, the central key is but a point of departure. The harmony is thickened by many seventh-chords; clashing dissonances abound, and abrupt modulations as well as simultaneous use of major and minor add to the freedom of the harmonic scheme. The consistent use of a few rhythmic motives and the rhythmic vitality of the whole relate the work—externally, at least—to the Baroque type of concerto. Yet the moods, including some occasioned by jazz idioms, are entirely those of the twentieth century.

The *Symphonie de psaumes* had been composed for the fiftieth anniversary of the Boston Symphony Orchestra, in 1930. Ten years later Stravinsky wrote a *Symphony in C* for the fiftieth anniversary of the Chicago Symphony Orchestra; and, in 1945, a *Symphony in Three Movements* for the New York Philharmonic-Symphony Society. The two latter works are, like the "Dumbarton Oaks" concerto, clear in texture, rhythmically alive, and somewhat tonal. The *Symphony in C* is, except for a few passages in the second movement, remarkably free of counterpoint; here, as throughout his career, Stravinsky has stressed the rhythmic element as few composers before him. Forceful and pounding reiteration of small patterns and a consistent shifting of accent and meter have remained striking elements of his style. Wide-ranging and angular melodic fragments are often rhythmically transformed on successive appearances; and the cold, objective, and often mechanical expression which animates the symphony is lost sight of in the interest of observing Stravinsky's processes of rhythmic manipulation.

The *Symphony in Three Movements* is even more dependent upon a percussive, impersonal type of expression. The work is characterized by long passages in which melodic fragments are interspersed in a predominantly rhythmic context, by syncopated chordal passages, by strong suggestions of jazz figures, and by a complete absence of warm, lyric expression. A short *Concerto in D*, for string orchestra, composed in 1946, contains the same rhythmic compulsion even where the percussive qualities are minimized. And the *Ebony Concerto* of the same year exploits the rhythmic elements again—this time in company with the functional sentiment appropriate to a work written for a dance orchestra.

A number of Stravinsky's post-1920 orchestral works have remained unmentioned in this account, notably a violin concerto of 1931 and four *Norwegian Moods* of 1943. In these as well as in the compositions discussed above, one sees a continuation of a general tendency which came to notice about 1920–1925. The extreme experiments of the decades 1900–1920 were largely abandoned, and a renewed interest in smaller media of expression became characteristic. But of primary importance was a rediscovery of the values, forms, and expressive ideals of the past, especially those found in the music of the Baroque period. As a foremost exponent of that tendency, Stravinsky altered his style radically, as we have seen. "Back to Bach" became a slogan in the years after about 1920, and many writers of the time began to speak of a "neo-Classical" period. In the revival of the Baroque concerto form, in the tentative return to a tonal scheme, in objective expression, and in the return of many composers to a somewhat contrapuntal texture are to be seen the style elements of this historically misnamed period.

The works of Béla Bartók (1881–1945) reveal yet another attempt to substitute a new type of expression for the decadent Romantic idiom. Bartók, too, was influenced by late-Romantic composers in his early works; the marks of Brahms are especially strong. But very soon (about 1904) he became imbued with a strong nationalistic feeling. Determined to assist in the creation of a truly Hungarian music, he set about the study of regional popular songs. He quickly discovered, however, that the latter were corrupt and were strongly overlaid with a Gypsy veneer. Then he extended his studies into the field of folk music proper and became an outstanding authority in that field; his interests were not confined to Hungary alone but embraced neighboring countries as well. Decades of work with the rich and almost unknown folk songs of eastern Europe gave him a profound knowledge of the scales, rhythms, and expressive types of that music, in which the sources of his personal style are also to be found. But unlike the typical nationalist composers of the nineteenth century, Bartók avoided descriptive music to a great extent. He became the first important composer to employ specific eastern European (and non-Gypsy) idioms in large-scale abstract compositions.

An early work, the *Kossuth Symphony*, written about 1903, remained unpublished. According to Haraszti,[3] its ten sections, reminiscent of similar scenes in the music of Berlioz and Liszt, already contain individual style traits. The *First Suite* for orchestra (1905) as well as the Rhapsody for piano and orchestra which preceded it

[3] Haraszti, *Béla Bartók*, pp. 55f.

(1904) are also Hungarian in their melodic content and expressive intention. These works fall into a period when folk song and nationalistic ideals exerted their strongest influence upon Bartók and when the separation of Gypsy elements had not yet been attained.

The *Second Suite* for orchestra, completed about 1907, discloses a throwing-off of purely local influences, a discarding of Lisztian techniques, and the first considerable appearance of the rhythmic "barbarism" that was to characterize much of his later work. Diabolical intensity, plaintive melancholy, and a pungent and tense harmonic scheme mark the suite. The *Two Portraits* for orchestra, also from 1907, reveal a new element: horizontal concerns have taken precedence over vertical ones, and the writing is largely melodic—but the melodies carry no harmonic implications, and are developed at will in a texture which can scarcely be said to contain the harmonic element. In Haraszti's words, Bartók "went through the same stage as Schoenberg and Stravinsky, that of violent reaction against the predomination of vertical harmony." [4] And in the *Four Pieces* for orchestra (1912) the rhythmic complexity is such that a polyphony of rhythms—in company with unmetrical rhythms as in Stravinsky's post-1913 works—may be spoken of.

In the period of the *Dance Suite* (1923) and the first piano concerto (1926), Bartók's individual and mature style took shape. That style had developed out of national idioms, it is true, and included such elements as whole-tone and pentatonic scales, modal patterns, and characteristic melodic and rhythmic turns. But these national elements were now blended with a personal harmonic system, a keen interest in contrapuntal writing, and a rhythmic vitality akin to Stravinsky's—to such an extent that Bartók's later works are "Hungarian" to only a small degree. The simultaneous use of major and minor chords (with both E and E flat present in a triad on C, for example); the consistent use of ninth-, eleventh-, and thirteenth-chords; chords based upon superimposed fourths or fifths; considerable chromaticism both in melody and harmony; and many added tones or chords composed of tone clusters—all these added up to a

4 Haraszti, *Béla Bartók*, p. 30.

dissonant style that was only rarely relieved by consonant chords.

This complex harmonic texture was thickened considerably by the use of contrapuntal techniques. Further, *basso ostinato* devices and double and triple pedal points—always striking elements of his style—now appeared in greater number; the consistent employment of such devices often gave rise to polytonal passages. A number of significant new instrumental effects became characteristic also: glissandos and passages in harmonics for the entire string section, extreme use of pizzicato and percussive bowing effects, and the like. The end result was an uncompromising, wonderfully flexible style which was consistently dissonant and occasionally brutal or ugly.

In later works these style elements were somewhat refined. Extreme objectivity in company with unrelieved dissonance tended to disappear. Short bits of suave lyricism and even warm sentiment are found in the violin concerto of 1938, for example. The *Concerto for Orchestra* of 1944 reveals a further softening of the severely dissonant harmony; but the rhythmic vitality and instrumental effectiveness of the style remains on a high level. And finally, in the third piano concerto (Bartók's last work, completed only a few days before his death in 1945), consonant tonality makes its reappearance. Many of the keyboard passages of this great work are strongly reminiscent of Brahms; the slow movement is essentially a chorale with interludes. Bartók's mastery of form, his disciplined imagination, and his keen rhythmic sense are revealed in every measure. With this last group of works Bartók solidified his position as one of the most important twentieth-century composers.

A survey of the dates of Mahler's, Strauss', and Reger's works reveals that post-Romantic composers remained active in Germany and Austria long after composers elsewhere had struck out in new directions. Not until the early 1920s did a significant new stylistic impulse emerge in Germany. This is not to say that that country remained entirely unaware of the requirements of the time. As early as 1900 Ferruccio Busoni (1866–1924), an eminent German-Italian pianist and composer long resident in Berlin, had taken steps to dispel the fog. Busoni sought to substitute a clarity of line and expression, economy, and restraint for the sentimental excesses of post-Romanticism. Thus he became one of the earliest exponents of what later was to be called neo-Classicism. His ideas came to expression primarily in his operas and in two of his orchestral works—a *Comedy Overture* (1897, later revised) and a *Rondo arlecchinesco* (1915). Soaring melodic lines set in a contrapuntal texture and a dry, unsentimental content are marks of Busoni's style. It must be admitted, however, that the style suggestions were of more lasting value than the music in which they came to expression.

Extramusical programs and subjectivity were cast out of this new German music, and the Romantic concept that music expressed feelings or psychological events was replaced by a concept through which a composition expressed merely the orderly, constructive processes of musical creation itself. Form and content were inseparable, and only musical laws governed musical composition. In the years immediately after the first World War, Paul Hindemith (b. 1895) revealed himself to be, by temperament and talent, the foremost exponent of the new ideal.

Hindemith's early works show that Reger's chromaticism, Brahms's control of form, and even Debussy's sequences of seventh-chords influenced him to some extent. But with such style elements, which scarcely any young composer could ignore, came a virility, an energetic quality coupled with humor and good sense, and evidence of a thoughtful musical mind. To a far greater extent than any other twentieth-century composer, Hindemith has always given the impression of knowing exactly what he was about. There is in the evolution of his style little of the backtracking and fruitless experiment that has characterized the careers of his contemporaries. Beginning with a series of chamber-music works in the early 1920s he has developed logically and intelligently to the present day.

The outstanding element of Hindemith's early style was its polyphonic texture. The melodic line, in works up to about 1924, had gradually freed itself from the dominance of the harmony, and had developed its own horizontal or linear tensions and releases without reference to harmonic (vertical) considerations. Simultaneously, the traditional formulas of nineteenth-century harmony, with its progressions from dissonant to consonant and its need for chord resolutions, were done away with; only the encounters (on strong beats of the rhythmic patterns) of the various melodies with each other determined the harmonies. The consistent domination of horizontal considerations over vertical ones is a feature of the "linear counterpoint" which Hindemith embraced wholeheartedly at this time. Fugal and canonic writing and various Baroque forms played an important role in Hindemith's works; and contrapuntal imitation became its chief structural principle. (Jazz elements, introduced into the works of about 1920–1922, found less employment in the later ones.)

Hindemith's style to this point had developed largely in the field of chamber music, notably in four string quartets. From about 1924 he turned to the chamber orchestra as a medium of expression and composed, as Opus 36, four separate concertos each with a different solo instrument: piano, cello, violin, and viola, respectively. A concerto for orchestra appeared as Opus 38. These five works, all written between 1924 and 1927, brought about a relaxation of the strict polyphonic style. It is as though Hindemith could not bring his vital rhythmic impulses to adequate expression in a texture that was exclusively polyphonic; and since expanded forms and virtuosic writing, which became characteristic in these works, were scarcely compatible with quartet style, he chose a less restricted instrumental combination. Among the most distinctive elements of content in these works are forceful and widespread melodies set in a boisterous rhythmic context, a variety of imitative figures over a moving *basso ostinato*, and a texture that employs short lyric melodies in a loose, relaxed contrapuntal style.

The gradual lightening of texture continued in the next group of works. With it came an increased brilliance in the solo writing and a growing warmth of expression. A concerto for wind orchestra (that is, a band), Opus 41 (1927), resulted from Hindemith's attempt to carry the new style into the field of military music. A masterful blend of contrapuntal writing and martial content was achieved, and the brass instruments, which are treated so skillfully in his later works, are here fully exploited. In two chamber concertos, Opus 46, for viola d'amore and organ respectively, written in 1928–1930, the element of free rhapsodic expression is characteristic.

These were followed by a *Konzertmusik* for solo viola and chamber orchestra, Opus 48; an important concerto for piano, brass instruments, and two harps, Opus 49; a *Konzertmusik* for strings and brass, Opus 50; and a *Philharmonisches Konzert*, written for the Berlin Philharmonic Orchestra. With these four individual works, written between 1930 and 1932, the balance of polyphony with free, impulsive writing was attained and Hindemith's future style took its definite shape. (It may be mentioned that after Opus 50 Hindemith discarded the device of opus numbers.)

The orchestral work for which Hindemith is perhaps best known is the set of three instrumental pieces (constituting a "symphony") drawn from his opera of 1934, *Mathis der Maler*. The pieces are, respectively, the opera's prelude and two interludes, and are translations into music of the three paintings which form Mathias Grünewald's famous Isenheim altarpiece at Colmar: the *Angel Concert*, the *Temptation of Saint Anthony*, and the *Entombment*.

The opera, according to Strobel,[5] is a symbolical work which clarifies the relationship between an artist and the populace. Mathis is an embodiment of the lonely, creative, artistic spirit. In the opera, laid at the time of the Peasant War (1524–1526), Mathis has given up his work to help the peasant cause. Disillusioned and forced to flee, he takes refuge in a forest. In the course of the work, the forces of ignorance, brutality, and murder which animate the mob whose cause Mathis has championed are revealed in all their ugliness. Mathis realizes that the artist contributes most by remaining true to his work. The opera places artistic activity in its proper place as

[5] Strobel, *Paul Hindemith*, 3d rev. ed., pp. 78–81.

a condensation or concentration of the creativity of the people. The three orchestral excerpts reveal a new richness of orchestral sound, a greater warmth of expression, and a further slackening of strict polyphony. *Mathis der Maler* remains one of Hindemith's finest works.

In a book written between 1934 and 1936 Hindemith explained the rules and principles which govern his method of composition: *Unterweisung im Tonsatz*, of which Book I, the theoretical section, was published in 1937.[6] There he made clear that his method is an expansion of the tonal system and has no relationship to atonality. Chords are not necessarily constructed out of superimposed thirds, however, and the concept of chord inversion is discarded in favor of a new definition of the chord's fundamental tone. He shows that chords may be arranged in the order of gradually increasing harmonic tension from a consonant chord to the most dissonant, and that the interplay of degrees of tension becomes one of the structural principles of the new music. An important element of the method is the two-part counterpoint that exists between the bass and the next most prominent voice.

The melodic basis of Hindemith's compositions has been stressed above. The polyphonic works written up to about 1924 had been almost entirely melodic, of course, and even in later works, where the strict counterpoint was somewhat relaxed, the melodies retained their important place. But development of melodic themes in the nineteenth-century sense finds little or no place in his works. Rather is there a continuous melodic expansion, as in Baroque contrapuntal compositions, or a juxtaposition of melodies of a similar type, as in the works of the period 1720–1780. These types of construction come to full realization in the next group of orchestral works: *Der Schwanendreher*, a concerto for viola and small orchestra, 1935; a set of *Symphonic Dances*, 1937; a violin concerto, 1939; and a cello concerto, 1940. The first of these is essentially a fantasy on folk melodies. The second brings melodic writing and rhythmic vitality

[6] In English as *The Craft of Musical Composition* (1942).

into effective and masterful balance. The violin and cello concertos are outspokenly virtuosic, but brilliant figurations are never allowed to interfere with the contrapuntal integrity of these works.

The dance legend, *Nobilissima visione*, is based on episodes in the life of Saint Francis of Assisi; the orchestral suite (1938) drawn from that work is one of Hindemith's most sensitive and profound larger compositions. A noble expression is achieved here in a texture that is full of cross-rhythms, concentrated polyphony, and glowing orchestral color. In spite of many melodic and harmonic devices which point back to an earlier period (the interval of a fourth plays a large part in the melodic construction throughout, for example), *Nobilissima visione* gives clear evidence that Hindemith's music has continued to grow warmer, more eloquent, and more significant with the passage of the years.

The term "symphony" has played a comparatively minor role in Hindemith's career to this point. An early sinfonietta, of about 1915, had remained unpublished; the Symphony from *Mathis der Maler* is to be understood in the early Baroque sense (the *sinfonia* was merely an instrumental piece found in a stage work); and the *Symphonic Dances* reflect merely a more serious treatment of dance music. In the latter work, however, one finds along with the seriousness a type of expression that verges on the imposing. A greater use of brass instruments, passages filled with pomp and sonority, a richer harmony, a free and expansive form, a balance of rhythmic energy and expressiveness—such elements come to the fore in the works from about 1940, and such elements are worthy of the term "symphonic."

The *Symphony in E Flat* of that year is typical of this turn in Hindemith's style. Small polyphonic detail is lessened, and wide-ranging two- or three-part contrapuntal writing is emphasized. A new interest in lavish display comes to notice, along with grandiose passages for brass instruments, and the warm, almost intense expression that had become ever more prominent since the 1930s here comes to its fullest realization. The *Symphonic Metamorphosis of Themes by Weber*, written in 1943, is, on the other hand, charming and rhythmically alive throughout. It is filled with touches of humor, an element that has never long been missing from Hindemith's works and that remains an important constituent of his style. Later works include a piano concerto and the *Symphonia serena*, both of 1946.

For over thirty years Hindemith has been a prolific, resourceful, and forward-looking composer. In consistency of style, strength of purpose, and technical quality he has few peers. A later generation must decide which of his many works are of enduring value. At the present time one can do no more than voice the belief that his high place in the musical history of the twentieth century is secure, and that he is one of the two or three most significant of contemporary composers.

XIII

CONTEMPORARY DEVELOPMENTS

THE FOREGOING brief, somewhat general, and necessarily super-ficial account of the principal twentieth-century styles has sought to give a picture of the diverse approaches of Debussy, Schoenberg, Stravinsky, Bartók, and Hindemith to the musical problems of their time. Many of the works mentioned were frankly experimental or tentative; as such they have all but disappeared from the repertoire. The new stylistic impulses and musical concepts they revealed, however, influenced scores of composers throughout the world. Lit-tle significant music has been written in recent decades that is not in some fashion indebted to them.

In some cases the new concepts were adopted and the styles imi-tated; in others, they were rejected. In all the major countries (in a musical sense) one may trace the rise of individuals or small groups whose creative output is a reflection of, for instance, Debussy or Schoenberg, or whose music combines the elements of two or more styles and thus leads to the synthesis that the major composers them-selves brought into being.

It is safe to say that each of those countries has its favorite sons. France, Italy, England, and all the others possess a body of music that is primarily of local interest; only small portions of that music have found places upon the international concert stage. This, aside from the fact that space limitations forbid a thorough discussion of all the works—even the most significant ones—written in those countries, determines the content of the following pages. The author can do little more here than list and describe a few of the twentieth-century compositions that transcend such local interest. No one at the present time may hope to undertake a complete aesthetic evaluation of all contemporary western music. The restricted aim of the present chapter, then, will be to show how the various styles of the principal composers have influenced each other and have given rise to a style and musical outlook which are fairly well distributed throughout the musical world today. Composers will be discussed by country of origin rather than in chronological order.

Paul Dukas (1865–1935) was among the earliest of Debussy's contemporaries to reveal a fondness for Impressionistic methods. His first important orchestral work, and the one for which he is best known outside France, is *L'Apprenti sorcier* (1897), a one-movement piece which is essentially a musical counterpart of Goethe's ballad. The rhythmic animation, colorful and brilliant orchestral sound, clear intentions, and humor which the work contains are carried by a harmonic scheme that is clearly tonal. Yet certain chordal effects are derived from Debussy, as are the shimmering texture, the chromatic figurations, and the free modulatory scheme.

Maurice Ravel (1875–1937) was, next to Debussy, perhaps the most important of early twentieth-century French composers. His earliest published orchestral work, the *Rapsodie espagnole* (1907), makes considerable use of Impressionistic devices: exotic atmosphere, flashing glissandos, series of parallel seventh- and ninth-chords, melodic and rhythmic fragments, and even single chords employed for their color effect. These devices also appear in the two series of "symphonic fragments" drawn from the ballet, *Daphnis et Chloé* (1909–1911). Iridescent passages alternate with strongly rhythmical ones, and glistening, undulating background figures provide flashes of ever-changing color.

These are not consistently subjective works, however, as the majority of Debussy's are, nor are their forms as free and impulsive. A certain respect for traditional forms and even traditional methods of thematic development marked Ravel's compositions from the beginning. And an objective, somewhat cold, and impersonal element was present also. Rhythmically more straightforward than

Debussy's works, Ravel's were often more artificially made; one senses the presence of an enormously skilled technician. Stylistic perfection, along with the irony which became characteristic, is seen in *La Valse*, a "choreographic poem" for orchestra written in 1920. According to a note in the score, "one sees, vaguely and intermittently, the waltzing couples. The mists disappear gradually; one distinguishes a large ballroom filled with dancers. The illumination comes to full splendor. An imperial court about 1855." A comparison of this program with Debussy's veiled and imaginative allusions to mist, foam, and elusive light allows one to see how Impressionistic techniques have, in Ravel's hands, been hardened and made to serve materialistic ends.

In 1928 Ravel composed, as an experiment for the dancer Ida Rubinstein, a piece consisting of a seventeen-minute reiteration of one rhythmic figure and two melodic fragments, set in the pattern of one great crescendo, and culminating in an enormous climax: the famous *Boléro*. The experiment was a sensational success. Here are neither Impressionistic nor other stylistic elements—nothing but "orchestral tissue without music," in Ravel's own words. The inexorable rhythm, the ceaseless melodic repetition, the unmoving C-major harmony, the cumulative growth in sonority as more and more instruments are added—these produce an almost hysterical tension. And at the point of greatest emotional impact, where frenzy is close at hand, the key changes from C major to E major—the only harmonic change in the work, and a tonal masterstroke. This is a tour de force, to be achieved once and thereafter to be weakly imitated.

The piano concerto of 1930–1931 reveals a stylistic change; for this three-movement, neo-Classical work is clear and neat in content, transparent in texture, and characterized by an abandonment of the tremolos, glissandos, and veiled harmonies which Impressionism had made its own. The incisive rhythms, clear phrase structures, and fine proportions of the concerto are far removed from the diaphanous, vague writing of his earlier compositions. This is also true—even if to a lesser extent—of the *Concerto for the Left Hand*, for piano and orchestra, written about the same period. Here the restriction imposed upon the solo part caused Ravel to employ flashing arpeggios as the chief element of texture—to the detriment of melodic clarity.

Throughout all Ravel's orchestral works, his genius in orchestration comes to full expression. In respect of flexibility, suitability, and variety of color and effect, Ravel ranks among the half-dozen great orchestral composers. A sensuous beauty of sound pervades especially the score of *Daphnis et Chloé;* and a brilliant, virtuosic technique is required of an orchestra which would play Ravel. Not only in quality of orchestration does Ravel's music reflect his gifts, however. Neatness, perfection of form, absence of unnecessary detail, and general standard of workmanship set it apart from that of his contemporaries. Much of it is contrived, cold, and even superficial; but for sheer glitter, refinement, and consistency of style it has few equals.

Albert Roussel (1869–1937) was in minor respects similar to Ravel. The influence of Debussy may be noted in his early works, along with exotic touches derived from his naval service in the Orient. Not until after the first World War did his strong, mature style develop; the works which were written after 1920 and which influenced a generation of younger French composers reveal Roussel at his best.

The *Suite in F* (1926), the piano concerto (1927), and the fourth symphony (1930) are the works of a dignified, even aloof, and meticulous composer. A dry and somewhat chromatic melodic line, thick harmonies verging on the polytonal, clear and traditional forms, reserved and refined expression—such elements are found. The quality of Roussel's workmanship is equal to Ravel's, even if the content of his music is not so colorful or brilliant. That music is restrained and elegant in details, its textures are mildly contrapuntal, and its fast movements are characterized by much bustling rhythmic activity with many cross-accents. It is attractive, and it is typical of a large segment of French taste.

In another group of French composers a forceful rejection of Impressionistic ideals may be noted from the start. Darius Milhaud (b. 1892) is prominent among them. Milhaud strove toward a style that eschewed vagueness, pretentiousness, and soft contours, and developed a simple, diatonic, and harshly dissonant manner of expression. A tour of duty at the French legation in Rio de Janeiro (1917–1919) brought him into contact with Brazilian music; upon his return to France he became acquainted with American jazz idioms; but eventually, and following the lead of Eric Satie (1866–1925), he embraced dissonant counterpoint and polytonal harmony. In a large number of works, including *Five Symphonies for Small Orchestra* (1917–1922), most of which are only a few minutes in length, a ballet entitled *La Création du monde* (1923), and the *Suite provençale* (1937), Milhaud became an outstanding exponent of polytonality. In the *Suite française* (1945) this device still finds expression.

To make certain that the separate tonalities are clearly perceived in a polytonal work, it becomes desirable to establish each tonality clearly; that is, diatonic writing in the various parts becomes essential. That type of writing, already a factor in Milhaud's early works, became more pronounced in later ones and led to the criticism that his melodic lines were perfunctory and overly simple. In works of the past decade, however, that diatonic simplicity has disappeared to a great extent; indeed, polytonality has become only one element of Milhaud's latest style. Among his recent works, the second violin concerto (1946) and the fourth symphony (1947) contain a rich variety of harmonic effects.

In company with the majority of composers in recent years, Milhaud has turned to a warmer, more emotional type of expression. Thus, in the above concerto, fervent and rhapsodic passages occur; the brilliant and rich figurations of the solo part in no way detract from the lyric expressiveness of the whole. In the symphony, however, the element of acrid and dissonant counterpoint adds a harsh tone to the prevailing moods of animation in the fast movements; a hard, uncompromising, and somber mood pervades the slow movement.

Milhaud has always written concisely. No superabundance of detail mars his works, nor any concern for the traditional manner of thematic expansion. The textures in his music are transparent and, quite often, atmospheric. His large output (well over one hundred and twenty works in about thirty years) has led him to develop certain harmonic and rhythmic mannerisms, no doubt. But the intelligence with which his compositions are constructed, the wide variety of content they reveal, and a general stylistic consistency make him one of the most important of French composers.

In the available works of Olivier Messiaen (b. 1908) we see that certain of Debussy's techniques still influence the younger composers of France—in some cases modified by a strong hint of Catholic mysticism. This combination of elements is seen in *L'Ascension*, a set of four "symphonic meditations," originally written for organ and later transcribed for orchestra. Each movement is prefaced by a Scriptural quotation. An Impressionistic play with one harmonic color or one melodic fragment is a striking element of Messiaen's style here, along with many tremolos, parallel chord formations, and the like. A Franckian kind of chromaticism and dramatic changes in range and texture are also present. But in general, Messiaen's music is characterized by "systems"; melodic patterns analogous to tone rows, complex rhythmic progressions based upon Hindu practices, and similar intellectually contrived devices are found.

The tendency to employ various combinations of stylistic elements may also be seen in Spanish and Italian compositions. Manuel de Falla (1876–1946), perhaps the most significant of recent Spanish composers, sought to express the spirit of his nation's music in company with Impressionistic moods. The rhythms, melodic mannerisms, modal patterns, and very atmosphere of Falla's compositions are Spanish—even though actual folk songs are seldom quoted; yet their forms, instrumental effects, and harmonic structures owe much to Ravel. The set of three movements for piano and orchestra entitled *Noches en los jardines de España* (about 1915) is Falla's most extensive orchestral work. Not merely descriptive, this music evokes melancholy and mystery as well as merriment and festivity. The rhythmic element plays an important part throughout and is often employed so elaborately that a true rhythmic counterpoint emerges. The concerto for harpsichord and quintet of wind and string instruments (1926), while not an orchestral work, may be mentioned here as evidence of Falla's early acceptance of neo-Classical stylistic concepts. This work is no less Spanish in its conception than his dances and stage works, but it reveals a clarity of form, an objective expression, and a sense for proportion that are no less striking for being accompanied by national idioms.

Ottorino Respighi (1879–1936) was foremost among a group of recent Italian composers who made notable contributions to the symphonic repertoire. Of more than a dozen large and colorful orchestral works, the two symphonic poems, *Le fontane di Roma* (1916) and *I pini di Roma* (1924), best represent the opulent, brilliant, and highly emotional aspects of his style. Here are "impressions" of, respectively, four fountains and four pine groves situated in and about Rome. Respighi did not merely describe the external objects, as Strauss might have done (he was for a short time greatly infatuated with that composer's music). His method was to relate in tones something of the emotions of the historically minded observer who recalls the past glories of the city even as he remains aware of the present.

Delicate poetic suggestion, riotous color, and deep melancholy are reflected in Respighi's music. His skill in manipulating the orchestra rivaled Rimsky-Korsakov's, whose pupil he was briefly. His tendency toward lavish display and inflated expression was not always held in control; and his resourcefulness in creating soaring, eloquent melodic lines was outstanding at a time when composers generally avoided eloquence of any description. The *Feste Romane* of 1929 is less restrained; being given over to impressions suggested by Roman festivals, it is somewhat obvious and noisy. Even in his most extreme moments, as in that work, Respighi remained firmly within the tonal framework of, say, early Debussy. An overabundance of chromatic detail lends a thickness to his most exuberant pages, but elsewhere a quality of superb craftsmanship and a rare poetic feeling for simplicity are characteristic.

Ildebrando Pizetti (b. 1880) and G. Francesco Malipiero (b. 1882) are Italian composers who have long since developed their own severe styles. Pizetti, essentially an Impressionist composer of operatic and other stage works in a style akin to Respighi's, is sparsely represented on concert programs in the United States. Malipiero, active in virtually all fields of composition and the composer of at least seven symphonies and half a dozen concertos, has remained virtually unheard until recent years. Available scores reveal him to be an atonal composer who writes meticulously and aristocratically in an individual, vigorous style that includes a neo-Classical manipulation of short motives as its chief melodic principle.

Another prominent Italian composer, Alfredo Casella (1883–1947), passed through several style periods before finding his mature manner of expression. A post-Romantic realism, of which the orchestral rhapsody, *Italia* (1909), is the best-known example, gave way to a polytonal, harshly dissonant style; the latter was followed, about 1924, by a diatonic, pungent neo-Classicism. In that style he composed several chamber-music works and a third symphony (1940). Tonal harmonies with chromatic thickening, occasional suggestions of Stravinskian rhythmic complexity, and passages in dissonant counterpoint combine to make a somewhat dry and severe manner of expression.

The works discussed to this point have been either French in origin or French-influenced to a small or large degree. All contemporary music, however, is not of that category; the twelve-tone system of Schoenberg, for example, has also made a considerable technical contribution to later composers. Among the direct pupils of Schoenberg were two Austrians, Anton von Webern (1883–1945) and Alban Berg (1885–1935). Webern carried the possibilities of the system to a point of compression or condensation at which musical substance and flow virtually ceased to exist. A scattering of single tones in an incredibly thin texture, a tenuous or nonexistent rhythmic pattern, and the briefest of musical forms sufficed for his ultrarefined expression. A short symphony, Opus 21 of 1929, disclosed a slight enlargement of the minute technical resources Webern required. But even here a succession of isolated tones, chords, and angular melodic fragments—the whole constituting scarcely more than a tonal skeleton—arranged in accord with the twelve-tone system, provides virtually the entire content.

Berg developed in quite the opposite direction; in his works an emotional richness and a feeling for large forms came to expression. His opera, *Wozzek*, completed in 1920, was among the first fully extended works to be written by a member of the Schoenberg school. An array of instrumental and vocal compositions ended with the violin concerto of 1935, completed a few months before his death. In the concerto, as well as in the instrumental portions of the opera, Berg demonstrated what Schoenberg had not: that eloquence, passionate warmth, and dramatic contrasts are possible in the twelve-tone system.

The texture of the violin concerto is, of course, largely contrapuntal. Above the thick, roiled orchestral accompaniment the solo violin spins a line of angular melodies that are composed of a few fragments which undergo continual transformation in rhythm and expressive content. A long and agonized cadenza (the work is a memorial to the young daughter of Alma Mahler) in the third section of the concerto leads to the statement of a somber Bach chorale; the latter is suitably elaborated in moods of gloom and resignation. Berg, to judge from the compositions mentioned here, did not employ the twelve-tone system exclusively; for sections of those works are consonant and definitely tonal in their harmonies. It is in the expansion of the tonal system along chromatic lines, making use of Schoenberg's systematic approach in some cases and transcending the methods of Mahler and Reger in others, that Berg's technical contribution to music may be found.

Nicholas Miaskovsky (1881–1950), an important Russian composer in the generation after Glazunov, occupied a unique transitional position. He wrote twenty-four symphonies between 1908 and 1943; although these works are in general within the limits of the tonal system, they differ widely in content and approach. The sixth symphony, in E-flat minor (1923), is the best representative of Miaskovsky's post-Romantic, subjective, and lyrically expressive early period. The seventh to the eighteenth symphonies, written between 1922 and 1935, reveal an increasing objectivity and a considerable use of Russian folk material. With these elements came a shift in the direction of "official" Soviet music: music which reflects social themes [1] and which, one may suppose, departs widely from the "decadent" influences present in the music of western Europe. Later works have gone far toward restoring consonant, sentimental—in a word, neo-Romantic—expression. Throughout Miaskovsky's symphonies, from the harsh and often gloomy early works to the lighter and more melodious later ones, one looks in vain for the influence, say, of Stravinsky or other leading composers. These works are in the direct line which extends from Tchaikovsky through Glière to Shostakovich. Tonal harmonies are thickened, abrupt modulations and free forms are typical; yet the hand of a nineteenth-century Russian sentimentalist is apparent in the great majority of his works.

The case of Sergei Prokofieff (b. 1891) is somewhat similar to Miaskovsky's—except that the differences between the composers' personalities are reflected in their music. Prokofieff's works have always been distinguished by rhythmic animation, bold and far-reaching harmonies—usually kept within the tonal system, however—and strong elements of the grotesque and the humorous. The well-known *Classical Symphony* (1917) was written for an orchestra that Mozart might have used; it employed Classical forms and textures and brought Prokofieff's irrepressible wit to expression. It may be looked upon as an early (and perhaps unconscious) example of the neo-Classicism which was to shape virtually all music a decade later. This work is not typical of the later Prokofieff, however, even

---

[1] Nicolas Slonimsky, "Nicholas Miaskovsky," in *The International Cyclopedia of Music and Musicians,* 5th ed., p. 1146.

though its abrupt modulations, wide melodic leaps, and employment of extreme ranges remained features of his style.

His first important orchestral work, the *Scythian Suite* (1914), derived from an earlier ballet called *Ala et Lolly*, had revealed a full measure of the rhythmic barbarism, harmonic audacity, and intense feeling that have marked later compositions. It is undeniable that the intensity of Prokofieff's expression often approaches sentimentality and mawkishness; yet it is equally true that he is among the few contemporary composers in whose music emotion and intellect are balanced.

In a number of ballets and operas written in the decade after the first World War, Prokofieff's search for new effects resulted in a hard, dissonant, and somewhat percussive or mechanical style. This phase passed in the 1930s when the element of lyric expressiveness assumed greater importance. The second violin concerto, in G minor (1935), provides perhaps the finest example of the changed style. Short melodic fragments are developed, and the moods range from quietly reflective to brilliant; the general freshness and vitality of the style are not lost, however. In this period Prokofieff returned to Soviet Russia after many years spent abroad as a pianist and a conductor; one may believe that he, like Miaskovsky, allowed the musical tastes of a political party to influence his composition.

The melodrama, *Peter and the Wolf* (1936), too well known to require extended comment, goes even farther in the direction of consonant, tonal writing. In recent works, notably in the fifth symphony (1944), a style that is rich, poetic, and full of warm sentiment has emerged. Throughout his career Prokofieff has remained faithful to a clear, forward-looking, and vital kind of writing. A highly developed sense of humor is present virtually everywhere that humor is appropriate; the grotesque instrumental effects, the comical leaps and twists in the melodic line, have in later works been subdued or refined. In the symphonies, the five piano concertos, and the many smaller orchestral compositions Prokofieff has revealed himself to be a skillful, versatile, and intelligent composer. Without indulging in fruitless experiment, without developing a "system," he has slowly perfected an individual style that is flexible, contemporary, and that allows him to write significant and enjoyable music.

Dmitri Shostakovich (b. 1906) is among the most prominent of younger Soviet composers. Like Prokofieff's, his later work seems to have been affected by political attitudes—to such an extent that one can come to no clear opinion about his real capabilities. His first symphony (1926) is a work of melodic charm, sly humor, and conservative harmony. Transparent textures and considerable solo writing for individual wind instruments allow him full opportunity to display the originality of his melodic and rhythmic ideas. Three additional symphonies and several ballets and operas, all composed between 1927 and 1936, give evidence of his attempts—not all of them successful—to write politically acceptable music.

Severely criticized because of his opera, *Lady Macbeth of Mzensk*, Shostakovich composed his fifth symphony according to the formula that had brought him success in the first. Two elements had contributed to that success: irrepressible humor, sometimes verging on the boisterous, and a sentimental, nostalgic melodic line. Those elements, plus a strength and dramatic power not always evident elsewhere, found enhanced expression in the fifth symphony and made it into perhaps his finest composition.

The seventh symphony (1941), on the other hand, composed during the siege of Leningrad, is an inflated and blatant piece of writing. Similar to the hysterical works of Tchaikovsky in its abandon and emotional excesses, it is redeemed only by a few quiet and reflective passages in the middle movements; it is as though Tchaikovsky's *The Year 1812* had been modernized and greatly lengthened. The ninth symphony (1945), in great contrast to the bombastic seventh and the moody and march-like eighth (1943), marks a turn to the style of Prokofieff's *Classical Symphony*. The work is short, requires a comparatively small orchestra, and is filled with a joyous, effervescent spirit. Shostakovich relied here, as he did in the first symphony, upon transparent textures and exposed groupings of a few instruments to carry his humorous or sentimental, forceful or limpid, traditional or grotesque musical ideas.

One may well deplore Shostakovich's adherence to the musical-political formulas that are imposed upon him. His undeniable gifts as an original and powerful composer would, in another cultural atmosphere, lead him into other directions and to a higher place than he now occupies. One senses the fact that he composes out of technical mastery, not out of conviction.

Brief mention may be made of a few composers in whose works national idioms are combined with elements derived from one or another of the major twentieth-century styles. Karel Szymanowski (1883–1937), born in the Ukraine but associated primarily with the music of Poland, is an outstanding example. His early works reflect, successively, the influence of Strauss, Debussy, and Polish folk composers. Among the works which have enjoyed performances in the United States is his second violin concerto (1930). Here Szymanowski attained a poetic, sensitive, and highly individual style in which elements of Impressionism, dissonant polyphony, and the spirit of Chopin are inextricably bound.

In the works of Georges Enesco (b. 1881), whose first *Rumanian Rhapsody* is well known, the idiom of Rumanian folk music comes to strong expression in a style that is technically superb and emotionally warm. Among Hungarian composers, Ernst von Dohnányi (b. 1877) exhibits a Straussian intensity of expression in a thick, highly colored, and essentially tonal style. A great mastery of counterpoint is one of his major characteristics, along with a refined use of Hungarian rhythms and inflections. The *Suite for Orchestra,* Opus 19, a set of *Variations on a Nursery Song,* for piano and orchestra, Opus 25, and much excellent chamber music reveal him to be essentially a post-Romantic composer. Zoltán Kodály (b. 1882), long associated with Bartók in the collecting of Hungarian folk songs, is even more strikingly nationalistic in spirit. In his best-known orchestral work, the suite from the opera *Háry János* (1926), he discloses a lyric gift and a delightful sense of humor; these are coupled with excellent craftsmanship and real ability in setting dramatic and picturesque scenes to music.

Bohuslav Martinů (b. 1890) has written much music in which Czech and Impressionistic elements occasionally come to expression; but these are combined with many other influences to the extent that an individual style of general attractiveness results. Martinů moved to Paris in the early 1920s and was affected both by the clarity and technical perfection of Roussel and by the harsh dissonance of Stravinsky; later, jazz idioms attracted him, along with polytonality and dissonant counterpoint. The amalgamation and synthesis of such elements, together with his own feeling for intensity of expression, has resulted in an energetic and rich manner of writing. Five symphonies, several concertos, a long list of chamber-music works, and a variety of compositions in other fields testify to Martinů's vigor and versatility. The *Concerto grosso* of 1938 and various smaller works with Baroque titles give evidence, in general objectivity and formal perfection of stylistic elements, that Martinů, like the majority of contemporary composers, has joined the ranks of the neo-Classicists. In his case, the content of the music has become ever more appealing, more consonant, and more consistently vital and significant.

Twentieth-century music in England represents, in its earliest stages, a mixture of Impressionistic and national ideals. Prominent among the sensitive, poetic composers of the time was Frederick Delius (1862–1934), a self-taught English musician of German ancestry who spent the greater part of his life in France. Working quietly in isolation, Delius absorbed certain Debussyian techniques —among them a play with individual chords, the creation of atmosphere, a virtual disregard for counterpoint, a minimizing of considerations of form—and added to them a rhapsodic, somewhat intangible kind of expression that is purely his own.

Many of Delius' tone poems and shorter pieces for orchestra are programmatic in content: *Paris*, 1899; *Brigg Fair*, 1907; *On Hearing the First Cuckoo in Spring*, 1912. It is here that his Impressionism is most clearly revealed. In larger works, notably in a half-dozen concertos, his lack of interest in problems of form leads to an episodic, halting type of utterance. Although his music has found great favor in England—due largely to the missionary work of one or two ardent enthusiasts—it has found little representation on the American concert stage.

For over forty years Ralph Vaughan Williams (b. 1872) has been among the most important of English composers, dominating the scene not only through the technical excellence of his works but also through his personal integrity and idealism. Vaughan Williams, perhaps to a greater degree than any of his contemporaries, has brought the essential spirit of English music to expression. Folk-song idioms, modal inflections, and polyphony in the manner of Purcell are factors of that spirit. Among the earliest of his larger works is the *Fantasia on a Theme by Tallis* (1910) for string orchestra; here the strength, austerity, and technical resourcefulness of his style are fully revealed. In the overture to *The Wasps* (1909), written for a performance of Aristophanes' comedy, a joyful and humorous tone is achieved. And in *A London Symphony* (1914) his approach is somewhat descriptive; London street cries come to expression, and atmospheric moods in the manner of Debussy are achieved effortlessly.

It is this versatility of expression that has always been among Vaughan Williams's chief characteristics. The separately derived style elements are unmistakable; yet the rich variety of his textures, the absence of a rigid harmonic system, and the great range of expressive content make him a composer difficult to classify. Vaughan Williams has kept abreast of the times, has even been somewhat in advance of them. In works written after the 1920s, the national spirit was impressed upon a harshly dissonant, thickly chromatic style which came close to atonality. The fourth symphony, in F minor (1935), is an uncompromising, ferocious work of tremendous power and rhythmic compulsion. Yet in the fifth, in D major (1943), a return to consonant, diatonic writing is to be heard in company with sonorous, ever-changing textures and serene, contented moods.

The sixth symphony, finally (1948), in E minor, is a dark and tempestuous composition, again rhythmically complex, chromatically inflected, and filled with passionate unrest; only in its last movement, a quiet and reflective piece that expresses resignation and a mood of farewell, is the somberness dissipated. One looks vainly, in the music of Vaughan Williams, for expressions of cloying sentiment or for passages that are designed to be spectacular or merely externally effective. He has made intelligent use of contemporary style elements and employed them in a highly individual manner to create music of universal appeal.

One composition by Gustave Holst (1874–1934) may be mentioned here to show that English composers were not immune to the grandiose and monumental. Holst's *The Planets* (1915), a work which enjoyed repeated performances for many years and which is heard only rarely today, is a suite of seven symphonic poems for a massive orchestra. Each movement of the suite is concerned with a single planet. Consistently post-Romantic in harmony and expressive content, it is distinguished by Straussian orchestral effects, considerable rhythmic reiteration, and tremendous power and sonority. Holst pays his respects to Impressionism in a few passages in the quieter movements; and in the last movement he employs a women's chorus to sing without text (as in the third of Debussy's *Nocturnes*). In later works, notably the concerto for two violins and orchestra (1930) he reputedly embraced the dissonant contrapuntal idiom of early Hindemith.

Among the younger generation of English composers, William Walton (b. 1902) and Benjamin Britten (b. 1913) have achieved important places. In an overture, *Portsmouth Point* (1925), Walton introduced a brilliant and satirical tone. A succession of short, sharply accented tunes in a pungent and polychordal texture, effervescent humor, and frequent changes of meter in the manner of Stravinsky—but without the soulless quality of that composer—characterize the overture. A set of pieces which accompanied the recitation of some of Edith Sitwell's satirical poems (1923) became successively a ballet and an orchestral suite (1936) known as *Façade*. Broad humor, sparkling wit, and impelling rhythms set in a mock-Romantic vein combine to make *Façade* a delightful piece.

Satire and rhythmic vitality are not the only distinguishing marks of Walton's music, however. In a viola concerto of 1929, and even more in a symphony completed in 1935, lyric breadth, serious purpose, and warm sentiment come to expression. An impulsive and powerful style akin to that of Sibelius, a brilliance of orchestral color, and a wealth of small rhythmic detail are revealed in those compositions. Always forward-looking in a harmonic sense and fully aware of contemporary developments, Walton has succeeded here and in the violin concerto of 1939 in creating an individual style that is only slightly reminiscent of other composers. The rhythmic vitality of Stravinsky, the harmonic resourcefulness of Hindemith, and the fervent expression of Schoenberg have been absorbed into a cool, competent and attractive personal idiom.

When a complete history of twentieth-century American symphonic music comes to be written, it will of necessity emphasize the following points: a gradual casting off of nineteenth-century German traditions; the importation and absorption of twentieth-century European styles; interest in independent experiment; the emergence of American idioms; and, finally, the appearance of a body of music which results from the amalgamation of foreign attitudes and native idioms and which enjoys international acceptance. Such a task obviously cannot be undertaken here; unavailability of and unfamiliarity with much recent American music, nearness in point of time, and space limitations are among the obstacles. It is possible, however, to set down a few details and to outline the probable course of that history.

The names and compositions selected here for illustration are not necessarily the most suitable ones, nor are they likely to be those which the future historian will emphasize. The American scene today is dominated by perhaps a dozen composers whose music is performed and whose scores are in print; to those we shall refer. But a future generation, in discussing the most representative composers of the present day, may, and very likely will, refer to others who remain unmentioned in the following pages. The whole course of music history indicates that present fame and future renown are by no means equivalent. One has but to recall that Telemann was the great composer of Bach's generation, that Stamitz was revered when young Haydn was indulged, and that Loewe's songs were famous far beyond Schubert's. Thus, the following may be taken as a general report on recent style trends rather than a thorough discussion of contemporary American composers.

The turn of the century witnessed the activity of a number of musicians in whose works a German Romantic outlook was dominant. Edward MacDowell (1861–1908), John Knowles Paine (1839–1906), and Horatio Parker (1863–1919) were the foremost representatives of the group. The music of MacDowell, in spite of its Celtic and Indian idioms, can in no sense be said to form a bridge from the nineteenth to the twentieth century. To a lesser extent this is true also of the works of Daniel Gregory Mason (b. 1873) and David Stanley Smith (b. 1877), among others. Mason, with three symphonies to his credit, reflects idealism and dignity in a conservative neo-Brahmsian harmonic style. Smith, who also composed several symphonies, adhered largely to traditional forms and minimized sentimental expression by substituting much structural detail. Henry Hadley (1871–1937), more prolific than many of his contemporaries, disclosed attractive melodiousness, great rhythmic vitality, and considerable craftsmanship in all details of orchestral composing.

A number of other men of that generation, however, were thoroughly attracted to twentieth-century musical styles. Impressionism, as the earliest of those styles, was also among the first to be represented in the United States; its principal exponent was Charles Martin Loeffler (1861–1935). Loeffler, an Alsatian by birth but a resident of this country from 1881, was an Impressionist parallel to rather than influenced by Debussy. His orchestral music is cool, delicate, and objective. He was much given to religious moods: the *Hora mystica* (1916), a symphony for orchestra and men's voices, is a case in point. Loeffler was fascinated by individual sounds and sonorities, experimented and refined ceaselessly to achieve the right shade of expression, and wrote with exquisite sensibility and attention to small detail. Considerations of form apparently interested him less. *La Mort de Tintagiles* (1901), for orchestra and viola d'amore, and *A Pagan Poem* (1903), are among his finest and most characteristic works.

Charles Griffes (1884–1920), although principally a composer of piano music in which the color and sound of Debussy are unmistakable, is remembered for the orchestral version of a brief piano piece, *The White Peacock* (1917), and the symphonic poem, *The Pleasure Dome of Kubla Khan* (1919). In the latter, Griffes's early Impressionism was modified. Sparse and contrapuntal textures, suggestions of polytonality, and a free formal style became typical.

In the music of John Alden Carpenter (1876–1951), the drift away from Impressionistic beginnings was still more marked. Carpenter's early songs revealed the influence of Debussy in their pale and tenuous style. In the delightful *Adventures in a Perambulator* (1915), however, he wrote with originality and strength; moods of humor and delicate feeling are prominent in this work. In a *Concertino* for piano and orchestra (1917) he employed syncopation in a manner suggesting ragtime. And in later works, for example in *Sea Drift* (1933), a poem for orchestra, he made a turn toward controlled and dignified Romantic expression.

The creation of music which, while it is not Romantic in mood or technique, yet avoids extreme dissonance and remains faithful to the tonal system, has occupied many contemporary composers of the older generation. Among them, Eric DeLamarter (b. 1880), Deems Taylor (b. 1885), and Howard Hanson (b. 1896) may be singled out. DeLamarter, a prominent organist and conductor, has written copiously in many fields. Four symphonies, two organ concertos, and many smaller works—including the well-known orchestral suite drawn from the play, *The Betrothal* (1919)—are among his contributions to the symphonic literature. These works, insofar as they are available, reveal a diatonic manner of writing, a subtle and expressive melodic line, and considerable rhythmic flexibility. Excellent workmanship and great knowledge of the orchestra are characteristic. A tonal harmony akin to Prokofieff's in quality and a content in which seriousness and humor are well balanced are found in DeLamarter's work. In smaller compositions a tendency to introduce folk songs may be noted; but the folk material is employed in a sophisticated manner, usually without literal quotation.

Taylor, widely known as a commentator and writer on musical subjects, is also an excellent if conservative composer. Two successful operas, several smaller works, and a series of delightfully humorous orchestral compositions—*Through the Looking Glass* (1922), *Circus Day* (1934), and *Marco Takes a Walk* (1943) are chief among them—testify to Taylor's craftsmanship and keen orchestral sense. In a harmonic scheme that is essentially diatonic and tonal, he sometimes employs whole-tone scales, rich chromaticism, and a variety of contemporary elements purely as harmonic color effects. The orchestral works of Taylor, while neither imposing nor serious, are engaging and enjoyable.

For more than two decades Howard Hanson has been one of the most prominent of American musicians. As administrator, conductor, teacher, and lecturer he has served the cause of American music wholeheartedly. And although he has championed and performed many varieties of music—including the most extreme—he has adhered to a moderate, even conservative style in his own works. His principal orchestral compositions are the *Nordic Symphony*, 1922; the *Romantic Symphony*, 1930; and two symphonies without titles, of 1937 and 1943 respectively. In works up to about 1930, a direct and vigorous manner analogous to Sibelius' was characteristic of Hanson. Young in spirit and romantic in feeling, the first two symphonies are expressive without being sentimental, strong without being overwhelming. Later, about the time of the third symphony, Hanson occasionally resorted to modal inflections, dissonant counterpoint, and a lighter orchestral texture. In the compact fourth symphony, the influence of Sibelius is again direct; short melodic lines, surging climaxes, and free, impulsive expression are typical.

Virgil Thomson (b. 1896) may be mentioned here. An opera, much film music, and a variety of smaller orchestral compositions are his principal works. Thomson's music reflects his several years of residence in France; it is said to resemble that of Satie in its satirical and tongue-in-cheek aspects. The hints of Impressionism, such as found in *The Seine at Night*, and the play with isolated chords, as in the orchestral suite drawn from the film, *The Louisiana Story*, are by no means characteristic of all of Thomson's works. The suite contains long passages with static harmonies, a passacaglia which is strangely noncontrapuntal, and a folklike movement in which chorale lines and a naïve tune are intertwined. It may be well not to judge this suite as concert music, but rather to keep in mind its original purpose—to illustrate a documentary film. In *Five Portraits* for orchestra, Thomson presents a series of unrelated sketches in a variety of styles, most of them simple to the extreme. Tonal harmonies, obvious counterpoints, elementary rhythms, melodic clichés—such factors make this into music which need not be taken seriously. And that is Thomson's primary intention: to compose music that is unpretentious, immediate, and entertaining.

A number of composers contemporary with Howard Hanson have written music which is not easily classified. Roger Sessions (b. 1896) and Walter Piston (b. 1894) are of this category. Sessions, in three symphonies and a violin concerto, has composed painstakingly and has remained aloof from any particular foreign style tendencies. Formal clarity and profusion of detail are characteristic of his music, and a clean-cut melodic line is usually in evidence. Other typical elements are a chromatically thickened harmony which adheres to definite tonal centers in some cases and is distinctly atonal in others, a complex rhythmic texture in which two or more rhythmic patterns may be employed simultaneously, and a cool and impersonal manner of expression. In its intellectual aspects, neatness, reserve, and attention to balance and proportion, Sessions's music resembles that of Schoenberg. Its complete objectivity, seriousness, and lack of mannerisms relate it to the neo-Classical school of the 1930s.

Piston, in a sense, summarizes the musical developments of his generation. In forms that are neo-Classical in their clarity and proportions, he writes objectively, dissonantly, and with great competence. Atonal harmonies, a melodic line which is rarely diatonic, and considerable rhythmic reiteration in the manner of Stravinsky—

such elements are basic to his music. Among his orchestral works are the *Suite* of 1929, the *Concerto* of 1933, the first symphony of 1937, and the violin concerto of 1939. In these he developed a style that became ever more conservative in all respects but harmony; and his harmony employed all contemporary devices uncompromisingly and skillfully. The suite from the ballet, *The Incredible Flutist* (1938), is only mildly dissonant, however, and is somewhat reminiscent of Stravinsky's *Petrouchka* in rhythmic aspects and in its mock sentimentality.

With the *Sinfonietta* of 1941 and the second symphony of 1943, Piston's manner of expression became warmer, but no less dissonant or energetic. Indeed, energy and concise utterance have characterized the majority of his works. His technical skill and harmonic imagination have not impelled him to lengthen his compositions unduly. Even if they are somewhat alike and predictable in style, it is only because Piston has found a manner of expression that is compatible with his interests and temperament.

European musical styles are reflected not only in the works of the foregoing composers, however. The principal representatives of those styles—Schoenberg, Hindemith, and Milhaud, for example—have long been resident in the United States. In addition to those men, a number of other eminent European musicians have come to this country, have been active as composers and teachers, and have identified themselves with the American scene. Among them, Ernest Bloch (b. 1880) and Ernst Křenek (b. 1900) have contributed many works to the symphonic literature.

Bloch, of Swiss birth but American by virtue of his intermittent residence here since 1916, brings a warm, Romantic expression to his music and makes considerable use both of Jewish idioms and Jewish subjects. The *Trois Poèmes juifs* and *Schelomo*—the latter a Hebrew rhapsody for cello and orchestra—both performed in the United States in 1917, are perhaps the best representatives of Bloch's avowed Jewish style.

In the *Concerto grosso* for piano and string orchestra (1925), as in the two symphonic poems entitled *America* (1925) and *Helvetia*

(1929), a lessening of the frankly Jewish expression is to be seen. In the violin concerto of 1937 that element is still less abundant. The rhapsodic, highly emotional, and richly melodic content of Jewish music have, nevertheless, remained striking elements of Bloch's style. That style is essentially tonal, with definite key centers, tonic-dominant chordal relationships, and the like. But Bloch has never hesitated to employ free dissonance, polytonality, thick chromaticism, and even quarter-tones to color his harmonies. He has remained an individual, adhering to no system other than his own, and his music contains little that can be traced to any other twentieth-century composer. Always expressive and given to noble and dignified or passionate utterance, Bloch has written with great strength, rhythmic freedom, and utmost fervor.

Křenek has passed through a number of stylistic phases, only the latest of which has been of long duration. At first attracted to a dissonant counterpoint somewhat in the manner of Hindemith, he then became an ardent exponent of jazz elements—especially in his successful opera, *Jonny spielt auf* (1927). Thereafter, for a short period, he composed in a restrained neo-Classical manner that contained also a degree of warm sentiment akin to Schubert's. About 1933 he discovered the twelve-tone system of Schoenberg. He has remained a practitioner of that system ever since—even though a few of his later works are atonal without being based upon tone rows. Křenek has been a prolific composer in virtually all fields, and much of his music has remained in manuscript. Four symphonies, several concertos, and a number of smaller works testify to his energy and competence; two books and many articles in music periodicals reveal him to be an uncompromising champion of atonal music.

The foregoing general discussion has sought to call attention to a large body of American music in which European characteristics are unmistakable. All the music produced in the United States has not been of this type, however; experimentation and innovation have come to expression also, even if not in great quantity. Significantly, the experimental work of Charles Ives (b. 1874) even came before that of Schoenberg and Stravinsky. After a Connecticut boyhood, Ives became a successful business man in New York; and between about 1906 and 1916 he composed four or five symphonies and many sets of descriptive pieces in an intensely personal style that owes nothing to European models.

Working in isolation and developing little self-critical sense, Ives sought to describe out-of-tune bands, choral groups whose ensemble was less than good, and a variety of extramusical sounds. Everything that could be expressed in musical notation—and some things that could not—interested him. Unrelieved cacophony, incredibly complex multi-rhythms, many types of polychordal and polytonal harmony, thick tonal clusters, experiments in form and acoustic effect —such elements are combined with lyric fragments, portions of gospel hymns, occasional extreme melodic angularity, and a great range of humor and caricature.

One sometimes feels that individual parts are conceived separately and bear not the slightest relationship to each other; the effect, in such cases, is that of several people reading different prose selections aloud simultaneously. Ives's music has become better known only in recent years. An "Ives movement" seems in the process of formation at the present time, and a number of his early orchestral works are now available in recordings: the *Four Pieces for Orchestra*, the third symphony, and the last of *Three Places in New England*. With all its realistic, anti-musical, and frankly burlesque elements, the music of Ives contains a strong, sensitive, and poetic content that relates it to the most significant contemporary American compositions.

Henry Cowell (b. 1897) is a prolific composer who has for several decades identified himself with the experimentalists. His exploitation of the tone cluster—used by Leo Ornstein (b. 1895) and Ives long before Cowell discovered it—has been one of his more spectacular achievements; a group of tones played with the closed fist, the forearm, or even a short piece of wood became a striking element of his keyboard style. Transferred to the orchestra, tone clusters were often employed polyphonically—one series of consecutive clusters forming a "melody" being set opposite another similar series. But this is only one of Cowell's technical devices. His experiments led to complex rhythmic structures, his free use of dissonance led to a further enlarging of atonal harmonic resources—and these became elements of a style that is sometimes consonant and even sentimental. In recent works Cowell has become increasingly an exponent of conservative harmony and traditional expression.

In the rise of an American music, American national idioms necessarily play an important part. Now, Indian tunes and rhythms had been employed by composers such as MacDowell, Charles Skilton (1868–1941), and many others. We have seen, further, that European composers had often adopted American dance idioms (ragtime and jazz, primarily) about the 1920s; and even Dvořák had thought to express the spirit of the "New World" in his later compositions. But such use of melodic or rhythmic inflections proved to do no more than flavor the music exotically. The content itself remained largely European.

Not until quite recently have American legends and idioms become factors of a style that is contemporary, indigenous, and significant. In that work, two composers from Latin-American countries have produced orchestral compositions which parallel or antedate the efforts of their contemporaries in the United States: Heitor Villa-Lobos (b. 1887) of Brazil and Carlos Chavez (b. 1899) of Mexico.

Villa-Lobos has long been concerned with the music of his country. He has been a tireless experimenter in the harmonic and rhythmic fields, in the formation of new scales, in musical form, and in instrumental effects. Mixed with these nationalistic and experimental interests is an easy mastery of contrapuntal techniques and a flair for programmatic writing. Out of this considerable array of elements, attitudes, and skills have come a number of large, sonorous orchestral compositions. One new form, to which Villa-Lobos has given the name *chôros*, results from the synthesis of Brazilian Indian and popular music, set in the composer's highly complex and dissonant style. A series of twelve works bearing this title, for various combinations of instruments, appeared between 1920 and 1944. Several of them are in the field of chamber music; but *Chôros No. 8* (1925) is for two pianos and orchestra, *Chôros No. 11* (1941) is a piano concerto, and *Chôros No. 9* (1929) and *No. 12* (1941) are for large orchestra in which Brazilian percussion instruments are utilized. An orthodox piano concerto (1945) may be mentioned here as evidence that Villa-Lobos has, with increasing years, minimized the relentless dissonance of his earlier works and restored a high degree of tonal feeling to a strongly lyric and contrapuntal texture. But the rhythmic vitality and driving power of his style have not been lessened.

Chavez resembles Villa-Lobos in his use of (Mexican) Indian idioms and of native percussion instruments, and in the employment of great rhythmic variety. A work that is typical of Chavez's preoccupation with national materials is the *Sinfonia India* (1936). It is rhythmic and percussive to a considerable degree; one finds few melodic lines as such, and scarcely a trace of contrapuntal writing. Four percussion players are added to the already large orchestra and are required to perform on a dozen Indian drums, rattles, and the like. The unmetrical rhythms in this composition are akin to those of Stravinsky (here, however, employed to bring Indian tunes to accurate expression). The barbaric power and emotional compulsion thus engendered reach overwhelming proportions. In all respects an original and significant composer, Chavez has been equally important in vitalizing and organizing the musical life of his country. As conductor, musical administrator, and educator, he has been of enormous service to the cultural life of Mexico.

At a time when jazz represented an exotic field into which composers of concert music dipped on occasion and when jazz idioms were used only as flavoring, George Gershwin (1898–1937) reversed the process. In a series of works which achieved great popularity he applied symphonic techniques to materials drawn from the dance-music field. The *Rhapsody in Blue* (1923), the *Concerto in*

F (1925) for piano and orchestra, and the orchestral suite, *An Amer-ican in Paris* (1928) are his principal orchestral compositions in this category.

From the standpoint of rhythmic sparkle, authenticity of content, and value as entertainment, these works serve their purpose ad-mirably. It is only when judged by the technical standards which one must expect of composers in the larger forms that they fail to satisfy. The ability to organize an extended composition, to achieve a sense of line and growth, and to provide significant variety in a restricted idiom—such abilities were not among Gershwin's gifts. Since Gershwin's time the application of symphonic techniques to the popular-music field has interested many composers. Ferde Grofé (b. 1892), Robert Russell Bennett (b. 1894), William Grant Still (b. 1895), and Morton Gould (b. 1913) may be mentioned in this connection.

In the music of Aaron Copland (b. 1900) and Roy Harris (b. 1898) we come, finally, to a quality that may be called authentically American. Copland and Harris have for many years been among the most prominent of native-born composers. In number of perform-ances, of published works, and of recordings they have probably fared better than any of their contemporaries. A later generation must decide to what extent this prominence is deserved; at the mo-ment we must recognize it and consider their works as representing American music to the world at large.

The jazz element found an important place in Copland's early orchestral compositions—but it was a sophisticated, self-conscious jazz such as Stravinsky and Milhaud had employed in the 1920s. His *Dance Symphony* (derived from an early ballet, *Grogh*), the *Music for the Theater*, and the piano concerto—all composed be-tween about 1924 and 1926—bring to expression the melodic idioms, the syncopations and cross-accents, the blues, and all the other ele-ments of the time's dance music. These elements were coupled with polytonal harmonies, a large and impressive sonority, and a certain harshness of effect. That style was of relatively short duration, how-ever. An interval about 1933–1935 is marked by several works in which textures became thinner and dissonance more extreme. Thereafter, Copland utilized American legends and strove for an amalgamation of stylistic elements that would express the American spirit—to such an extent that a period of nationalism may be spoken of.

The principal orchestral works of that period (1936 to about 1945) reveal by their very titles the direction of Copland's new interests: *Music for Radio*, with a subtitle "Saga of the Prairies," *El Salon Mexico, Billy the Kid, Rodeo, A Lincoln Portrait, Appalachian Spring*. Several of these works were written for ballet performances and only later were made into orchestral suites. And even in this "nationalistic" period of Copland's career, the influence of Stravinsky was not completely shaken off. Their content is based upon folk tunes and folk-dance rhythms; a warm, at times sentimental, and always vital expression is characteristic. The complexity and extreme dissonance of the music written before 1936 is not always found in these later works. Rather is there a tendency to write ever more simply, more clearly, and with more immediate appeal.

Copland's third symphony (1944–1946) is more contrapuntal, more objective, and of course more highly organized than the theater works of the previous decade, but it contains the same attractive, warm, and unsentimental expressiveness. The percussive, free rhythmic effects which have characterized his compositions since the 1920s are still in evidence, along with the rich orchestral sound that most of the earlier works possessed.

Roy Harris's musical career has not developed parallel to Copland's and the two men have little in common, stylistically speaking. The majority of Harris's early orchestral compositions (1925–1932) have remained in manuscript. To judge from the published chamber-music works of that period, however, he adopted an aggressively dissonant style, wrote contrapuntally with long and somewhat awkward melodic lines and in forms that made few demands upon symmetry or recapitulation. Since about 1932 Harris has called himself a Classicist (not a neo-Classicist, be it noted) and has made full use of the resources of tonality without embracing any atonal or chromatic system. Modal scales appear in his works, and polymodality is often introduced. The *Symphony 1933*, an overture entitled *When Johnny Comes Marching Home* (1934), and the second and third symphonies (1934 and 1937, respectively) are representative compositions of the period.

The third symphony, one of Harris's most successful works, contains one movement divided into five contrasting sections. One is struck by the sparseness of the textures, by the absence of external effectiveness. Much of the writing, even in the contrapuntal sections, is vertical. There is little of the rhythmic variety and sparkle which animate so many American works of the time. A mixture of tonal and polytonal writing, a general absence of chromatic inflections, and a certain static quality characterize the harmony through long sections. The orchestration proceeds by blocks or by families of instruments rather than by individual lines, and considerable monotony of color results. Yet the whole is a strong and concentrated work.

About 1939 Harris entered into his period of nationalism and turned to the field of American folk song and legend. This phase is seen more markedly in fields other than the orchestral, however. The new content is reflected in several compositions for band, in the choral works, *Five Songs for Democracy* and *Sons of Uncle Sam*, and in the ballet, *What So Proudly We Hail*. But in a few orchestral works the same direction may be surmised: in the fourth symphony (1939), subtitled "Folk-Song Symphony," in the *American Creed* (1940), and elsewhere. Such works, directed to a larger audience, are necessarily more conservative in a harmonic sense, more compact, and less strident than the compositions of the earlier periods. But the strength and rugged individuality that Harris revealed in the early 1930s have not abated. The fifth and sixth symphonies (1942 and 1944, respectively) and a concerto for two pianos and orchestra (1946) are still American in spirit without relying upon overt use of folk materials.

There remains the orchestral music of the present generation of composers, of men born since about 1910, of those who have profited

by the work of Bloch, Piston, Copland, and others. The quantity
of that music, representing the intense creative activity of scores,
perhaps hundreds, of sincere and accomplished musicians, is large;
many pages would be required merely to list the composers and their
works.[2] Much of it is heard once and not again; large portions of
it have remained in manuscript and hence are not available. Some
has achieved prominence, but not all of it is significant. One might
single out such men as Normand Lockwood (b. 1906), Samuel
Barber (b. 1910), William Schuman (b. 1910), Norman Dello Joio
(b. 1913), and David Diamond (b. 1915); or, among the still
younger men, Lukas Foss (b. 1922 in Germany), Peter Mennin (b.
1923), and Clifton Williams (b. 1923). But no discussion of a selected group of these composers would be representative of the
whole, nor could it hope to do justice to the variety, good workmanship, and promise reflected in the music of those who remained unmentioned.

It becomes necessary, therefore, to make a series of generaliza-
tions broad enough to encompass the music written since about 1938
by the younger American composers. In spite of great differences
in the individual styles, personal interests, and capabilities of these
men, their music does reveal characteristics which allow the following observations to be made. It must be understood, however, that
a few composers and many compositions can never be subject to a
generalization, no matter how broad its terms.

The first obvious characteristic is that—at least in the case of
newer works that have come to performance—a return has been
made to the tonal system. The most recent compositions reveal
definite tonal centers, and the diatonic scale has come back into
its own. However, the tonic-dominant relationships which were
basic to tonality have remained free, and the term "modulation" has
lost much of its nineteenth-century restrictive force. The diatonicism
is often chromatically inflected, and a use of the chromatic scale
within the diatonic framework is customary. Chordal structures are
again composed of superimposed thirds, but tones added to the re-

[2] See, in this connection, Reis, *Composers in America*.

spective triads continue to thicken the somewhat dissonant harmony. In this sense, the very concept of dissonance has lost much of its former "unpleasant" connotation, and a dissonance is simply a factor that supplies more harmonic tension than a consonance can provide. Contrapuntal and homophonic textures are equally acceptable; and the counterpoint, following Hindemith's lead, is employed freely and often with linear considerations uppermost.

The tendency to employ Baroque forms continues to be characteristic of many recent composers, and nineteenth-century methods of thematic development are again in evidence. The rhythmic vitality and freedom introduced by Stravinsky and Bartók have been modified and controlled, it is true; but few composers have remained immune to the rhythmic concepts so strikingly revealed in the period about 1913–1925. Cross-accents, the virtual ignoring of bar lines, the use of unmetrical patterns—such elements give evidence of the contemporary approach to rhythm.

Of perhaps greater importance, however, is the emotional effect of much recent music. Lyric expression, impassioned utterance, and overt sentiment have again become respectable. Indeed, the term "neo-Romantic" is heard with increasing frequency at the present time,[3] and neo-Classicism has become largely the province of the older composers. Subtle or broad humor is often employed, pretentiousness and monumental forms are missing, in general, and the orchestra has usually been reduced to the size that Brahms, for instance, found compatible. A direct approach to the lay audience has again become possible. The extreme angularity and the mechanical qualities which concert-goers up to about 1930 found so repellent are seldom contained in contemporary scores.

Such, then, is the music that has been composed in the past decade, and upon such foundations the younger composers (as well as many of their seniors) are building at the present time. The expressive possibilities of the styles represented by that music are vast; no con-

---

[3] But among some writers the term includes those whom we have called "post-Romantic" in Chapter XI of this book. Contemporary composers would be the first to deny their kinship to Mahler, Strauss, and Reger.

temporary musician need feel hampered by the lack of harmonic, melodic, or rhythmic resources. Composers today are working industriously and intelligently to bring those possibilities to light. The precious attitudes, the posturing, and the lack of good sense which characterized many earlier composers are seldom in evidence. Whatever shape the music of the next few decades may take, one may be sure that it will be written with technical competence, imagination, and regard for the emotional factors in human life. The musical sincerity of the contemporary composer cannot be denied. He writes with keen awareness of his responsibility toward the cultural life of the day, and he has become conscious of the social importance of the art. One may confidently await the future.

BIBLIOGRAPHY

REFERENCE WORKS

Altmann, Wilhelm. Orchester-Literatur-Katalog; Verzeichniss von seit 1850 erschienenen Orchesterwerken. 2 vols. Leipzig: F. E. C. Leuckart, 1926–1936.

Apel, Willi. Harvard Dictionary of Music. Cambridge, Mass.: Harvard University Press, 1944.

Baker, Theodore. Baker's Biographical Dictionary of Musicians. 4th rev. ed. New York: G. Schirmer, 1940.

Grove, Sir George. Grove's Dictionary of Music and Musicians. 4th ed., by H. C. Colles. 5 vols. and Supplement. London: Macmillan, 1940.

International Cyclopedia of Music and Musicians. 5th ed., by Nicolas Slonimsky. New York: Dodd, Mead & Co., 1949.

Koechel, Ludwig, Ritter von. Chronologisch-systematisches Verzeichniss sämtlicher Tonwerke Wolfgang Amade Mozarts. Rev. 3d ed., by Alfred Einstein. Leipzig: Breitkopf & Härtel, 1937. Reprinted by J. W. Edwards, Ann Arbor, Mich., 1947.

Sonneck, Oscar G. Catalogue of Orchestral Music in the Library of Congress. Washington: Government Printing Office, 1912.

BOOKS

Abraham, Gerald, ed. The Music of Schubert. New York: W. W. Norton & Co., 1947.
—— The Music of Sibelius. New York: W. W. Norton & Co., 1947.
—— Tchaikovsky: a Symposium. 2d ptg. London: Lindsay Drummond, 1946.

Adler, Guido, ed. Handbuch der Musikgeschichte. 2d ed. 2 vols. Berlin-Wilmersdorf: H. Keller, 1930.

Barzun, Jacques. Berlioz and the Romantic Century. 2 vols. Boston: Little, Brown & Co., 1950.

Bauer, Marion E. Twentieth Century Music. New York: G. P. Putnam's Sons, 1933.

Bekker, Paul. Gustav Mahlers Sinfonien. Berlin: Schuster & Loeffler, 1921.

Berlioz, Hector. Memoirs. Tr. from the French by Rachel and Eleanor Holmes. New York: Alfred A. Knopf, 1935.

Brahms, Johannes. Johannes Brahms im Briefwechsel mit Joseph Joachim. Ed. by Andreas Moser. 2 vols. Berlin: Deutsche Brahmsgesellschaft, 1908.

Bukofzer, Manfred. Music in the Baroque Era. New York: W. W. Norton & Co., 1947.

Carse, Adam. The Orchestra from Beethoven to Berlioz. Cambridge: W. Heffer & Sons, 1948.

———— The Orchestra in the XVIIIth Century. Cambridge: W. Heffer & Sons, 1940.

Copland, Aaron. Our New Music. New York: McGraw-Hill Book Co., 1941.

Cowell, Henry, ed. American Composers on American Music. Stanford University, Calif.: Stanford University Press, 1933.

David, Hans Theodore, and Arthur Mendel, eds. The Bach Reader. New York: W. W. Norton & Co., 1945.

Demuth, Norman. César Franck. London: Dennis Dobson, 1949.

Einstein, Alfred. Mozart, his Character, his Work. Tr. from the German by Arthur Mendel and Nathan Broder. London: Oxford University Press, 1945.

———— Music in the Romantic Era. New York: W. W. Norton & Co., 1947.

———— Schubert, a Musical Portrait. Tr. from the German by David Ascoli. New York: Oxford University Press, 1951.

Evans, Edwin, Sr. Handbook to the Chamber Music and Orchestral Works of Brahms. 2 vols. London: W. Reeves, 1933–1935.

Finck, Henry T. Richard Strauss. Boston: Little, Brown & Co., 1917.

Flower, Newman. George Frideric Handel, his Personality and his Times. Rev. ed. New York: Charles Scribner's Sons, 1948.

Geiringer, Karl. Johannes Brahms, Leben und Schaffen eines deutschen Meisters. Vienna: R. M. Rohrer, 1935.

———— Haydn: a Creative Life in Music. New York: W. W. Norton & Co., 1946.

Girdlestone, Cuthbert M. Mozart's Piano Concertos. Tr. from the French by the author. London: Cassel & Co., 1948.

Grout, Donald J. A Short History of Opera. 2 vols. New York: Columbia University Press, 1947.

Grove, Sir George. Beethoven and his Nine Symphonies. London: Novello & Co., 1903.

Haas, Robert. Die Musik des Barocks. Vol. IV of Ernst Bücken, ed., Handbuch der Musikwissenschaft. Wildpark-Potsdam: Akademische Verlagsgesellschaft, 1928.

Haraszti, Emil. Béla Bartók. Paris: Editions de l'Oiseau-Lyre, 1938.

Hasse, Karl. Max Reger, Mensch und Werk. Berlin: Bote & Bock, 1938.

Hill, Ralph, and others. The Symphony. Harmandsworth: Pelican Books, 1949.

Hindemith, Paul. Unterweisung im Tonsatz. Mainz: B. Schotts Söhne, 1937. Translated into English as The Craft of Musical Composition. 2 vols.: Book I tr. from the German by Arthur Mendel; Book II tr. from the German by Otto Ortmann. New York: Associated Music Publishers, 1941–1942.

Howard, John Tasker. Our Contemporary Composers. New York: Thomas Y. Crowell, 1941.

Indy, Vincent d'. César Franck. Tr. from the French by Rosa Newmarch. London: John Lane, 1910.

Jahn, Otto. W. A. Mozart. 6th ed., by Hermann Abert. 2 vols. Leipzig: Breitkopf & Härtel, 1923–1924.

Kretzschmar, Hermann. Führer durch den Concertsaal. I. Abtheilung: Sinfonie und Suite. 6th ed. Leipzig: Breitkopf & Härtel, 1921.

Lang, Paul Henry. Music in Western Civilization. New York: W. W. Norton & Co., 1941.

Latham, Peter. Brahms. London: J. M. Dent & Sons, 1948.

Leichtentritt, Hugo. Händel. Stuttgart: Deutsche Verlagsanstalt, 1924.

Mahler, Alma. Gustav Mahler; Erinnerungen und Briefe. Amsterdam: Albert de Lange, 1940.

Moser, Hans Joachim. Geschichte der deutschen Musik. 3d ed. 2 vols., 3 parts. Stuttgart and Berlin: J. G. Cotta, 1923–1924.

Nef, Karl. Geschichte der Sinfonie und Suite. Leipzig: Breitkopf & Härtel, 1921.

Newlin, Dika. Bruckner, Mahler, Schönberg. New York: King's Crown Press, 1947.

Niemann, Walter. Johannes Brahms. 13th ed. Stuttgart and Berlin: Deutsche Verlagsanstalt, 1922.

Oxford History of Music, The. 2d rev. ed. 7 vols. London: Oxford University Press, 1938.

Pincherle, Marc. Antonio Vivaldi et la musique instrumentale. 2 vols. Paris: Fleury & Cie., 1948.

Reis, Claire R. Composers in America. Rev. ed. New York: Macmillan, 1947.

Riemann, Hugo. Geschichte der Musik seit Beethoven. Berlin and Stuttgart: W. Spemann, 1901.

Riemann, Hugo. Handbuch der Musikgeschichte. 2d ed. 2 vols., 5 parts. Leipzig: Breitkopf & Härtel, 1920–1923.

Riezler, Walter. Beethoven. Tr. from the German by G. D. Pidcock. New York: E. P. Dutton & Co., 1938.

Saint-Foix, Georges de. The Symphonies of Mozart. Tr. from the French by Leslie Orrey. London: Dennis Dobson, 1947.

Salazar, Adolfo. Music in Our Time. Tr. from the Spanish by Isabel Pope. New York: W. W. Norton & Co., 1946.

Schweitzer, Albert. J. S. Bach. Tr. from the German by Ernest Newman. New ptg. 2 vols. London: A. & C. Black, 1935.

Scott, Marion M. Beethoven. 2d ed. London: J. M. Dent & Sons, 1937.

Shore, Bernard. Sixteen Symphonies. London: Longmans, Green & Co., 1949.

Specht, Richard. Richard Strauss und sein Werk. 2 vols. Leipzig: E. P. Tal, 1921.

Spitta, Philipp. J. S. Bach. 3d ed. 2 vols. Leipzig: Breitkopf & Härtel, 1921.

Strobel, Heinrich. Paul Hindemith. 3d rev. ed. Mainz: B. Schotts Söhne, 1948.

Terry, Charles Sanford. Bach's Orchestra. London: Oxford University Press, 1932.

Thayer, Alexander W. The Life of Ludwig van Beethoven. Ed. by Henry A. Krehbiel. 3 vols. New York: The Beethoven Association, 1921.

Thompson, Oscar. Debussy, Man and Artist. New York: Dodd, Mead & Co., 1937.

Tovey, Sir Donald Francis. Essays in Musical Analysis. 6 vols. London: Oxford University Press, 1935–1939. Vols. I and II: Symphonies; Vol. III: Concertos; Vol. IV: Illustrative Music.

Ulrich, Homer. Chamber Music: the Growth and Practice of an Intimate Art. New York: Columbia University Press, 1948.

Veinus, Abraham. The Concerto. London: Cassel & Co., 1948.

Wolff, Werner. Anton Bruckner. New York: E. P. Dutton & Co., 1942.

ARTICLES

Avery, Kenneth. "William Walton," in *Music and Letters*, January, 1947, pp. 1–11.

Bellaman, Henry. "Charles Ives: the Man and his Music," in *The Musical Quarterly*, January, 1933, pp. 45–58.

Berger, Arthur V. "The Music of Aaron Copland," in *The Musical Quarterly*, October, 1945, pp. 420–47.

Broder, Nathan. "The Wind Instruments in Mozart's Symphonies," in *The Musical Quarterly*, July, 1933, pp. 238–59.

Cherniavsky, David. "The Use of Germ Motives by Sibelius," in *Music and Letters*, January, 1942, pp. 1–9.

Chrysander, Friedrich. "Händels Instrumentalkompositionen für grosses Orchester," in *Vierteljahrschrift für Musikwissenschaft*, III (1887), 6–11.

Evett, Robert. "The Harmonic Idiom of Roy Harris," in *Modern Music*, Spring, 1946, pp. 100–107.

Fischer, Wilhelm. "Zur Entwickelungsgeschichte des Wiener klassischen Stils," in *Studien zur Musikwissenschaft*, III (1915), 24–84.

Heiden, Bernard. "Hindemith's System—a New Approach," in *Modern Music*, January–February, 1942, pp. 102–7.

Herrmann, Bernard. "Four Symphonies by Charles Ives," in *Modern Music*, May–June, 1945, pp. 215–22.

Hill, Richard S. "Schoenberg's Tone-Rows and the Tonal System of the Future," in *The Musical Quarterly*, January, 1936, pp. 14–37.

Křenek, Ernst. "New Developments of the Twelve-Tone Technique," in *The Music Review*, May, 1943, pp. 81–97.

Leichtentritt, Hugo. "Ferruccio Busoni as a Composer," in *The Musical Quarterly*, January, 1917, pp. 69–97.

Mendl, Robert William. "The Art of the Symphonic Poem," in *The Musical Quarterly*, July, 1932, pp. 443–62.

Šafránek, Miloš. "Bohuslav Martinů," in *The Musical Quarterly*, July, 1943, pp. 329–54.

Salzer, Felix. "Die Sonatenform bei Franz Schubert," in *Studien zur Musikwissenschaft*, XV (1928), 86–125.

Stein, Erwin. "Schönberg's New Structural Form," in *Modern Music*, June–July, 1930, pp. 3–10.

Tiersot, Julien. "The Berlioz of the Fantastic Symphony," in *The Musical Quarterly*, July, 1933, pp. 303–17.

Urbantschitsch, Victor. "Die Entwickelung der Sonatenform bei Brahms," in *Studien zur Musikwissenschaft*, XIV (1927), 265–85.

Wellesz, Egon. "Anton Bruckner and the Process of Musical Creation," in *The Musical Quarterly*, July, 1938, pp. 265–90.

——— "The Symphonies of Gustav Mahler," in *The Music Review*, February, 1940, pp. 2–23.

Wiesengrund-Adorno, Theodore. "Berg and Webern, Schönberg's Heirs," in *Modern Music*, January–February, 1931, pp. 29–38.

PERIODICALS

Modern Music. Minna Lederman, ed. 23 vols. New York: League of Composers, 1924–1946.

Music and Letters. Eric Blom, ed. London: Music and Letters, 1920–.

Music Review, The. Geoffrey Sharp, ed. London: W. Heffer & Sons, 1940–.

Musical Quarterly, The. O. G. Sonneck, Carl Engel, Gustav Reese, Paul Henry Lang, eds. New York: G. Schirmer, Inc., 1915–.

Revue de musicologie. Paris: Librairie Fischbacher, 1917–.

Rivista musicale italiana. Milan: Frotelli Bocca, 1894–.

Sammelbände der Internationalen Musikgesellschaft. 15 vols. Leipzig: Breitkopf & Härtel, 1899–1914.

Studien zur Musikwissenschaft: Beihefte der Denkmäler der Tonkunst in Österreich. 21 vols. Vienna: Artaria & Co. and Universal Edition, 1913–1934.

Vierteljahrschrift für Musikwissenschaft. 10 vols. Leipzig: Breitkopf & Härtel, 1885–1894.

Zeitschrift für Musikwissenschaft. 17 vols. Leipzig: Breitkopf & Härtel, 1918–1935.

MUSIC

Bach, Johann Sebastian. *Werke.* 47 vols. Leipzig: Bachgesellschaft, 1851–1894.

Beethoven, Ludwig van. *Werke.* 25 vols. Leipzig: Breitkopf & Härtel, 1862–1888.

Berlioz, Hector. *Werke.* 20 vols. Leipzig: Breitkopf & Härtel, 1899–1907.

Brahms, Johannes. *Sämtliche Werke.* 26 vols. Leipzig: Breitkopf & Härtel, 1926–1928.

Denkmäler der Tonkunst in Österreich. 83 vols. Vienna: Universal Edition, 1894–1938. Abbreviation: *D.T.Ö.*

Denkmäler deutscher Tonkunst; erste Folge. 65 vols. Leipzig: Breitkopf & Härtel, 1892–1931. Abbreviation: *D.D.T.*

Denkmäler deutscher Tonkunst; zweite Folge: Denkmäler der Tonkunst in Bayern. 36 vols. Leipzig: Breitkopf & Härtel, 1900–1931. Abbreviation: *D.T.B.*

Handel, George Frederick. *Werke.* 96 vols., 6 supplements. Leipzig: Deutsche Händelgesellschaft, 1859–1901.

Haydn, Franz Joseph. *Sämtliche Werke.* Leipzig: Breitkopf & Härtel, 1908–. (Publication continued by The Haydn Society, Inc., Boston, 1949–.)

Liszt, Franz. *Musikalische Werke.* 39 vols. to date. Leipzig: Breitkopf & Härtel, 1908–.

Mendelssohn-Bartholdy, Felix. *Werke.* 36 vols. Leipzig: Breitkopf & Härtel, 1874–1877.

Mozart, Wolfgang Amadeus. *Sämtliche Werke.* 24 series in 75 vols. Leipzig: Breitkopf & Härtel, 1877–1905.

Schubert, Franz Peter. *Werke.* 40 vols. Leipzig: Breitkopf & Härtel, 1888–1897.

Schumann, Robert. *Werke.* 34 vols. Leipzig: Breitkopf & Härtel, 1886–1893.

INDEX

Abel, Carl Friedrich, 105
Academic Festival Overture (Brahms), 212
"Academies" devoted to public performances, 54
"Accursed Hunter, The" (Franck), 229
"Adelaide" concerto (Mozart), 85*n*
Adventures in a Perambulator (Carpenter), 314
Ala et Lolly (Prokofieff), 306
Albéniz, Isaac, 255
Albinoni, Tommaso, 20
Alpine Symphony (Strauss), 265
America (Bloch), 317
American Creed (Harris), 324
American in Paris, An (Gershwin), 322
American scene, music in which European characteristics are unmistakable, 312-17; European musicians who have identified themselves with, 317-18; experimentation and innovation, 318-24; use of national idioms, 320; Latin-American composers, 320; present generation, 324 ff.; return to tonal system, 325
Antar (Rimsky-Korsakov), 250, 251
Antiphonal singing, 14
Appalachian Spring (Copland), 323
Applausus (Haydn), 69
Apprenti sorcier, L' (Dukas), 297
Arabian Nights, 251
Architecture, influence in formation of Rococo style, 51
Art of the Fugue, The (Bach), 27, 230
Ascension, L' (Messiaen), 301
Aus Holbergs Zeit (Grieg), 253
Aus Italien (Strauss), 262
Austria, exotic strains in music of, 66

Bach, Johann Christian, 63, 79; influence upon Mozart, 85

Bach, Johann, Sebastian, 5, 22-39, 49; B-minor Mass, 4; *Passion According to St. Matthew*, 4, 22; his style undermined during his lifetime, 6; relationship to standard repertoire, 6; *Christmas Oratorio*, 8; way prepared for concertos of, 21; culmination of seventeenth-century musical development, 22; instrumental resources, 24 ff.; formal perfection of works, 27; achieves balance and contrast simultaneously, 28; conductor for Telemann's Collegium Musicum, 35, 54; summarized and refined Baroque style tendencies, 37 ff.; transformer of compositions, 48; resolved dilemma between homophonic and polyphonic textures, 98, 99; use of chromatic lines, 102; use of cyclical-form principle, 230
— Brandenburg concertos, 24-32; violin and keyboard concertos, 32-35; suites or "overtures," 35; *sinfonia* in F major, 37
Bach, Karl Philipp Emanuel, 34, 64 ff.
Bach, Wilhelm Friedemann, 34
"Back to Bach," slogan, 287
Balakirev, Mili, 247
"Ballet of the Sylphs" (Berlioz), 193
Ballets, Stravinsky's for The Ballet Russe, 283
Ballets de cour, 11; overtures, 12 f.
Banchieri, Adriano, 8
Banister, John, 54
Barber, Samuel, 325
Baroque style, 3-49; town bands, 7; changes in instrumental music, 10; Bach's music the culmination of, 22; tendencies summarized and refined by Bach, 37 ff.; decline of, 50 ff.; influenced by doctrine of the affections,